Getting the Best Out of College

GETTING THE BEST OUT OF COLLEGE

A PROFESSOR, A DEAN, AND A STUDENT TELL YOU HOW TO MAXIMIZE YOUR EXPERIENCE

PETER FEAVER, SUE WASIOLEK,
AND ANNE CROSSMAN

TEN SPEED PRESS
Berkeley | Toronto

Ten Speed Press
PO Box 7123
Berkeley, California 94707
www.tenspeed.com

Distributed in Australia by Simon and Schuster Australia, in Canada by Ten Speed Press Canada, in New Zealand by Southern Publishers Group, in South Africa by Real Books, and in the United Kingdom and Europe by Publishers Group UK.

Cover design by Laura Milton
Text design by Linda Davis, Star Type, Berkeley

Library of Congress Cataloging-in-Publication Data
Feaver, Peter.
Getting the best out of college : a professor, a dean, and a student tell you how to maximize your experience / Peter Feaver, Sue Wasiolek, and Anne Crossman.
     p. cm.
Summary: "A guide to optimizing all aspects of the undergraduate college experience, written for students by a professor, a dean, and a recent college graduate"—Provided by publisher.
  Includes index.
  ISBN-13: 978-1-58008-856-5
  ISBN-10: 1-58008-856-2
1. College student orientation—United States. I. Wasiolek, Sue.
II. Crossman, Anne. III. Title.
  LB2343.32.F433 2008
  378.1'98—dc22

                                                2007039776

Printed in Canada on recycled paper (100% PCW)
First printing, 2008

1 2 3 4 5 6 7 8 9 10 — 12 11 10 09 08

To the faculty mentors who helped me get the best out of my college and graduate experience, and to the mentorees who help me get the best out of being a professor.

PETER

To my mom, who continues to inspire me to become a well-educated person. Thanks for studying with me, taking me to the library every Sunday, and buying me every book I ever wanted.
(Just think, you won't have to buy this one!)

SUE

With heaps of gratitude to my parents and grandparents for their tireless love and sacrifice in propelling me toward my dreams, and to my husband for helping me make them a reality.

ANNE

Contents

Acknowledgments

We are grateful, first and foremost, to and for each other. Writing this book has been an adventure all its own and a great learning experience—rather like college, actually. Peter and Sue built up the idea for nearly a decade, advancing it by baby steps because most conversations took place at the gym or at loud college social functions. It was not until indefatigable Anne joined the merry band that we got this book steadily under way.

That said, we could not have written the book without the countless students, faculty, and administrators who, over the years, have shared with us their lessons learned the hard way. Some, like Mel Baars, will easily find themselves in the anecdotes we have included. Others will have to look a bit harder, but we assure you that you're here—in the stories, in the counsel, and in our most sincere gratitude.

We eagerly thank all those who read the draft manuscript, in whole or in part, and gave us the kind of trenchant feedback we needed. We especially thank Dorothy Lou Bailey, Autumn Bonner, Nick Bonner, Barbara Carlson, Josh Crossman, Lisa Disbrow, John Feaver, Ruth Feaver, Carol Fidler, Arunabha Guha, Beth Whitehead, and John Zink.

And we thank Sheila Curran, who led us to the good people of Ten Speed Press, particularly Aaron Wehner and Brie Mazurek.

Above all, we would like to thank our families, who were supportive and patient (not to mention long-suffering!) through this process. A special apology to Karen, who too many nights caught

Peter sending furtive emails of chapter drafts after a long hard day at the White House. And a special thanks to Josh for giving up kayaking for a year of weekends to watch their son so Anne could warm a seat at the Seattle Public Library. (Josh—Thank you for your tireless cheerleading, feedback, and support both in this writing venture and the others. I could not—and would not—have done this without you. —Anne)

Introduction

Everybody knows that college is expensive—it doesn't take a fancy degree to understand that. And yet somehow or another most people who are able to get into college find a way to pay for it. The premise of this book is that, as hard as it is to select and pay for college, most people figure that part out. The unexpectedly hard part—the part that in our opinion most people get wrong—is getting their money's worth. Yes, paying tuition is a challenge. But making the most of that tuition is harder still.

As a prof, a dean, and a recent grad, we have advised thousands of students on how to get into the college they want and how to get out of college what they need. We have learned that few students (and even fewer parents) appreciate a fundamental secret: it matters less where students go than what they accomplish once they get there.

There are lots of books telling students how to get into the college they want and how to pay for it once they do. This is not one of those books. This book begins where they leave off.

Bright, eager students work unbelievably hard to get into college and are willing to shoulder an enormous financial burden along the way. Then, after that huge investment of time and money, those same students settle for a mediocre college experience. Some even graduate without the skills or glowing recommendations they need to succeed at the next level. Every spring we hear the graduate groan, "I wish I had known that as a freshman." But, not you. This book is, in a way, an antidote to the uneven advising that afflicts most colleges—even the most prestigious ones.

Designed to help you start well and finish strong, this book is aimed at the incoming first-year student, beginning with the most common freshmen concerns about dorm life, leaving home, and deciding the fall schedule. But we guarantee that even seniors will find helpful tips as we discuss how to decide between the summer internship or paying job, how to balance the desire for an attractive GPA with a respectable course load, when and how to ask professors for that glowing recommendation (and how to actually earn one), and how to make memories as an undergrad that you'll enjoy remembering. After decades of collective experience advising students, we have learned—and watched others learn—these lessons the hard way so that you don't have to.

Since parents tend to believe the purpose of college is to gain an education, while students tend to see it as a rite of passage into adulthood that includes a few classes, we have built our chapters to appeal to both points of view. The chapters explore both curricular and extracurricular topics and are organized somewhat chronologically, based on how students will most likely encounter them, which enables them to be read at random or as a progression.

What qualifies us to help you get the best out of college is a distinctive blend of perspectives and a shared passion for making higher education worth the price tag. Peter Feaver has won two teaching awards as a professor of political science at Duke University. He is prominent in research and public policy–making circles in the area of American foreign policy, but he has written this book because some of his most rewarding experiences have been interacting with students inside and outside the classroom. Sue Wasiolek, assistant vice president for student affairs and dean of students at Duke University, is known as "Dean Sue"—a seasoned administrator who has been mentoring students and troubleshooting student life for twenty-eight years. She has regularly taught classes during that time but is best known on campus for her deep engagement with students in the extracurricular parts of their college experience.

Anne Crossman, a recent Duke alumna, founded a student group as a freshman to mentor first-year students as they slalom through the college scene. She is also passionate about helping students achieve their best, and taught both public high school and college students before retiring to become a full-time mom and author.

Most importantly, we are people who have spent a long time helping students get more out of their college experience than they would have otherwise. We are honored to be joining you in your journey.

CHAPTER 1

"You Expect Me to Live with a Stranger?"

Managing Life in the Dorm

It's been played countless times across the theater of your imagination. Perhaps desperately—inspired by those days when your little sister plucked your last nerve. Perhaps wistfully—when she wrote you that sentimental birthday card and you got misty-eyed thinking that you wouldn't get to watch her grow up. Heck, maybe you tried a dry run when you were six, filling your Snoopy suitcase with Pop-Tarts and getting as far as the mailbox. And now you are leaving home for real. Your parents' car is packed to the hilt, your welcome packet is at the ready, and any minute now you will be pulling up to what will be home for the next four years.

You are not alone. Tens of thousands of peers are heading in the same metaphorical direction. And one (or more) is heading quite literally to the exact same place you are.

Life with a roommate will be full of surprises—from a scenario so awful it's worthy of a novel to best friends who found a multibillion-dollar company and whose children later intermarry to form a dynasty, and everything in between. What to expect is anyone's guess.

Here is our confident prediction: your roommate will be another flawed human being with complementary strengths as well as aggravating weaknesses. Shocker, we know. Learning to manage this is probably the first hurdle a freshman faces (which is why we begin the book here). It is a big part of the rite of passage that college has become. But you should not let it determine the success or failure of your college career.

Sharing personal details, inadequate space, and possessions can be tense at times—and that's assuming both parties get along. Yet, after a brief period of adjustment, most students describe their residence experiences on campus as being a highlight of their college careers, enabling them to find timely support that often led to friendship.

> **Life with a roommate will be full of surprises—from a scenario so awful it's worthy of a novel to best friends who found a multibillion-dollar company and whose children later intermarry to form a dynasty, and everything in between. What to expect is anyone's guess.**

A positive experience can make your college career gleam while a negative one can feel like a literal disaster; our goal is to help you avoid the latter. The former is kismet, meaning there is only so much you can do to make it happen. The latter is also partly a matter of luck—bad luck—but that doesn't mean you need to build a shrine with magic trolls to keep evil at bay.

The wise student learns how to manage this relationship *before* any crises occur so it never becomes so tense that it leads to discord. There are lots of areas in this book where we will encourage you to push yourself to get the best out of college; however, in this chapter we will advocate the opposite philosophy. As influential as your roommate experience might be on your day-to-day happy meter, of all the areas of college life needing your attention we recommend this area be low on your list of priorities. Rather than maximize the upside, minimize the downside.

It's not that the roommate relationship doesn't consume your life; it's that it shouldn't. We wouldn't dare suggest that your roommate isn't worth your time; a meta-theme of this book is that relationships matter and they certainly hold priority. But the natural inclination of most students is to invest too much time in this piece of the college experience and not enough in the others, which is why we tilt against it and advise heaps of thoughtful communication early on so the relationship will continue smoothly and require little course correction from there. Stay tuned for more on how to go about that.

Night Owl or Early Bird?

Filling Out the Questionnaire

Shortly after mailing in your acceptance card saying "I choose YOU," you'll receive a rather plump packet in the mail most likely full of brochures on classes, student rights on campus, and, somewhere within the ream, a roommate questionnaire. *Don't blow this one off.*

This is one of those applications that parents love to fill out and oftentimes—with the best intentions, of course—parents will answer the questions the way they wish their child were in the hopes that their roommate will fit this description and rub off on them. Or, students will fill out this form afraid of what their parents will read and so they don't really tell the truth, particularly when it comes to smoking. This is not the time for subtlety. If there is something you feel adamant about concerning your roommate or your own personality, be as clear as possible.

Sometimes the questions are elaborately creative, like "If you were a toaster pastry, what flavor would you be?" while others are the basic "Do you study late at night or early in the morning?" Unless you know someone in the residential life office, you probably won't know which questions are the decisive ones, so put equal effort into each of them. One of the most critical questions is whether or not the roommate smokes, and it's typically a key decider in the matching process

This is not the time to compromise. The most basic rule of filling out this form is honesty. Don't answer questions as if you were the person your parents think you are, the person your parents want you to be, or the person you wish you were—stick with who you are. If need be, send it in without sharing a copy with Mom and Dad. On the other hand, if you have an open, candid relationship with your parents, let them have a peek; more than anyone else, they know what it is like to live with you and they may have key points to emphasize. If you're a glutton for punishment and really want honesty, you might even share it with a sibling.

Granted, you will change in college. We all did. But start out by telling your interests. If you like leaving your room messy, say so. If you think having a non-color-coded sock filing system is a near cardinal sin, say that too. Some forms ask about sleep schedules and others musical preferences. (Please—just tell the truth, even if it is a horrible truth like you can't get to sleep without listening to *Love Songs on the Accordion.*) It leads to a much better chance of matching you with an appropriate roommate, and, should conflicts arise later, your resident advisor (RA) may refer to what you wrote on this form as a starting point in reaching a compromise. The key is not to agree to something on the form that you aren't willing to do, because you will most likely be held to your word if a problem arises later.

One last point: be considerate. We know of an RA who was called in to referee a particularly thorny dispute. Apparently some young woman had strongly requested a nonsmoker on her roommate questionnaire and was granted one, but she didn't bother to mention that she was a smoker herself. What was she thinking? She later told the housing staff that she requested a nonsmoker because she thought two people smoking in one room would have been too much.

Back Away from the Kitchen Sink
Packing for College

Ridiculous as it may sound, a couple of years ago a student arrived on campus with a U-haul on freshman move-in day. As he backed it up to the entrance and rolled up the door everyone was in suspense—what could he possibly be bringing that required a moving truck? Out came his dolly with a full-sized fridge. It got as far as the dorm's front stoop and was wisely sent back by an insistent RA.

What many freshmen may not realize as they pack is they can't duplicate what they have at home, and all that stuff won't be necessary in order to feel at home either. Assemble what you feel like you can't live without, then pack only 60 percent of that. Try to imagine how you will store your stuff in the off-season once your parents' minivan isn't around and you have to pay for every cubic foot you fill. Take an honest look at each memento and be sure you absolutely need it—and that you are willing to pay (over and over again) to store it for the next four years.

Besides hauling it, a key factor in deciding what to pack is whether or not your school is located near a Big Mart. If yes, then it's probably worth erring on the side of taking too little. Other than a toothbrush, a change of clothes, and towel, it is very unlikely that you'll need absolutely everything from day one. You can always shop for the right stuff once you figure out what that is.

> **In packing for college, assemble what you feel like you can't live without, then pack only 60 percent of that.**

Okay, maybe you need a little more than a toothbrush, but you certainly need less than you may initially want to pack. Even if there isn't a Big Mart, most on-campus stores will have what you need. The bookstore is a mini department store of sorts, though probably more expensive and not as extensive a selection. It's also cheaper to have Mom and Dad mail you something later on than it is to have overloaded your small room and then *you* have to mail multiple items back home.

To combat this "kitchen sink syndrome," some colleges mail a brief list of what you will need to bring to campus: typically a set of sheets, a bath towel, a warm coat, toiletries, and a pillow. It's pretty basic. You won't immediately need Christmas decorations. Or scrapbooks. Or your library. Or a sofa. And you most certainly won't need your antique guitar or your grandmother's diamond earrings . . . belongings get damaged or lost, and it's best to leave the valuables at home with the folks. Clay *did* bring his brand-new acoustic guitar and discovered his roommate etching his frustration into it one day with a cafeteria knife. If you play a musical instrument and want to bring it, please do, but make sure it's not a family heirloom. Even the most practical of valuables can get dinged, such as Michele's laptop, which ingested half a can of beer when an inebriated hall mate stopped by to say hello. $*^@!

One off-the-wall suggestion we can offer: don't arrive with a full year's wardrobe. To start, the closets are super tiny (as most things in your room will be), and yours won't hold all you're used to storing at home. Even more so, there tends to be an abrupt style shift that happens in the second half of the year as people return from studying abroad and from holiday shopping. Whereas high school sort of melded together one academic year at a time, spring and fall have a very split feel to them, almost as if they were separate years of study. Clothing styles make a notable adjustment come spring, regardless of the weather. If staying au courant with fashion is important to you, hedge your bets and save your money and some closet space for January; there will most likely be a new look and you'll want to be ready for it. (These deep wardrobe insights were brought to your attention by none other than the coiffed and fashionably astute Peter Feaver—as they say, those who can't do, teach.)

If you are the type who really must have every T crossed before you arrive (and don't worry, we are more empathetic with that sort than we sound—if pressured, one of us could be forced to admit she even packed crates of soy milk when she moved into her freshman dorm), a lot of schools now provide the dimensions of the rooms and even CAD drawings online so you will have fewer surprises about what fits where. Be forewarned that your roommate might have her own ideas about how to arrange the furniture and may not want to sleep in a bunk bed just so you can fit the love seat in the room. One thing you'll definitely want to know is whether or not the residence hall is air-conditioned. If not, and you are going to college in a steamy climate, a fan or two or three is a must, even starting the first night.

One final note, and we'll leave you to return to your suitcase. It's worth mentioning that some students may feel pressure to buy everything up front while they can still saddle Mom and Dad with the bill—a wise economic strategy from the student's point of view. However, it creates perverse incentives to buy stuff you don't need and may tax your folks' budget. The compounding purchases may cause them to balk at some spending where they might have been generous otherwise. Consider making a deal with them. Ask what they have set aside for your dorm purchases and whether or not they intend for you to pay for everything else once your feet hit your dorm stoop. Depending on their expectations, you may be able to split the amount and spend 60 percent now and 40 percent later. Or perhaps they would be willing to set up a bank account where they automatically deposit some fraction of that amount each month, minimizing discussions about your spending habits. We realize that an enterprising student might say that he would like 100 percent now and then another 50 percent in January. Of course, we can't recommend that. This book is about getting all that you can out of college, not out of your parents.

How Sweet Is a Suite (or a Single)?

Of all your years, freshman year is the best time to have a room-mate. Deciding on how many roommates to have (or if you want a roommate at all) . . . now that's a good question. Some colleges give you a choice, and some surprise you with a threesome in a double-sized room just because they are short on space. (Another GREAT reason to pack less.) Regardless, unless you have some sleeping disorder that causes you to wake screaming each night at 2 a.m. and you are worried about it harming your relationship with a roommate, consider opting for one or more roommates and save the single for grad school or your senior year.

Steve opted for a single by accident when he filled out his roommate questionnaire. For some reason, he thought he was checking the box requesting a single roommate as opposed to two or three roommates. It turned out to be a very lonely experience the first few weeks, and it was harder to win friends in the dorm because his hall mates assumed he was antisocial by opting for a single. Their assumptions were wrong, and Steve admits the year wasn't as interesting as it could have been had there been someone to share his space.

You'll find that it's easier to move from a double or suite into a single than the other way around. Another incentive is that hav-ing a roommate will bring social traffic into your room, which will in turn broaden your circle of friendships on campus. The bottom line is you'll be missing out on one of the fundamental elements of the college experience if you decide to room alone. And, anyway, it's only for a year.

On the other hand, opting for a four-person suite may be more than you bargained for. The number of roommates you request is a highly personal decision that depends entirely on your capacity for delightful entropy. A lot of it depends on how many siblings you have or wish you had, whether you consider yourself an introvert or extrovert, and what sort of setting will make you feel most at home.

Two housing alternatives offered by some colleges are campus apartments or student cooperatives. Since the value and challenges of each vary from campus to campus, it's difficult to make a recommendation here. No matter how wonderful these alternatives might be at your school, we would advise living in a dorm your first year on campus because it's nearly always the strongest hive of activity and networking. Beyond that, if you are interested in campus apartments or co-ops for the future, spend the year talking to upperclassmen about the ups and downs of living there. Ask questions about parking (will you need a car or is there adequate bus service for buying groceries and getting to class?), safety (what kind of police or security surveillance is provided?), how people interact (is it just a large group of cliques that never intermingle?), and trends of being involved on campus (do students seem to disappear from campus life once they leave mainstream housing?). It could be a winning combination or a bomb, and your sleuthing will be able to determine what the best fit is for you.

Steel-Toe Boots or Flip-Flops
First Impressions and Putting Your Best Foot Forward

Some colleges give students the option to contact their roommates before the school year starts, while others prefer the sink-or-swim approach and save the introduction for freshman orientation. If you're given the choice, our advice is to opt for a conversation beforehand but to limit it to very superficial sorts of topics to get to know each other. Don't dive right in to the nuts and bolts of life just yet. Though we recognize we're in the age of email and online chats, we recommend you handle the first couple of conversations by phone. Here's why.

THE PHONE IS YOUR FRIEND

Zia was a freshman from Bangladesh who was attending college on a student visa. After being on campus just a few weeks, he admitted to us that he and his roommate had met online earlier that summer, and that it hadn't gone well. (As is true with all of our anecdotes, the names have been changed to protect friendships, but the details are oh so true. Honest.) His roommate was an African American from New York who was enthralled with hip-hop. After swapping images for their blogs, he gave Zia the online nickname "Z-dog." Needless to say, Zia wasn't big on this particular nickname, and though he would listen to hip-hop from time to time, his passion for it wasn't anything close to his roommate's. Their exchange of emails that summer (which often centered around hip-hop) left Zia feeling completely out of his comfort zone, and he worried that, come move-in day, they would be polar opposites. Miracle of miracles, after a little face time and a few conversations around campus-related topics, the two are getting along famously. Much to his relief, "Z-dog" now goes by "Zia" again, and he gladly admits that he had the wrong impression of his roommate before coming to campus.

Email is such a delicate medium. You may have experienced how difficult it can be to decipher (or express) emotion accurately, whether there are emoticons or not. Zia's experience is not all that uncommon, and since you don't have any goodwill to spare in this relationship just yet, we suggest you prevent any potential miscommunication and stick to the phone. See this phone conversation as a great opportunity to practice the standard spiel you will give a couple hundred times over the next few months about who you are, where you're from, why you came, and what you want to do with the next seventy years of your life.

But, what about that awfully uncomfortable, eternal-feeling pause when no one knows what to say? Consider scheduling the conversation via email so that you can have your head in the game when you sit down to talk. And—this may seem a bit like overkill but you will thank us later when silence erupts—consider writing a list of five to ten questions you want to ask during the call and then perhaps a nice line or two so you know how to end the call. It will help you remember which details you want to cover, such as if he's bringing a fridge and does he mind sharing.

Your first conversation should be about interests at home and what you hope to do while you're in school (such as wanting to audition for a play or find a crazy work-study job). Dorm gadgets are also a safe topic as well as a great money saver, since you may not need two coffee pots. If your roommate seems willing to share (and you are able to give as well as take) then synchronize. Printers, refrigerators, microwaves, coffee pots, a sound system, and NASA-quality video gaming equipment are cumbersome and there is lit-tle reason to have two of each. You may want to discuss potential room configurations or the notion of borrowing. Some students enter with the mind-set that there are certain items they are will-ing to share from a practical standpoint and others they are not. Even if you don't resolve this question entirely during the first conversation, it's okay to at least get the topic on the table. Hoping, of course, that microwaves are allowed in the dorm, you can pur-chase one and bring it to campus unopened. Once you've met your roommate in person and worked out the details about shared space, your folks can return it if necessary. Just save your receipt.

Other conversations, such as how to handle overnight guests or whether or not you should institute a lights-out curfew, are probably better discussed in person. Your dorm will have informa-tion and regulations on these topics and others when you arrive, so there is no need to go into them beforehand.

Feel free to share some generic background about yourself, like whether or not you go to church or if you're gone every weekend playing golf, so that your roommate can calibrate what to expect. Keep the info minimal, and as you listen to your roommate's side of things, be careful of forming too strong an opinion. It's difficult to know how the freedoms of college will affect a person, and he may not even realize himself how much he will change. Also, figure his parents—who want to know all about you too—are standing nearby as you talk, so he may not be as candid as you might think.

If your faith is important to you and influences a lot of who you are, mention it in a nonthreatening way just so your roommate is aware that it will be a noticeable part of your life. This is not the time to try and convert him to your way of seeing the world. Those sorts of conversations are encouraged in college, but when it comes to a new roommate, you want to give that conversation at least a couple months. You'll have plenty else to talk about.

It's best to treat this person as a prospective friend, not an automatic one. Don't set expectations (either with yourself or promises to each other) of how close this friendship will become. What often happens when those sorts of expectations are made and folks don't click is that someone gets miffed or hurt, and then the situation gets awkward. Instead, let the friendship develop naturally as you will all your other relationships on campus.

SHOULD YOU ROOM WITH A FRIEND?

If you are attending a college in state along with other graduates from your high school, you may be given the option as a freshman to room with someone you know. We've had a number of students query us on this point, and our answer is that we've seen mixed results. We know of some students who were great friends before becoming roommates but then were terribly disappointed by the experience and it dampened their friendship. And then we know of others where rooming together galvanized their friendship all

Rolling Out the Red Carpet
Move-In Day

It's your first and probably only "freshman move-in day." However new it may feel, since you are not the first freshman ever, don't feel like you're encountering this new phase alone. Your college has done this many, many times before and most likely will have some sort of plan to help you overcome the initial hurdles. Read their instructions. Follow their instructions. Show up where they say and when they say. There's no need to arrive super early, but don't be late either.

While we're handing out "don'ts," here's another one: don't trust the first impressions you draw of your roommate or his family, especially if they are negative. Chances are he has endured an awkward car ride with parents, great physical strain trying to defy several laws of thermodynamics in moving things that space will not permit into his room, is a slight bit nauseated about what the year will hold, and is trying to help his parents deal with their own emotional upheaval—it's an emotional powder keg. Make a promise to yourself that you'll hold those initial impressions lightly. Also, try not to focus too much on what your parents think of your new roommate. They don't have to live with him—you do!

While you're at it, you may want to hold your furniture hopes lightly. If you haven't had a chance to coordinate with your roommate in advance—or even if you have, people have been known to change their minds—you will most likely have two of some items when you really only need one. The first day as roommates offers up an unnecessary test of who will give up their whatever-it-is first. Be the first one to compromise if you find that your coordinated plans with your new roommate fall short of the mark. Avoiding small battles early could make a big difference in preventing larger skirmishes later in the year. It's not that you need to roll over for every minor complication, but it doesn't hurt to be the generous one up front so you have a greater say on the big-ticket decisions that may come later.

the more. It can go either way. Since there is no way to know, we advise students to venture out. Consider this high-school buddy a person already in your friendship circle and seek to add someone new to make the circle even bigger.

Compromise Isn't a Four-Letter Word
Writing Your Roommate Agreement

Yes, we know you can count as well as spell, but some people don't recognize compromise for the art form it truly is. Offering to go the second mile is a good first-day move. It is also a useful frame of mind to have for the first couple weeks. It's a mistake to approach discussions like you are the United States and she is North Korea. At least with roommates, compromise can be a show of strength and will not inevitably lead to international nuclear blackmail. If things get rough, you can always appeal to the RA, who is a lot more capable of effective action than the UN.

One of the most important things you will do your first week of school is fill in some sort of roommate agreement, typically given out by your RAs, to help guide you over the next year. Some schools may not provide a formal agreement but will just encourage you to establish some ground rules and then talk with your roommate whenever there is any sort of misunderstanding. (If that's the case, you may want to use some of the headings in this chapter to outline your discussion.) Putting your roommate agreement down on paper can certainly help identify any potential misunderstandings before they occur, but whether it is written or not, it is important that you discuss expectations ahead of time in order to avoid conflict. Topics to discuss might be whether or not you have a food or animal allergy, if you want to have an agreed time for lights out and music off, whether or not it's okay to have family members sleep on the floor when they visit from out of town, and, if the setup of the room is less fair to one of you, what changes can be made to balance the score for second semester. Feel free to ask your RA for help in either identifying potential concerns or in mediating your discussion should conflict arise.

CULTURAL DIFFERENCES

Should you be assigned roommates from a different cultural background or a different country, recognize that they may have unique forms for expressing dislike and working out compromises, so keep your radar up. Although you and your roommates will have a lot in common as college students, you'll also want to remain sensitive to how you are different.

Allie grew up in a small town and was excited to discover on move-in day that her roommate, who had a name she wasn't sure how to pronounce, was from Thailand. What Allie didn't realize was that, as an international student, Prasert had arrived days earlier. She had been enjoying her solitude when an entourage of parents and boxes arrived and overwhelmed her with clutter. As the year wore on, Allie learned that "okay" didn't always mean okay and that Prasert valued saving face and a type of humility that meant not standing up for oneself whenever they discussed areas of disagreement. She also learned that when Prasert gave her a gift, it was important to display it in a place of honor for a time as a way of showing gratitude, regardless of whether she liked it or not. This might seem an unfair burden on Allie, but given all that Prasert was adjusting to in living in a new country, it was a very small burden, if that. Having Prasert for a roommate also gave Allie the privilege of introducing her to college football and the pregame bonfire, not to mention the opportunity to escape campus with Prasert to explore the city nearby when her engineering and computer double major got to be too much. It was an unforgettable year for both, with a lot of great memories.

Whether or not she is an international student, your roommate will most likely arrive with needs or communication styles that won't be like yours, so it's best to assume that up front. Should you find yourself living with a Prasert of sorts, recognize that she may find it odd and more than a little alarming that students paint themselves in school colors and prance half-nude in front of tens of thousands of other people, not to mention the television cameras. Collegiate athletics is an American thing. Try to see it through an international student's eyes. And, consider yourself fortunate, since having an internationally astute roommate could become a valuable part of your college education.

OVERNIGHT GUESTS

There are bigger questions as well, such as whether romantic guests should be allowed and, if so, how to notify each other to prevent an embarrassing situation. Students usually try to be very understanding of their roommates' requests but often don't know how to respond when those requests get way out of hand, which they can do in a short matter of time. It's best to be clear about your expectations up front and to hear your roommate's side of things as well, and then to go with the highest standard—meaning, if one of you says, "No overnight guests," then consider the rule concrete even if you disagree and move on. Your room is a shared space where both of you should feel at home and welcome to return at any time. It's actually not that unusual for roommates to choose the "no vacancy" policy, so if that's what you decide to go with, think of it as helping to prevent any potential miscommunications that could result in embarrassing, painful, or risky situations.

ALCOHOL

Alcohol can become an issue when a drinker and a nondrinker room together. The drinker wants to make the room party central and uses the nondrinker's blender for margaritas or, worse, returns to the room quite ill. There are people on staff to help with that, particularly the latter scenario. Grab the closest RA and ask for help or even a quiet place to sleep while your roommate recovers from his hangover.

In a situation where you are uncertain how much alcohol your roommate consumed, it is most important that you let someone on staff in your hall know that your roommate is not doing well. RAs are less concerned about underage drinking than they are about the potential for alcohol poisoning, and unless you have been trained to make that sort of diagnosis it's best to bring in some outside help. (In fact, to encourage students to protect each other's health and to prevent alcohol-related deaths, many colleges provide a sort of backdoor policy so you can take a friend to the ER without anyone being penalized.) After all, the risk of getting your roommate in trouble should be the least of your worries.

Diagnosing whether or not your roommate has had "too much" to drink will be complicated by your not knowing his health history or if he's taking meds that react negatively to alcohol. Your safest bet is to assume your roommate needs help if he is unable to tell you coherently why he does not.

We know of one freshman named Pat who returned to his dorm room clearly ill after a party one night, but whose roommates assumed he was simply hungover. What they didn't realize was that, along with having had too much to drink, Pat also had a very fast-developing form of meningitis. Tragically, once they did get help, it was too late and he died a few hours after being taken to the ER. Given the possibility that your roommate may be at risk—and this may sound harsh, but it's true—it's better to brave looking like a tattler than to be selfish by prioritizing your feelings over your friend's health. More than likely he will feel bad for putting you in the awkward position of having to choose what was best for him and will appreciate that you were looking out for his safety. If he isn't, tell him we said he should be.

DRUGS

Most colleges reflect the prevailing view in society: drug infractions are taken far more seriously than alcohol infractions. You and your roommate will come to some understanding about drugs and whether you will or won't allow them in your room. Whatever your agreement, remember that the responsibility (and culpability) for what happens in the room rests with *both* of you. So, your decisions about drugs could have consequences for both of you, even if you don't plan to partake. Some schools hold students accountable for the deeds of their roommates. The honor code may require that you report or otherwise take action if you witness your roommate or hall mates partaking. Beyond medical implications, your roommate smoking pot in the room can also have consequences for your academic record. Even if you have agreed with your roommate to be a passive participant, your role as an observer could spell trouble, so be wary what you agree to. There are ways to toe the line without feeling like a rat, and your RA is a great resource on this question. Not to worry, your RA doesn't have to report everything, especially when you're just looking for info and asking hypothetical questions. For instance, you might ask the RA, "What if a student is using drugs in his room and his roommate knows but doesn't join in—will both of them get in trouble?" or "What if the roommate isn't in the room at the time drugs are being used—will both still be penalized?" While you're at it, you might want to ask similar questions about alcohol.

VALUES

One issue that typically isn't an issue, though some might assume it would be, is religious or political values. It's easier to share a room with a flaming politician from the "wrong" side than it is for the über-organized to live with the organizationally challenged. Intellectual differences can be bridged far more easily than lifestyle. While you may converse in polite terms on these sorts of subjects, there may be a point when you don't want to discuss them further. Your roommate—like you—will most likely have an opinion about everything in your life, and since you are living together will know more about you than you may want to reveal to most people. Figure out an appropriate boundary for sharing opinions. Agree on some sort of code or response that wraps up the conversation when one of you has had enough so you never have to resort to punching the red button. Sometimes, it's best to agree to disagree, and this can be acknowledged with something as simple as, "Well, we've danced around this issue before, and I'm sure we'll talk about it in the future, but I need to put it on pause for now so I can get some sleep before my test tomorrow."

Most Common Roommate Complaints

We began our discussion of roommates by talking about the value of compromise, but at times compromise is not possible or is not enough. In digging for anecdotes on this topic, we've ended up with some fairly anemic examples—not for lack of drama, of course, but because we lose something in translation. Most scuffles between roommates tend to be so petty that it's ridiculous to put them into print. Something happens early on in the relationship that sets the melee in motion, and the straw that turns the proverbial camel into a paraplegic is that one roommate used the other's dishwashing detergent without asking. Of course, more lurks beneath the issue than stolen soap, but that's all that exists on file and so what results is a set of bitter roommates whose complaint can't be truly resolved because it can't be pinpointed.

COMPLAINT #1:
DIFFERENT DEFINITIONS OF "CLEAN"

Hygiene may not appear on the roommate agreement, but, hands down, it wins the dubious honor of being roommate complaint #1. The slob and the neatnik tend to butt heads. If you find yourself in this situation, you may feel tempted to draw a line down the center of the room, demarcating "your" territory and "his" territory, but that kind of compromise rarely works since odors don't respect boundaries. The problem will be further exacerbated if the neat roomie decides to straighten up for the cluttered roomie and ends up losing or misplacing something the cluttered roomie needed (and surprisingly had organized in some entropic method for sorting.) Aim for a preventative agreement on this one—like who vacuums which weeks or where the dirty dishes will be stored to keep the room from reeking. And, by all means, come to an agreement about this early in the game while your room is still relatively clean!

COMPLAINT #2:
DIFFERENT STUDY HABITS

If hygiene is complaint #1, then study habits is #2. There are two key components: when to study and how to study. Are you an early riser? Do you plan on setting your alarm for 5 a.m. so you can head to the library? This might cause your roommate some frustration considering she was up studying until 3 a.m. and just entered her sleep rhythm as you started bustling around the room. Do you require absolute silence, or do you need to hear the plaintive whine of bagpipes when you hit the books? Do you take frequent breaks, or do you need a marathon of uninterrupted intensity? Differential workloads may also be a cause of contention, since the lit major appears to be lounging around reading on her bed while the bio chem major is hunched over her desk crunching numbers. The easiest solution to this scenario is to suggest that neither of you use your room as a primary place of study.

COMPLAINT #3:
DIFFERENT BEDTIME RITUALS

Complaint #3 is differing sleep patterns. One roommate may want to sleep with the window open in the dead of winter while the other is from Arizona and thinks anything under 74°F is uncomfortable. Or, one roommate may need to fall asleep to white noise while the other prefers dead silence.

The good news is that, should you someday marry, these roommate sorts of discussions will come up again, so consider them great practice. It may be that you need to help buy your roomie a down comforter or suggest he listen to soundscapes on his headset instead of the stereo. We could fill the remainder of the chapter with suggestions, but you're smart enough to come up with them on your own. The point is that the two of you should reach some sort of compromise that is equally unsatisfactory to you both (that's how you know it's a true compromise) and try to get some shut-eye.

COMPLAINT #4:
DIFFERENT MESSAGE-TAKING EXPECTATIONS

Roommates not delivering messages is often the fourth complaint. Like everything else, set some reasonable expectations about taking messages. If you plan to have a landline and you aren't willing to play secretary, get voice mail and ask the caller to call back and leave her message. On the other hand, mature adults take useful messages for each other. You have not become someone's tool just because you record the date, time, name, and number of the caller. The same is true of visitors who drop by and leave notes. Have a designated location for sticky notes and ask the visitor to leave it there. Being clear about your willingness to participate in messaging is far better than attempting it halfheartedly and failing.

ADDRESSING ROOMMATE COMPLAINTS

In general, the most successful strategy for dealing with a disagreement is to speak up long before the issue becomes so painful that it cannot be resolved. A great deal of that will be knowing your own limits and asking for help when it's needed. You may even want to invoke the "serenity prayer" over yourself, that you would accept the things you cannot change, have courage to change the things you can, and have the wisdom to know the difference.

Feel free to propose your RA as a mediator early on in a conflict. It doesn't need to sound like a threat, such as "If you don't stop, I'm going to tell the RA," but more of "Hey, let's talk with the RA and see if he has any advice." If your roommate is unwilling to see the RA, then go to him on your own. Though it may seem like you're talking about your roommate behind his back, even that is preferable to suppressed rage, which can end catastrophically.

On the little stuff, early sacrifices and early gestures pay off in bigger dividends than you might think. And they don't necessarily lead to doormat status either. Should you be in one of those incredibly rare circumstances where you have a strange roommate who sees these gestures as weakness and takes full advantage of them, your RA is just a couple doors down.

At the end of the day, talk is just talk and actions are actions. If the talk doesn't lead to actions, try to restrain yourself from making a beeline to the housing office to request a new roommate. It's very unlikely you'll be given a new roommate after a few weeks for the simple reason that the dorms are packed and there may not be other options available. Sure, it doesn't hurt to ask but prepare yourself for a no. Even if there are rooms available, the housing office is often unwilling to participate in roommate exchanges because they consider the art of compromise part of the college experience. In some senses, they're right. There is something very meaningful about learning to live with people different than you, both in finding commonalities and in learning to respect and overcome your differences.

However, if the situation hinders your ability to perform in your classes or you start sleeping elsewhere just so you don't have to return to your room, then it's time to take the matter to the authorities. Amy had to resort to applying for a change in roommates the second week of her freshman year when her roomie's reverse sleep habits and consistent pot use within their room made a compromise impossible. For a case such as this, the university was happy to move Amy into a healthier situation and did so within the week. If it's not that bad, stop fretting.

There's a Reason the First House Meeting Is Before the Activities Fair . . .

Before classes start, your residential staff will assemble your dorm for a house meeting. It will probably be the longest one of the year, since they will need to discuss various rules that govern your dorm, identify fire escapes, make introductions, and "Oh! We need to elect officers." Now's your chance to get involved in your dorm. Before raising your hand, be sure you know a few of the ins and outs of taking on a position of dorm leadership.

First off, becoming the president of your dorm is a great way to feel like you are established and to get to know people quickly. We give it props for that. If you don't want to be president, there are a host of other responsibilities. Kim signed up to help organize the semiannual blood drive. It turns out she ended up needing surgery later that year, which became an added incentive for dorm mates to donate blood. In fact, Kim made a game out of it and kept her blood type a secret until the end so people of all types would visit the blood bank. She spent the rest of the year being called by various blood-related nicknames but enjoyed that it helped her get to know folks. Even so, she invested very little time into the program beyond what was necessary since it wasn't a major focus for her college career.

The same points we recommend later on in chapter 4 about extracurricular activities hold true here in terms of time investment. Most dorm activities—even leadership positions—are probably modest payoff activities. On the positive side, they offer a ready opportunity for leadership and getting to know administrators (which might lead to good letters of recommendation.) On the negative, dorm activities are neither the noble humanitarian work of community service nor the intellectually stimulating experience of serving as a research assistant—the kinds of extracurriculars that produce great anecdotes for job interviews or expand your mind in new directions.

Getting involved in dorm life is great. But most students will want to take advantage of the opportunities colleges offer beyond residential life, so you will want to pace yourself. Get involved in residential life but at a minimal level. There is a unique level of community you experience just by living in a dorm, so enjoy it and maximize it for all it's worth.

Real Life Lessons, Compliments of Your Dorm

View college life as a round-the-clock learning experience. (Understandably, that's what happens when you live at school.) Even your dorm will offer up nuggets of insight. Let's take, for example, the often-overlooked service the university performs in cleaning up after you. If you live in a residence hall, it is likely that the university provides housekeeping services for public areas such as hallways, bathrooms, and lounges. (Don't get too excited, you're still responsible for cleaning your own room.) It happens without asking for it, just like magic. Only it isn't magic. It is hard work performed by real human beings with hopes and dreams and feelings—not unlike you, actually. It can be nasty work too, made all the nastier because—dare we suggest it—college students can sometimes appear to be most ungrateful. (In reality, they're probably just oblivious, but puddles of vomit after Friday night's party are rarely left with an apology note for the guy who has to clean it up.)

Even if they were all too familiar with doing chores at home, most students quickly acclimate themselves to the luxury of a housekeeping service, and since it's "part of tuition," never give a thought to cleaning up after themselves. As a result, the dirt and disregard can make for a demeaning experience for the housekeeping staff. We've taken a tangential rant for a reason, and it isn't just to invoke the rights of the underpaid.

What we are suggesting is that you take these next four years to notice the people who are providing those services and to show yourself grateful. Their work is valuable in helping you focus on your studies—find ways to respect their dignity. Not only is it a valuable life skill and an admirable sign of character, it will hold into your future career. The parking attendants, the security guards, the sanitation service, the grounds folks, the dining hall staff—all make our lives a little easier, and many have not had the opportunities you have to further yourself. Consider it a sign of wisdom and maturity that you have recognized it.

"This Is Not What I Had in Mind When I Left Home"
Worst-Case Roommate Scenarios, Just in Case

Much as we hate to plant the thought in your mind, we would be remiss if we didn't hit upon a few roommate situations that could complicate your year. The chances of you actually encountering any of these are almost the same as those of you being elected homecoming queen (and just to be clear, unless you attend a very small college, we mean to say that the possibility is very, very small).

However, chances are more likely that you may know of someone who is in this situation. So, for their sake and for the enhancement of your own wisdom, read on. Here are five situations that could make for a complicated residential experience.

POSSIBILITY #1:
SHE FORGETS THE "DO NOT DISTURB" SIGN

You walk in on your roommate and the love of her life in what lawyers call "in flagrante delicto" (or, an embarrassingly passionate entanglement). This is not a teachable moment. This is not a moment for a lengthy explanation of your schedule, your embarrassment, and your intention not to tell anyone. This is a moment for a one-word apology and a hasty retreat. Give the situation about an hour to cool off and then consider it safe to come home. Knocking might not be such a bad idea. Be sure to spend the hour thinking about what sorts of activities should take place in your room. If you'd rather this not be repeated, then be up-front about it. Couples have been making whoopee in campus hideaways for years, so it's not like they'll be deprived. This room is your home too, and you need to have the freedom to come home when you want.

POSSIBILITY #2:
HE LOSES HIS WILL TO LIVE

Your roommate attempts or threatens suicide. It goes without saying that this can be devastating for all who know this person. First off, get professional help for you and for your roommate assuming he is, we pray, unsuccessful. These are deep waters and you should not try to navigate them for any length of time without a professional guide.

A few things to consider while you are seeking help: First, your roommate's decision to end (or attempt to end) his life is not your fault. Figure that a lot has gone into this person becoming who he is and don't count yourself to blame. Once you've taken yourself off the dartboard, look for opportunities to reach out to your roommate and his family. It's probably obvious, but this is not the time to be Mr. Popularity by regaling the dorm with tales of your room-mate woes. It's best to be discreet; this discretion will prove you to be not only a mature individual but someone that your friends (troubled or not) will be willing to trust even more so in the future. Consider silence a booster of your respect points.

What will most likely happen is that your roommate will take time off from school and you will be assigned a new roommate. Give that person a clean slate and refrain from placing the burden of assumptions on him—it's a whole new world. Of course, your roommate could also choose not to leave campus but to stay and seek out help. If that's the case, then you will definitely have points to discuss with him about expectations for the rest of the year. Since he is going through a rough patch, it might be best to offer "Hey, do you mind if I bring our RA in on this conversation? I don't want to say anything stupid, and I really don't even know what to expect about your recovery. I'd like to hear his advice." Undoubtedly your roommate will feel like EVERYONE is talking behind his back, so being up-front will hopefully be a relief for him and will start you both back on the right foot.

This advice also applies to other health issues, such as noticing your roommate is struggling with depression or an eating disorder. Be a friend and get help. Ignoring the situation will only allow it to escalate. The same discretion we mentioned earlier of consulting your RA as well as the campus counseling center (as opposed to the dorm blog) applies here. In the end, you and your roomie will thank you for providing vital assistance and doing so in a way that did not expose him to public embarrassment.

POSSIBILITY #3:
SHE COMES OUT OF THE CLOSET

Your roommate decides to tell you that she is a lesbian. Every college we know of assigns same-sex cohabitants, at least initially. The premise behind that pattern is that it takes the sexual dimension out of the equation to allow students to focus on studies. It assumes that students have a right not to have sexual undertones to their rooming situation, unless the roommates have chosen to be in that sort of setting. Even though many mixed male/female roommate situations won't inevitably end up in a sexual relationship, nevertheless the powers that be have decreed that students have a right not to risk it simply because the potential is there.

It follows logically that students have a right not to be rooming in a situation where there is a potential for same-sex romance. It doesn't make you homophobic any more than choosing not to room with someone of the opposite sex makes you heterophobic. However, some colleges do not see it this way. They tend to view it as no different from living with someone from another country—thus, no reason for a roommate change. Of course, other colleges may be able to accommodate everyone involved—you never know until you ask.

In such a situation, we prescribe personal integrity. Communicate openly with your roommate and talk about your concerns. If the issue is raised initially by an "I have something to tell you" conversation, then you cannot avoid it. Your roommate has told you for a reason about her lesbian identity because she wants you to know, and she probably anticipates some sort of response. Feel free to go back to her after you've had a few days to think about it and say just that: "I've had a few days to think about it and I was wondering if we could talk more about how you see this influencing our roommate situation or whether you plan on having your partners over during the night or ways you can help me feel more comfortable with this change in our friendship." All are part of a mature way to proceed forward.

If you are the gay or lesbian roommate, our advice is likewise to be honest about this. You may feel absolutely certain that there is no reason for your roommate to feel awkward, but it is presumptuous of you to make that decision for her. It might be worth checking with the RA or an administrator about what room-swapping options are available before you tell her just so you can offer your roommate the most mature options possible as a friend.

POSSIBILITY #4:
HE *CAN'T* QUIT WHENEVER HE WANTS

Your roommate is a frequent drunk, and not a happy one at that. If you find your roommate is overly prone to this sort of behavior, you would be wise to lean in the other direction. Heck, you might even be able to save your roommate from a life-changing mistake. Be assuaged that you won't need to clean up his vomit for the rest of the year, but a sacrificial gesture early on is wise on a number of accounts. After you've seen what's in store for the year, begin to discuss ways for him to either manage his drinking or have some of his drinking buddies care for him in his stupor so you aren't his designated Girl Friday for every hangover. Repeated binge drinking is not a sign of a fun-loving party animal: it is a sign of alcoholism. Your roommate has a disease and he needs professional help. You aren't that professional help, but you can point him to it, starting with your RA.

POSSIBILITY #5:
SHE'S A HOUSEHOLD NAME

Your roommate is someone famous. She could be "Someone's" daughter, a teen TV star, or a rising athlete. Just to put it in perspective, this situation is almost as likely as the others above—rare, so don't get too excited. But should you end up rooming with a recognizable name, first consider how you would like to be treated were you that remarkable person. (When all else fails, the golden rule makes for a nice fallback plan.) Everyone needs downtime. Everyone needs space where they can relax and be themselves.

As you put yourself in her cleats, you'll come up with some likely scenarios of what to do and not to do. (We're sure you won't line her desk with carbon paper so you can get handwriting samples to sell on eBay.) No matter what this person has done or whom she's related to, chances are she'd just like you to treat her like she's normal.

"My Roommate's a Neanderthal . . .
Am I a Loner for the Rest of the Year?"

Take heart, a bad rooming situation doesn't destroy your chances of a decent collegiate social life. In fact, it doesn't even need to ruin your year. On the other hand, if you expect to be best friends forever it could cause problems. A substantial number of roommates swap after their freshman year. This is not a life sentence or even a marriage. It's more like dating. Even in the rare instances that roommates become the best of buds, it's exceedingly rare (not to mention a tad bit unhealthy) that they become each other's entire social life.

Should you have a less-than-ideal roommate, it is understandable that your expectations of the next one will be a bit higher, especially if you were able to pick that roommate yourself. As big as that balloon of hope might be, don't let it carry you off into some never-never land fantasy that your next roommate will fit some dreamy ideal. We—human beings in general and the writers of this ever helpful guide especially—are not quite as easy to live with as we wish we were, and hence cannot expect those living with us to make our lives speed-bump free either. We all have social flaws of some kind, so it's best you prepare yourself for your next roommate just as you did for this one—expect anything and nothing and everything.

Should you be one of the lucky ones—one of those kindred-spirit-finding roommates—all of this chapter still applies to you. As much as you will love your roommate, there will be things she does that drive you to the breaking point. There will be some hobbies you share and others you positively don't, some habits you appreciate and some you could easily do without. There is no such relationship that is without its kinks, and if there is, well . . . it isn't real.

For the vast majority, the roommate relationship is a good experience. For as many horror stories as there are out there, there are many more stories of roommates being bridesmaids and godparents and lifelong friends. And forging these friendships is itself a learning experience. We all have to learn to work with people, share office space, and perhaps share a home with a spouse. The roommate situation is a wonderful laboratory for refining these skills. Remind yourself (often) that you are learning life skills that will be useful for a number of work, home, or military settings where you are forced to live in close proximity. Experts call all of these skills "emotional intelligence," and this kind of intelligence may be as important or even more important than old-fashioned smarts in determining how successful you will be in life. College will expand your mental intelligence, for sure, but you should also expect to develop your emotional intelligence along the way.

Leaving Home, Phoning Home, and the First Trip Back to the Mother Ship

Maintaining Relationships Back Home

Home is one of the toughest parts of college. Many students discover that maintaining healthy relationships and connections with the old home while getting established in the new home stretches—and sometimes stresses—them in surprising ways. Some miss home too much and stagger around campus like a weepy Hallmark commercial. Others don't miss home enough, or at least feel guilty that they don't, and strain against the proverbial umbilical cord like it was a noose. Still others find that home is changing almost as fast as they are and don't know what to make of it. The truth of the matter is, whether you're enrolled in state or studying three thousand miles away, relationships back home will affect how well you transition into this new phase of independence.

> Whether you're enrolled in state or studying three thousand miles away, relationships back home will affect how well you transition into this new phase of independence.

Things have changed. Your room has possibly been turned into a craft center for Mom. Your high-school friends may seem immature. Your kid sister no longer acts as though you hung the moon. And though you have only been gone a short time, upon returning you find your parents remarkably smarter than when you left them.

Leaving the nest can be a bit rattling for everyone involved, and well-meaning parents can have as hard a time as any (mistakenly

keeping the cord a bit too tight or cutting it a bit too completely.)
Even the most self-sufficient of students can find themselves day-
dreaming of home when they should be studying. If any of this is
starting to sound familiar, don't worry—you're not an alien, and
you're not alone.

"How Do You Explain School to a Higher Intelligence?"
Relating to Your Folks as an Adult

Most likely you grew up hearing stories about the good ol' days
when your mom and dad were in college livin' the high life. Their
tales of meeting each other in the cafeteria line or skipping class
on a Monday just because it was a nice day at the beach or visiting
Chinatown with a Chinese roommate and finally understanding
the menu have probably been romanticized a tad. Okay, bump that
up to *a lot*.

Just because they are nostalgic and oh so old doesn't necessarily mean their suggestions will be irrelevant. Human nature has
not changed dramatically since they were in college and, though
your major may not have existed back then, a lot of their wisdom
may be sound. That said, the college campus *has* changed dramatically in the last twenty years, so some of their advice may no longer fit the situation. For instance, they might not be
aware of the depth of support staff available to students, but they are probably more aware than their
own parents were that you will need help with big life
decisions.

What we are trying to say (delicately, if possible—
who knows who may be reading over your shoulder) is
this: the natural undergrad reaction that Parents Don't
Know A Thing is only *a smidgen* true.

> Before you file
> your folks under
> "antiquated," keep in
> mind that of all the
> people in your life, your
> parents have thought
> about your future longer
> than anyone else.

Here's the kicker: you are changing in ways that neither you
nor your parents fully appreciate—possibly in all senses of that
term. Before you file your folks under "antiquated," keep in mind
that of all the people in your life, your parents have thought about

your future longer than anyone else. Just picture them standing over your crib, you only one day old, and them musing over who you will become. Then, out of love for you and wanting you to become your very best, they sacrificed the upgrade on the car, a vacation here or there, and even the wardrobe they would have liked just to make sure you had braces, tutors, soccer uniforms, and a whole host of other gifts. That long-range perspective is what drives their interests and actions. And, while that may at times feel like they are trying to control your decisions or prevent you from steering your own future, being aware of this dynamic will help put your conversations in perspective. Most likely, they have your best interests at heart.

We doubt you will be surprised to hear that there may be moments of conflict as you differ with your parents about how to make a success of your future. On the whole, parents don't typically care what their child does at college, but they *do* care that what he does might have lingering negative effects on his future. As one wag put it: they don't worry that you will make mistakes, they worry that you will make the w   rong mistakes.

"You Could Be Happy Here—I Could Take Care of You"
The Growing Pains of Leaving Home

"The day I drove off to college was the most emotionally charged moment of my life—even more than my wedding a few years later," said Kyla. "It was almost like attending my own funeral the way my mother kept avoiding eye contact so I wouldn't see her crying, or how my brother was angry because he'd just realized that I was going to miss every one of his band performances. I was excited and then felt guilty that I was excited. I was frightened and then giddy with the possibilities ahead of me. It was exhausting and I nearly wish I could do it again."

Kyla's experience of leaving home may have been more of an emotional roller coaster than yours will be, since she was the first child to leave the nest and the only girl. This heightened response tends to be true if you are the first, last, or only child leaving home.

All parents are usually very proud of their children, regardless of birth order, for taking on new challenges and bettering themselves (as in going to college), and as a result they may experience some mixed emotions—panic, resentment, pride, and maybe even envy—all at the same time. Students whose parents did not go to college could just as well have intense emotions of their own. Perhaps their pride in blazing a new path is tinged with embarrassment that their parents do not have the same educational achievement. The best advice we can offer up front is:

- Be aware that this will be an emotional time for everyone involved.

- Try not to take your family's reactions personally.

- Don't feel like you must make them understand everything you are going through.

There will be time for decompressing and debriefing after the flurry of emotions has died down a little. For the time being, focus on the journey that is ahead of you and know that, in the end, your family wants the best for you.

Unless you have attended boarding school, this is most likely the first time you are leaving home. As a result, how your family actually responds (as opposed to how you expect them to respond) may come as a bit of a shock. Maybe there won't be tears, but we would be surprised if there weren't some frayed nerves and a terse word or two.

What all graduating high-school seniors need to realize is that their grand entrance into college life is (typically) much more bitter than sweet for their parents. Certainly both students and parents will miss each other to some extent. But if the relationship was a healthy one to begin with, parents will experience the "empty nest" as a major loss of closeness and a dreaded change—things will never be the same again.

Your parents will be doing their best to negotiate their own transition into this new condition of life—made even more painful, as

> What all graduating high-school seniors need to realize is that their grand entrance into college life is (typically) much more bitter than sweet for their parents.

Parents' Weekend

Are They Really Going to Come?

You go, and before you know it, they come. The boxes are unpacked, you have your route to class figured out, and the emotional dust has started to settle. Now it's time for parents' weekend. Whether your parents will attend is not automatic. It's not fair to say that no one comes, but on the other hand, it isn't required by the university that they attend. Even the best parents' weekends are to some extent artificial. For instance, because it's on the weekend, your profs won't be around, so your parents will only see the extracurricular side of life. Whether or not they come is up to them—and you.

Assuming they are coming, it would probably help to establish the notion ahead of time that you won't be able to spend every minute of the weekend with them. Most likely you will have work to do—it's not unusual for students to have test prep or papers to write by this point. On the other hand, you owe it to your parents to do as much of your work ahead of time as possible so you can host them around your university. (Don't slack off the week before they come so you can plead a heavy workload and avoid them all weekend!) If you don't think it's worthwhile for them to come either because of your workload or a lack of campus offerings, then say so up front. But if you'd like them to be there, do all you can to make the weekend a fun one.

To improve your chances of a positive weekend, here are a few dos and don'ts we've gleaned from years of observation and experience:

- Introduce your parents to your friends and their parents—other than coming to see you, it's why they're attending the weekend.

- You might prep a tour to walk them through your typical weekly paces so they can see just how far your chem lab is from your writing course, or where you grab your morning bagel. These will make for a nice mental gallery as they picture you in your new life.

- Clean your room. Even if your parents aren't coming, your roommate's parents might be and they will want the full tour. You never know what sort of relationship you will have with these people down the road, and it doesn't hurt to put your best foot forward.

- If you have formed a close working relationship with a couple faculty members, arrange well in advance to introduce your folks to them. It need not be as painfully embarrassing as you imagine. (But be aware that your faculty mentors may have even more awkward social graces than you think your parents do!)

- Even if you don't have a lot of work , don't feel obligated to spend every waking minute with your folks. It's okay to meet up after breakfast or to not sleep over at their hotel room.

- Most campuses offer special shows or programs during parents' weekend, but the tickets can only be purchased by students. If this is something you think they'd enjoy, you'll want to buy tickets in advance since shows tend to sell out quickly.

- Make the good-bye easier on Mom and Dad by sending *them* a care package or putting a nice note in their car—show your maturity by thinking of them first. It will not only remind them how much you love them but will also help them see you as an adult.

- Email them any photos you may have from your weekend together once they're on the road so they're waiting for them when they return home.

we said earlier, if you are the first, last, or only child to leave home. In some respects, they are losing a child and gaining a friend. Your parents may struggle to accept your newfound freedom; and you may find it difficult, at times, to accept your new responsibility to make decisions about your life and to be held accountable for those decisions. This struggle is normal. It will take time for your relationship with your folks to make the transition.

None of this is to make you feel guilty. By all means, go off to college. It is not only a privilege, it's a rite of passage into adulthood that is good and necessary for jump-starting your life. We only mention all this about your parents' emotions so that you can begin the transition well by being that friend they hope you will become.

The permanence of this new stage in life may not have even hit you yet. After all, you can go home whenever you want, right? It's only a drive or plane flight away. The thing is that unless they beg or plead or strong-arm you into that seat belt, each of your trips home will be by your doing alone, and your folks probably realize that. In some ways, any tribulations of adolescence are nature's way of preparing everyone for this change. Sadly, by freshman orientation some parents are barely on speaking terms with their children, yet somehow not even that tension can dull the sense of loss the parents feel.

Your parents' view of your college experience will be a combination of what they hear from you, what they read in the media, and any newsletters your college sends home—all filtered through their own experiences from years ago. It's a bit of a jambalaya. In almost every case they will be wiser than you, but increasingly you will find yourself more knowledgeable than they are—and not just in the trivial areas of pop culture.

In college, the knowledge gap (note, we emphasize "knowledge gap" not "wisdom gap") starts to approximate where you thought it was when you first crossed puberty: you actually *do* start to know important stuff that your parents don't know or can't remember. Though they might surprise you by how well they can hold their own in a conversation on transcendentalism, most likely you will be sharper on the subject since you just completed two hundred pages of reading on it last week.

So far we've mentioned the emotional isolation and physical distance your parents are braving. Let's tack onto that the financial pressure of footing the bill for this adventure. Ah, so here you may chime in that you will be helping chip away at the debt by pursuing a work-study job. That may be true, but in most cases parents are shouldering a big part of the load. Even if your parents can somewhat afford writing the tuition checks, each signature still represents luxuries they are sacrificing to send their baby far, far away so she can be happy. The joy of seeing her happy is tinged by that loss—losses some parents may never communicate but you can bet your mini-fridge they are feeling. This, combined with their long-term perspective we mentioned earlier, will set the stage for a lot of their conversations with you.

For most parents, their child's college opportunity represents the largest investment they have ever made besides the family home. For you, the investment may seem secondary to the rite of passage that college represents (and perhaps you feel you deserve). When the two perspectives collide, expect them to weigh in heavily on getting the biggest return on their investment.

To sum all this up, the two typical parental reactions to look for as they prepare to send you on your way lean toward the extremes of either neediness or dismissal. Either you may feel smothered toward the end because they fear the empty nest or worry about you getting the best out of college, or you may feel disconnected if they emotionally distance themselves from you to help buffer their feelings. (This may have even been going on since you started your senior year and "the end" was in sight.) Sometimes it is a combination of the two. And sometimes parents are able to disguise these emotions and put on their best face so that you will head off to school none the wiser about how much duct tape they are using to keep themselves together. A good thing to remind yourself in all of this is that they have been extraordinarily patient (or at least tried to be, anyway) with your insane pubescent emotional roller coaster for the last eight years, so cut them a little slack. Be loving, be gracious, but go.

What to Do When the Mother Ship Gets a Makeover
Adjusting to Change Back Home

The three things that tend to be the most difficult news from home are parents separating, a newly diagnosed illness of a family member, or some tragedy befalling the family pet. Students expect that while they are in college, life will remain the same at home. It seems a reasonable expectation after all, since life at home hasn't changed that much over the years. Home will always be home. Mom will have the same haircut. The house will be the same color and the furniture will be in the same place—the expectation provides a sense of stability.

Sadly, however, this is an unrealistic expectation since your departure altered the family dynamic. Your parents might buy a new car without telling you, and when you arrive home for fall break you may be surprised and wonder, "What else are you hiding from me?" If the change influences you directly (such as them cleaning out your room), it will hopefully have been communicated by them in advance. But there is no guarantee. In some ways, the safest bet is to expect your family will have changed as much as you have since you've been away at college; that way you won't be surprised by any makeovers and may be comforted to find that a few things stayed the same.

PARENTS SEPARATING

A new car is easy, but some bombshells are not. The most heartbreaking change is death or divorce. We aren't suggesting that your parents are about to die or file—in fact we hope they don't. But both do happen and, sadly, it's likely that someone you know on campus will be going through this misfortune, so it may be helpful for you to be aware of the possibility. In fact, divorce may even be a bit more likely *because* the kids have gone to college. Many parents in troubled marriages "hold on" until their child has left high school. Other folks don't even realize they are in a troubled marriage until the one thing they still have in common—their child—is gone. The sad truth is that the psychological costs of divorce are not lessened just because the children are living away from home, and in the worst cases we have seen divorce destroy students' college careers.

A word for parents—if bad news of any kind must be given, please engage the help of the residence life staff or the dean's staff before delivering the news. If you are willing, the staff can be there when the news is shared.

Hopefully, if the parents are adamant that a divorce is necessary, they will wait to tell their student until they can do so face-to-face. This word is for parents—if bad news of any kind must be given, please engage the help of the residence life staff or the dean's staff before delivering the news. If you are willing, the staff can be there when the news is shared. If a student is going to encounter any sort of family tragedy, it's best to work with the counseling services on campus, where they can be ready and available at a moment's notice.

To the student, we recommend you have the counseling services on campus help you evaluate how this news is affecting your course work. From there, talk with your academic advisor and your profs as soon as possible. Profs may not make good counselors, but they *do* need to know why your performance is impaired so they can be more supportive.

RECENT DIAGNOSIS IN THE FAMILY

Family illness is another big blow. Again, we hope that all of your loved ones remain healthy, but in the event a friend's mom has just been diagnosed with breast cancer, you might be able to offer some helpful counsel (or at least have him read this chapter). Our biggest suggestion on this front is to take some time off from school if it is a family member you are particularly close to. Since your head won't be in the game anyway, it's the healthiest thing you can do to give yourself a break and go home to support your family, saving your tuition for when you are better able to focus. Most schools will recognize the benefit of taking a leave and will work with you to make certain that your scholarship or other financial aid will not be adversely affected.

Heck, you can even get a job stocking shelves just to pass the time while you are home. Most schools are very accommodating and willing to work with students so they don't lose academic ground in these situations. There may even be a way to finish one or two classes from home and withdraw from the rest. This is where it is important for the student to communicate with the appropriate people on campus *immediately*, if only so you know where to find the eject button. (The best way to figure out who those "appropriate people" are is to start with your RA and academic advisor so they can steer you in the right direction.)

Your parents shouldn't feel that they need to arrange all this for you—it should be something you take care of so that every decision is your most comfortable decision. That doesn't mean you shouldn't consult your parents, but that ultimately the decision is up to you.

Often in the case of divorce, some students want to stay as far from the battle as possible and remain on campus. That's totally fine. It's all about what works best for you. Our big point here is simply that you not go the distance alone. Sadly, most deans and professors complain that they find out about a troubled family situation or illness too late in the process, when the student has already dug himself a hole so deep that no one can help.

Most faculty and staff take the stance your future employers will: it is up to you to make sure your home life does not undermine your work. The responsible thing to do if home life is consistently affecting your work is to tell the folks in charge. They don't need to know all of the details, but if it affects your work, it's your responsibility to let them know so expectations can adjust accordingly.

THE FAMILY PET

As for the last heartbreak of losing a beloved family pet, there is probably little comfort we can give. While the situation is not typically significant enough to warrant time taken off school, the initial news may make it feel that way. During his junior year, one student of ours—Philip—lost Max, "the most wonderful dog in the world," the dog that had stayed with him through eight childhood moves. He admits that the news hit him hard for a couple weeks but that he recovered eventually. He didn't feel like going home, but he did visit some friends who had a dog he could at least play catch with to help him deal with his grief. For some, the loss of a pet is no big thing, while for others it is a symbol of the home life disintegrating. Whatever your take may be, reach out to friends around you (whether furry or not) so they can help.

Paving the Way

This is one of those sorts of sections we recommend you and your parents both read and talk about one night over pizza. (We bet they may sneak a peak at other chapters too, especially the one about sex and alcohol!) There are three times in the life of a parent where there tend to be unspoken expectations about their child—going to college, getting married, and having the first grandchild—and these seasons of change tend to flow much easier when all of you are on the same page and talking about it ahead of time.

Is There a Vaccine for Homesickness?
Missing What You'll Miss

Oh, how we wish there were. In prepping for this section, we realized we would be talking out of both sides of our mouth. On the one hand, homesickness is normal and definitely not shameful or childish. On the other hand, it's not something to indulge.

Even if you want to, and even if home is only a short drive away, our biggest push on this point is that you shouldn't go home every weekend—certainly have some planned trips home but also plan some diversions for those other weekends. Try not to be pulled home by that overwhelming urge to be in the familiar again (see how the word "family" is inside the word "familiar"? There's a reason for that . . .), because it actually makes it harder for both you and your folks to adjust to you being an adult and on your own.

Another bonus to staying on campus is that you are able to focus your attentions not only on your studies but also on your second family that you will develop by getting to know roommates, hall mates, and colleagues. Even hanging around on a weekend with no plans allows for the opportunity to engage in campus life and make unexpected connections, and that will never happen if you keep going home. Sorry.

> There are three times in the life of a parent where there tend to be unspoken expectations about their child—going to college, getting married, and having the first grandchild—and these seasons of change tend to flow much easier when all of you are on the same page and talking about it ahead of time.

If you're looking for ideas of what to do (especially on the cheap), check out your campus visitor center. Many college websites also list cultural and sporting events in the area so students can get involved in life where they live. (And if not, check out your college city's home page to see what's happening.) Don't feel like you have to discover every cool book nook, market, theater, and museum on your own—at the very least, the visitor center will help you weed out places that would have been a waste of time.

But what about going home to see your friends? That's a tricky one, and it varies from student to student. Some neglect their high-school classmates entirely and dive into new friendships on campus. Some stay connected with former classmates and do it in a healthy way that still enables them to connect with new friends on campus. Some try desperately to maintain their high-school friendships in exactly the same form and priority that they were before graduation, which rarely turns out well. While there is nothing wrong with the first two scenarios, the last one clearly hinders personal growth. Friendships should enable you to become the best person you can possibly be. What you will likely find over your undergrad years is that you will naturally prune your high-school friendships. Some will fall away to be revived in fun ways at future reunions as you desperately try to remember the names of people who were the sun and moon and stars for you in high school. Others will grow and may even deepen, but perhaps in ways you did not expect and could not have planned.

Speaking of planning, "Don't plan on the hometown honey lasting all the way through college." That is what one prof we know tells her advisees at the beginning of each year, and most of the time she's right. But there are exceptions. One student in particular—we'll call him Stuart—was a smart football player with a bit of a sarcastic wit. Upon hearing his advisor's pronouncement, he challenged her and said not only would he graduate a math major (she had just finished the spiel about changing your interest in majors a couple times), he would also keep his high-school girlfriend. The complication in this budding romance was that his girlfriend attended school forty miles away, which is an unmanageable distance when you don't have a car. The happy ending is that four years later, Stuart graduated a computer science major and a math minor (close enough!) and his advisor flew to Texas to attend their wedding and eat crow. Now, a couple years later, she was invited to the baptism of their new daughter and she is thrilled to admit they are happily married.

It's a sweet story (and not an altogether impossible hope, for those of you with high-school sweethearts out there), but we would be remiss if we didn't tell you that it is an exceptional case. The futures market on high-school romances is bearish. (Take an econ class if that analogy makes no sense to you.) Over the next four years, the two of you will grow and change a ton—even if you attend the same institution. In some cases, being on the same campus makes it even more difficult since your interactions can become smothering and not allow for the personal growth you need.

Of course, don't feel like you need to break up with your boyfriend upon finishing this chapter. (And if you do, please do not tell him that it was because of what we wrote.) We are not trying to be Dr. Kevorkian-meets-Dr. Phil. These relationships tend to follow a natural life cycle of drifting apart, and as a result, they don't require drastic steps toward euthanasia. If it dies, let it die naturally.

It isn't healthy to cut off all home ties and immediately expect college to be your entire life. This is true across all fronts—family, friends, interests, and significant others. A healthy perspective is to blend your former and current lives, beautifully marbling the best relationships in each so they can survive and become a foundational part of who you are.

Your Cell Phone—Life Preserver or Anvil?
Communication Strategies That Build
Healthy Adult Relationships Back Home

What may be one of the hardest adjustments of all is that while your parents will be deeply involved in your college experience (in most cases psychologically if not financially), they cannot be intimately involved in your day-to-day life as they were in high school. At least, they shouldn't be.

As much as we would like to offer some lifesaver advice, there is no perfect equation directing contact between parents and students—perhaps that it's always in some sort of flux is what keeps it healthy. Thanks to modern technology, it's far easier to stay in contact with your parents than it was for previous generations of freshmen, and the nature of contemporary middle-class society sees a lot more instant communication than we dare describe without dating ourselves. The technological arm seems to stretch farther and faster every day.

> It isn't healthy to cut off all home ties and immediately expect college to be your entire life. A healthy perspective is to blend your former and current lives, so they can survive and become a foundational part of who you are.

As a result, this is one area where you must be exceptionally wise and sensitive to your folks. If you find that your parents need more contact with you than you need with them, it shows your maturity to compromise in your parents' direction. Part of being an adult is respecting someone else's needs rather than merely assuring that your own are met. You may think that being an adult means being independent—and it does, to a certain extent—but all the more, it means transitioning from "taker" to "giver." It doesn't mean you are letting your parents control your life, it just means you are checking in to see that they are doing well for their sake. At the same time, parents need to understand that there are some limits on how often they should expect to hear from you. For instance, multiple times a day is probably unrealistic and unhealthy.

On the other side of the equation, if you are the needier one, then our advice is to resist the temptation to check in as often as you would like—especially if you find you are speed-dialing home multiple times a day. Perhaps our basic message is that this area cries out for moderation, so lean against your natural inclinations and you will likely get the balance mostly right.

Students who phone home too much can find they have created trouble in the form of parents who are a bit too involved in their new lives. If you are calling home with hourly updates, you're asking for it! By stringing your parents along on your yo-yo days of ups and downs, don't be surprised when they call your advisor or dean or roommate's parents to iron out snafus and be supportive.

There are multiple ways to interact with folks back home, and it's best to think through the advantages and disadvantages of each before communicating absentmindedly. The cell phone is convenient and it's oh so easy to dial your mom after class to let her know how your test went—but are you missing an opportunity to talk to your professor or teaching assistant (TA) as you both meander the same direction to lunch? Okay, so you opt for the text message. That is certainly expedient, but then neither of you gets the warm fuzzies of hearing a live voice. Maybe there is a better time you can catch up with her so that your interactions are more meaningful and so you have a better handle on your emotions. Or maybe by scheduling only a few conversations a week you will have more to tell her than what you just ate for lunch. As you set a communication pattern for calling home, try to make it flexible to accommodate the various schedule changes you will encounter in your college life, as well as sustainable for the long haul.

> As you set a communication pattern for calling home, try to make it flexible to accommodate the various schedule changes you will encounter in your college life, as well as sustainable for the long haul.

To close off this topic, here's a little FYI that might save your neck from the chopping block someday. In our techno-centered age, it is not uncommon to see people multitasking with email while on their cell phone and ordering lunch at a diner simultaneously. In fact, it's almost encouraged. Be forewarned, however, that there are varying receptions to this sort of behavior depending on the generation you are communicating with at that moment.

The student generation probably expects this to be the case and may not think it's rude to hear you typing in the background during a phone conversation (though, some would disagree and say they are still offended). However, step back one generation (such as your parent's age group): while they may suspect you are multitasking, there is still the hope that you will attempt to mask it so that it doesn't look like you find the conversation boring. Step back two generations (between your parents' and grandparents'—think CEO): multitasking can be seen as the height of rudeness.

This can create intergenerational tensions not only at home but in the workplace as well, so keep your radar tuned to make sure you aren't sending the wrong signal. After all, you don't want your sixty-year-old hostess to spit in your burger because you were curt with her while trying to text message your roommate about your urgent change in flight plans while on hold with the airlines.

"Me human. Boy. Elliot. Ell-i-ot."
For the Male Reader

Indulge us as we take a brief detour onto the quicksand of gender stereotypes. Taken from personal experience over the last twenty-five years, it is the parents of males who tend to complain the most about their child's lack of communication. It doesn't seem to matter which parent is speaking either. Both seem to find their son less talkative than they'd like. Parents are generally more surprised by news from sons than they are daughters, since their daughters are more likely to have kept them informed of little progresses along the way. For good or ill, the parents of males say they are the last to know when their sons have a new girlfriend, but they seem to know immediately if their daughters have a new boyfriend on the scene.

Certainly the old adage of "boys will be boys" is clanging somewhere in the background and you may not want to change. If nothing else, be advised that you may be erring on the side of non-talkative and your folks may need a little more tele-time. If you aren't willing to communicate for their sakes, do it for your own; emotional intelligence (that is, reading and responding appropriately to the needs of others) is just as important as mental intelligence, and it's a critical lesson to master as early as possible.

Avoiding the Worst-Parent-Ever (WPE) Award

(Word to the wise: We think parents should read this section. However, if you plan on sharing it with them, it would be best if you restrained your enthusiastic highlighter and notations of "Right on!" in the margins.)

Loving your child is not and should never be a crime. However, the way parents go about expressing that love can be complicated at times. The Worst-Parent-Ever Award could easily go to parents who respond to their children leaving by becoming "too distant," but in our experience most finalists are in the "too involved" camp.

THE TOO-INVOLVED PARENT

The typical worst parent is the one who feels that the only thing his son or daughter should be doing is studying. Period. Therefore that parent does everything the student needs up to the point of taking her tests and writing her papers for her. This parent calls to handle his son's bounced check or his daughter's speeding ticket, or calls his daughter's professor to find out how she can improve in class. Though their parents' motives are admirable, students don't learn how to manage the day-to-day distractions of life while accomplishing a greater goal.

True to life, there was one parent of a recent freshman who was practically awarded a WPE plaque as a result of her behavior the summer before her student ever stepped foot on campus. Between two administrators, they tallied fifty emails they had received from her covering every worry a mother could face about her child leaving home. Her son was away from home for the summer and the whole time he was gone she fretted about his course deadlines, whether or not he had registered for the right classes, if she could get the syllabi in advance, and so on. While administrators are typically prepared to receive one or two emails of this sort from parents (especially parents sending their first or only child off to college), they were overwhelmed by the quantity of emails from this one woman. Generally, her son's courses looked fine and they tried to reassure her that he would have a two-week window like all the other students to make sure they were a good fit. Sadly, their reassurances did little to assuage her. The message most colleges send home to the folks is that, while they are available should parents ever have a concern, the parents should consciously try to develop new outlets for their time now that their children have left home.

In keeping with the idea of helping their student focus on studies, parents will often come running when their child calls in sick. Too many parents have a propensity to come to campus and shepherd their child through the medical system at the first sign of minor illness. (For major illness or surgery, this sort of help may be warranted—but not for bugs that can be knocked out with a quick prescription or two.) This is another example of an opportunity to develop a new life skill—one that is sadly lost when Mom or Dad shows up with the best intentions. In order to help your parents keep whatever illnesses in perspective, the onus is on you to communicate it in a way that doesn't send them into a tailspin of panic.

At this point, it may be helpful to note that, historically, colleges have had an implicit understanding termed *in loco parentis* (L., "in the place of a parent"). The idea is that undergrads are not children but are not yet adults and so still require some sort of parental guidance; since the parents are not there to provide it, the responsibility falls to the school. In ancient days, the faculty acted in loco parentis on behalf of their students by chaperoning parties, monitoring curfews, and the like.

Students and professors both happily celebrate that this is no longer the case now that campuses have developed a huge complex of student life administrators who are able to provide advice, support, and a measure of accountability. Sure, the bureaucracy can be a bit more bewildering than a quick call home, but it's a fairly apt halfway point between on-call parents and real life as an adult—like a climbing harness as opposed to a safety net. The staff will not mother students but are certainly available to provide more hands-on care than students would receive if left on their own.

Like any new venture, there is a possibility of little failures along the way—expect them. One student exemplified *not* accepting this fact. Julie asked her professor if she could call over break to discuss her final grade with him, and he agreed. The conversation went something like this:

Julie: Now that semester grades are out, what grade did I get on the final?

Prof: You got an 85.

Julie: [Whispering in the background.] Well, what was the grade for class participation?

Prof: An 87. It works out to an overall final grade of 85 when combined with your other papers and tests.

Julie: [More whispering.] What is the weight given to quizzes?

Prof: 10 percent

Julie: [More whispering.]

Prof: Would you like me to talk with your mom directly?

Julie: Yes! [Hands the phone over.]

Mom: Now, I was a sociology major in college—why did my daughter get this grade in your class? You don't understand, my daughter is not like the other students. She is studying in the library on Saturday nights, she reads all the material, she . . .

We didn't make that conversation up—scout's honor. It really happened just like that. While the mother may have a greater understanding of her daughter's performance as a result of that call, most likely she undermined her daughter's sense of independence or confidence by returning her to the days of high school. The mom did less damage to the professor's perception of the student than one might think—in fact, the professor had some sympathy for her and her relationship with her too-involved mom as a result. Which reminds us to remind you once more: as strange as your professor may seem, we can state with utter certainty that your professor has been a student before and has dealt with parents before (and may even be a parent himself), so whatever you are going through, chances are the professor can relate at least a bit.

In situations where parental control is too great on subjects of future importance—like choosing a major, career, or grad school—it is not inappropriate to have your professor talk to your parents. We can't promise that your professor will be willing, but don't be so embarrassed that you forsake asking altogether. Have your parents call him during office hours (on their nickel). Because the prof is an adult (and may even be a parent—certainly he had parents of his own), he will most likely be aware of the challenges you face, and sometimes a conversation like this can go a long way.

Be forewarned in all this that there are various federal laws that restrict communication between the school and the parent. A student's educational record can generally not be shared with anyone—including the parent—without the student's authorization, so parents should not be surprised if college officials or faculty will not share details about the student's performance. On the other hand, the law *does* allow info to be shared regarding alcohol and drug violations, so it is in the student's best interest to call home before the dean does if such violations have . . . ahem . . . occurred. Most profs don't keep abreast of privacy law and so they may be willing to talk with your parents without your knowledge, but that may be the exception to the general privacy rule. Understandably it frustrates parents when they feel barred from the conversation, and one father told us, "It's like I just bought a new car that I will never be allowed to drive."

THE TOO-DISTANT PARENT

So far, these bits of wisdom have been aimed toward the most prevalent scenario: the too-involved parent. But what about the other possibility—the one where Mom or Dad seems to have lost all interest or concern for their child now that he has left home?

Liam was a student raised by well-educated parents that were supportive of him as a youngster in his many academic endeavors. But once his treads hit the college campus and they had unloaded their minivan, they went home to clean out his room (without telling him) and to return to life as it was before he was born. In their desire to send him off into adulthood, they didn't write letters, they didn't call, and they didn't send care packages. They waited for all communication to be instigated by him. And, while this fostered a spirit of independence in the lad, it also left an unsettling feeling of abandonment. Partway through his education they made it known to him that, though they had the means to continue to financially support his basic needs, they were pulling all funds and tuition checks so he could learn to make it on his own. Like our other stories, this is true. Sadly true. Liam had very little time to transition into life as an adult and as a result it placed an undue amount of emotional and financial stress on him. The stress was so great that it eventually caused him to drop out of college.

So parents can fall off the horse on either side. Just when they think the constant fretting about whether or not they are raising Junior properly was over, they find themselves maneuvering the most delicate tightrope of all. We tip our hats to any and all attempting this feat and we wish them the best.

Avoiding the Worst-Offspring-Ever (WOE) Award

It wouldn't be fair to hand out such a dubious award to parents without making one available to their offspring as well, now would it?

Just as your parents want the best for you (even if you think they have an odd way of showing it at times), we suspect you are grateful that they birthed, fed, and raised you. Chances are, however, that you may have odd ways of showing your gratitude at times as well.

The best place to start is to be extra sensitive to your parents' feelings. The WOE Award goes to the student whose self-centeredness chokes off all sympathy or empathy. No matter how hard you try, it will be obvious when you come home for the first holiday (often Thanksgiving) that your first priority is seeing old high-school friends and your second priority is expressing how much you miss being with your new college friends.

We ask you to consider a third priority: reconnecting with Mom and Dad. When your mom apologizes that her wardrobe is outdated, or if your dad tries to ask your advice on a topic that may or may not be of interest to you, try to hear their underlying message: they miss you, they are proud of you, and now that you are on your way to adulthood they want *you* to be proud of *them* too. Prove how much of an adult you are by being mutually encouraging.

Ultimately, be teachable. Just because you've reached college doesn't mean you should no longer ask for (or take!) advice. Folks will be dishing it out for the rest of your life (heck, we do it for a living), so whether it comes from parents or faculty or the custodian or a book, hear what they have to say and then sift. Just because you may think you know it all doesn't mean you should act like it.

But what if you *do* have a better idea of how to spend your future than your parents? Delana came to us complaining that her parents wanted her to take a high-paying job whereas she wanted to travel and study abroad. They argued that they paid her bills and she insisted that it was her life—and both are right. Whose argument wins? First off, this should be a conversation and not a fight (slamming the door or the phone are clear winners for the WOE Award, by the way). But it is a conversation that will need to reach a conclusion. At the end of the day, certainly, it *is* your life and *you* have to take ownership of it—that's appropriate. But part of taking ownership and being an adult is living with the consequences of your decision. If Delana chooses to give up an opportunity to take a well-paying job so she can teach English in Asia, she can't very well expect her parents to wire her a couple grand if she gets stranded in Vietnam.

If you haven't had "the conversation" (no, not the birds and bees!) with your parents yet, be sure to ask what they believe their financial role to be as you work through school. Some stop doling out the dough in high school, some go through grad school, some pay for up to a year after college. It's much better to have that conversation early on in your career. That way you can adjust your expectations and set your course from there.

We've talked a lot about talking in this chapter. It's something you will live and die by. The big rule of the day is that when there is big news, be sure to share it with your parents—consider it a sign of respect. That's probably a no-brainer.

We've also made a lot of generalizations about parents in this chapter, some stemming from the types of parents we've had and others from the types of parents we've seen. We tried to hit the extremes. Yours may fall somewhere in the middle, and that's great. Maybe none of this chapter applied to you because you have already struck the perfect balance. In that case, just remember that a college education involves learning lots of stuff that, so far as you can tell, has no direct application to you right now—that might also apply to sections of certain books about college.

CHAPTER 3

"I Have the Perfect Schedule– All My Classes Are on Wednesday!"

Writing the Personal Narrative Called Your Transcript

Unlike the other college study guides out there, we are going to suggest that you *not* pick your courses.

That's right. From our perspective, and the perspective of your future employers, you are not picking courses, you are writing a story—a narrative of your educational journey (your school calls it a "transcript"). The narrative doesn't need to be ploddingly linear, but you should be able to make some sense out of it in retrospect. If there are mistakes, they should be balanced by subsequent successes. If there are successes, they should culminate in conquests.

Beyond writing your own *Pilgrim's Progress*, you are choosing professors rather than choosing courses—since the professor you pick can make or break any course.

Let's say you enter college thinking you will be a business major. Logically you'd start off with some econ and accounting courses. But halfway through the term, you can barely keep your eyelids propped open and you wake up every morning dreading the day's classes. Shock of all shocks, the course "Intelligent Design from Cells to Snakes," which you are taking to complete your science requirement, has turned out to be fairly fascinating. You like the professor so much that you take another class from him and get his recommendations on other profs in the department you should consider.

By junior year, you are happily majoring in evolutionary biology. Remember those business classes that turned out to be a dud? Well, you are starting to notice some parallels—it turns out the survival of businesses reflects a lot of evolutionary dynamics. Add to that a couple literature courses you took—"Darwin and Race in the Modern Era" and "Tribal Stories of Origin"—as well as perhaps fulfilling your PE requirement with "Aboriginal Dance"—and you are looking pretty learned.

While that may not be your personal narrative of choice, the point is that the resulting transcript is one of breadth and depth; there is a broad range of courses but also a deep engagement in one or two areas. To turbocharge this sample transcript, you might take a couple grad-level courses to show real mastery beyond merely fulfilling graduation requirements.

What if venturing out into unknown fields of knowledge leads to a couple landmines (also known as bad grades)? Good question. The fear of bad grades often prevents students from getting the best out of college, and it shouldn't. Bad grades in your freshman year are more easily explained than they are in your senior year—so in the scenario above, that graduate could easily explain how losing interest and failing in his business major led to a newfound passion in the economics of survival. However, had this student waited until his junior year to admit defeat in his business courses and experiment elsewhere, it would have been much harder to explain.

Should you fall short of the ideal GPA, try at least to build an interesting narrative. The example we gave showed a rather obvious pattern. Obvious is nice, however it isn't necessary.

We have seen transcripts that at first blush suggest total random whimsy. However, it turns out the students took as many courses from "star professors" as possible, resulting in a hopscotch across the pantheon of the university. What they lost in systematic progression, their narratives more than made up in quality of individual chapters. A diverse transcript with a spectrum of profs across your major department and across departments in the university will speak well of you even if your GPA is a bit lower than another student who took a safer route, since it shows you are not afraid to take calculated risks. And if you can perform well in at least one or two of those classes, then you can get a strong letter of recomendation that can emphasize your intellectual courage and put the rest of the GPA in context.

Pick your courses according to the following priorities:

1. Reputation of the professor as a teacher/scholar
2. Reputation of this particular course as a course
3. Your intrinsic interest in the topic
4. Level of difficulty so you can balance out your schedule
5. Any graduation/distribution requirements
6. The applicability of the time slot for the course

Most students naturally go by exactly the opposite priority. Most students, of course, are not getting the best out of college.

Beyond your own satisfaction at having gotten the most bang for your buck in your college experience, the overall goal in building a narrative via your course selection is to present a thoughtful, well-educated, well-rounded individual to future employers. While they do tend to look at an applicant's GPA, the transcript coupled with your resume are in some ways a teaser that will hopefully make you an intriguing prospect for an interview. Then, should you make it as far as the interview process, the opportunity to discuss the themes behind your educational narrative will make your application all the more interesting. And, as we all know, the more interesting the candidate, the more interested the employer in hiring that individual. The same holds true of applying to grad schools.

If you aren't a top-down thinker (meaning that you find it difficult to plan beyond next semester), don't panic. We've got some bottom-up strategies spelled out later in this chapter to help you secure your footing as you make your way through the course guide. As long as you are intentional in choosing courses for their value (as opposed to a convenient time slot or location, or rumor of the prof grading lightly), it will be hard to stray too far from a compelling narrative.

"I Refuse to Take a Class That Starts Before Noon"
The Best Way to Pick a Course

Granted, you may have pushed yourself through endless mornings of 5 a.m. alarms in high school with the promise that when you got to college you wouldn't roll out of bed until noon, but we're about to break some sad news to you: choosing your schedule by how late the courses allow you to sleep in is not the breakfast of champions.

Your best bet in selecting classes is to start off by asking your peers which professors to take. Be sure to set aside a fair chunk of time to do this (meaning, not the night before registration begins) since you will need to ask advice from a wide range of students to hedge against the possibility that one or two had a trivial pet peeve. You'll want to ask questions that are specific about the students' likes or dislikes in terms of course load, timing, teaching style, grading scale, fairness, availability, and so on—and weight their teacher preferences accordingly. Your best bet is to look for first-hand advice from upperclassmen as opposed to hearsay from newly minted freshmen.

Other questions to ask:

- What were highlights/lowlights of the course?
- What seems to excite this prof?
- How manageable is the workload, and do you have any advice on making it work?
- What was the quality of feedback for grading (and did your final actually have grades/comments on it, or did you not pick it up)?
- Did you feel prepared for this course?
- Did you find that the information taught in this course was worth your investment of time and tuition?

Other sources of information on professors include, not surprisingly, professors! But while profs may know more about the background of other professors than students do, they won't necessarily know any more about how that professor teaches than students would. In fact, for professional reasons, they may be reluctant to tell you what they know about the professor's reputation—like, "avoid that prof"—but they may be willing to suggest colleagues you might enjoy.

There are also online evaluations to consider. Be wary here. These sorts of tools are fairly skewed; they cater to the extremes, especially when those students who have had a bad experience use them to vent (and sometimes they come back multiple times posing as different users to exact their full revenge). We have even heard of profs who subscribe and write recommendations about themselves. If it is an evaluation program run by the university, there will be a bit more quality control, but it still may not present an accurate picture.

Finally, once you have narrowed your search to a few potential professors, consider attending one of their lectures a semester beforehand to observe their style and how the students respond in class (panicked, attentive, snoozing, on the edges of their seats, and so on). You might even be able to walk out with a couple students after class and lob them a few specific questions about their experience with this prof and whether or not today's lecture was typical. Should you decide to follow our advice, take two things into account: First, please choose a large lecture where your presence will not be noted (and thus disruptive). Second, give very little value to the fact that you will feel completely lost in the content—and don't hold it against the professor that you haven't attended previous lectures or completed the readings.

If the professor you are interested in observing doesn't offer lectures but is primarily a seminar instructor, keep reading. We have some advice later on about registering for one too many courses so that you can see a prof in action for a week or two, and this would be a great way to decide whether or not to take in his seminar.

"I Learn Best When Profs . . ."

No matter what advice you hear, remember that it's only advice, not divine command (nor popular vote). In fact, we have some advice about the advice you will be getting: filter it through a screen called "know thyself." Two anecdotes make our point.

Without realizing what she'd done, Sarah requested "Literature in the Arts" to fulfill her freshman writing requirement first semester, primarily because the description of the course sounded fascinating. However, once she arrived on campus, other students started to warn her that she had picked the hardest freshman lit class at the university and that it would be a ton of work and she should try to switch immediately—actually, multiple sources agreed. She panicked. But the textbook looked so amazing, and the one day of class she had attended made her want to record everything the professor said. In the end, she found one former student who admitted that the course was a lot of work but also argued that it was well worth it. He gave her a few tips on how to balance the load and how to discern the must-read from the nice-to-read on the syllabus, and with that she kept the class. Now that she's graduated, if you ask Sarah what was her favorite course of her college career, she will cite "Literature in the Arts" as an easy winner.

By the way, she *did* make good use of her peer's advice. Rather than being caught unaware and later being overwhelmed by the impossible workload, she was ready for it and knew a few moves to keep herself afloat.

Here's another course-hunting anecdote.

Jerry was looking for a good course in the history department, so he began asking around about a professor whose course description sounded interesting. Of the two or three people he asked, all adamantly disliked the professor. They said her teaching style was mind-numbing because she used PowerPoint slides with bullets for every single point she made, that her syllabus was color-coded, which was insulting, and she assigned a ton of reading to compensate for only having two lectures a week. Jerry signed on immediately. Why? After asking very specific questions about this professor, what he heard was that her teaching style didn't match his friends' learning styles, but it *did* match *his*.

He had been having difficulty following some previous professors' lectures, so the idea of a PowerPoint outline was a relief. And, not willing to admit it to his friends, he color-coded his lab notes because it helped him stay organized and ahead of his deadlines. Sure, no one likes a ton of reading, but since he'd already taken a look at the subject matter, it didn't seem as daunting as they made it out to be. It turned out to be a great match for him.

The key is discovering early on how you learn best. Part of that discovery will be learning which teaching styles definitely *don't* work for you. But rather than learning the hard way—stuck in a course you dislike for a whole semester—you could swing by the counseling center in the first few weeks of the semester to have them help you pinpoint your learning style. A quick test or two should do it (rest assured, it doesn't require any needles).

Are you a visual learner? Auditory? Kinesthetic? Once you find out, look for profs who teach as closely to that learning style as you can. You will undoubtedly be stuck with a few professors who are the absolute opposite of your learning method of choice, but even knowing yourself in that situation will give you ideas for compensating.

In short, picking courses that fit you is a trial-and-error process. Shop carefully and deliberately.

"Since I Took Eight Courses in High School, I'll Take Seven in College"
Blunders Best Avoided in Weighing Your Course Load

Every university has a different way of counting credits and course hours. Whatever that number may be, do your best to stick with the average recommended by your advisor for your freshman year: too few courses and you'll probably get bored and run the risk of working inefficiently; too many courses and you'll run the genuine risk of burnout, not to mention have little possibility of building friendships.

Professors understand the way courses are weighted at their university and for the most part will stick to that definition in assigning workloads in their courses. Unless you've got a particularly devious prof, she won't grant her course a low number of credits and then assign work as though it was worth the greatest number of credits possible. Of course, the real challenge is that not all equivalently weighted courses are, in fact, equivalent in workload. Across departments and within departments, some courses are harder than others.

It takes great skill to balance the number of time-intensive courses each term (such as labs or lit courses with a ton of reading and writing assignments) with "easy" courses. (Be aware that even though these "easy" courses are meant to lighten your load, they still require diligence, and a poor grade here will carry the same weight as a poor grade in a harder course.) Also, taking five "easy" courses is not the same as three "hard" courses, even though both scenarios may add up to the same amount of total credits. The more courses you sign up for, the more professor relationships you will need to manage, the more syllabi you will need to track, the more classes you will need to attend, the more finals you will need to ace. Your advisor is there to help you strategize your semester lineup, so why make the process unnecessarily difficult by trying to figure it out on your own?

Knowing yourself as you do, if you really think you can handle an extra course above the average for a semester, then give it a go. Register for the class and use your one- to two-week window to practice balancing all those courses at once, and then ask yourself if it's doable.

Be sure to communicate your intentions with the prof of this extra course in advance, and explain that you are trying to choose courses cautiously. This will build a professional rapport with your prof. Should you have to back out at the end of week two and take the course next term, you will have begun a mature relationship with the professor and possibly have earned his respect as a result. Of course, this means that if you decide to back out, you do so at the university's appointed time. Waiting until a few weeks from the end of the semester to beg forgiveness for your frailties and ask that you be deleted without record from the course won't go over so well. At most schools, it can't be granted regardless of how smoothly you request it.

If location is an issue with close scheduling (meaning that taking two courses back to back will make you either miss out on the end of one or be consistently late to the other), work it out with your profs in the first week of class so that their responses to your behavior don't come as a surprise.

It almost goes without saying that this trial period only works if you are in fact doing all of the assignments and attending every class. Since most profs don't take attendance or require weekly homework, it is easy to shirk some of the workload and give yourself a false sense of confidence that you can handle the load. The amount of work in the first two weeks may be less than what is ahead for the rest of the term (only the course syllabus can tell you that); be diligent and make the trial as close to realistic as possible. If there is a paper due in a month, start it now just so you can see how well it works into the routine.

"I Want to Finish All of My Grad Reqs by Spring of My Sophomore Year"
And Why This Is a Bad Plan

Though the labels vary from school to school, there are almost always two sets of grad requirements: general education (that everyone has regardless of major) and major requirements (that vary from department to department). Each involves a prescribed series that looks like a Chinese restaurant menu (take one from column A, two from column B, and so on) The level of constraint imposed on general requirements varies from college to college (or school to school, if you are at a university that has both a liberal arts and an engineering or business school). The level of constraint imposed by majors varies from department to department.

Though they may seem utterly random, both sets of constraints were developed through an agonizing political process involving faculty and administrators. A lot of smart people (and probably some dumb ones too) invested hours of committee time and enormous thought and effort into designing a horse, and in the process created a camel. And, every set has its own implied narrative. It aims to take students along an intellectual journey, visiting places that students might not otherwise visit, and dwelling in some places longer than students might otherwise stay.

Undergrads tend to have one of two equally bad reactions to general education requirements. Some view them as an insult to be resisted as long as possible and then only grudgingly indulged. Others view the requirements as a game of speed chess, racing as fast as they can from the dinging of freshman day one to fulfill the requirements with no thought whatsoever as to the quality of the courses.

Don't be like most students.

View requirements as an invitation to embark on a variety of intellectual excursions that you otherwise would not have taken. As much as you can, grab only good classes as they become available rather than accepting whatever is offered this semester just so you can check off that box. If you choose your grad reqs well, you may be surprised to find years later that some were among your favorite and most memorable courses.

> View requirements as an invitation to embark on a variety of intellectual excursions that you otherwise would not have taken.

Some students take comfort in finishing their grad requirements early but have no idea by the end of them what they are majoring in or where their interests lie. There is no harm in spreading out general requirements over four years. In fact, it might be advisable to save a couple for your last year if that means you will be better able to use the requirements as they were designed to be used—to help you find your major in the early years, to complement your major in the later years, and to broaden your academics throughout. Though there is certainly the danger of having fewer choices if you leave many until your senior year, chances are that you will fulfill more reqs along the way than you realize just by taking courses (strategically) for your major.

You should make it a goal to choose the most vibrant courses possible when it comes time to fulfill a requirement. Go for the best courses, whatever they might be at your school: "Ancient Egyptian Literature," "Social Dance," or "How the Harmonica Shaped the American South." A priority should definitely be placed on discovering your major and possibly using your general ed reqs to do so. We have much more to say on choosing your major—in fact, a whole chapter's worth (in chapter 9)—but for now let's just say that your major is the cake and the general education reqs are the frosting.

Plan to take at least one course within your potential and then actual major each semester to build depth. Over a couple years, you will have banked some considerable knowledge in your field, not to mention discovering some great profs early on so you can spend the next couple of years getting to know them better. However, too much of a good thing can be just plain too much. Don't take more than two courses in a department in a semester except, perhaps, for one intensive semester in your junior or senior year.

"If the Course Title's a Snoozer, I Won't Take It"
Unveiling the Mystery behind Course Listings

If only bad courses came with a "truth in advertising" label like those on hot-dog packages that tell us what's actually inside (not that we *really* want to know, right?). It is, alas, not that simple. For one thing, much of what will make or break a course for you will be your personal learning style.

We can, however, still offer a few tips.

AVOID SUMMER QUARTER

Be wary of taking summer courses unless it is absolutely, unequivocally, most definitely necessary. While we've known our share of great profs who teach in the summer, the courses are typically of lower quality. The top students will most likely be gone doing exciting things for the summer (and don't kid yourself—your peers are an asset in your courses), and your profs may be a little weary from the year.

"Law Schools and Employers Require High GPAs, So I Won't Take Anything Hard"

If grad school is your aim, you need to do some serious planning early on. Begin with an advisor in that department. If you specifically have law school in mind, see an advisor in the law department early on for suggestions on how to craft your transcript. Some schools hold LSAT scores and GPA of equal value, so it will help you plan your transcript if you know your options.

Ideally you want a 4.0 with a challenging course load. Who doesn't? But don't be fooled by the glamour of a high GPA. Once you are over the hurdle of the minimum GPA, schools will evaluate what went into that GPA. A 3.8 with an array of tough courses is more impressive than a 3.9 with a lighter course load.

The earlier you know you will be applying to law school, med school, or grad school, the better you will be able to tailor your transcript accordingly. However, if you have built a transcript that amounts to an interesting narrative on its own terms, then it probably doesn't matter all that much. Each type of graduate school has its own special requirements, so you will need to research your course-selection needs as they apply to that school. For instance, a senior thesis is important if you want to apply to a PhD program, but it matters less for law school; certain science classes are requirements for medical school, whereas law schools are less interested in what classes you chose (as long as they were challenging) and more concerned with the overall GPA.

Knowing which specific schools you would like to attend and what their requirements are will be your best guide. We feel your stress. This probably seems like a lot to ask of you early on, especially if you are not yet a freshman or sophomore and graduation feels so far away (not to mention it feels like you *just* figured out what college to attend!) But it isn't far away. And your top-choice schools will expect to see forethought on your part when it comes to meeting their expectations.

RECONSIDER "UNPOPULAR" COURSES

Beware of sexy titles and convenient times. Sometimes they mask a professor who has difficulty drawing quality students without these superficial attractions, or they may attract so many students that you won't be able to get any face time with your prof.

Take a close look at courses taught at unpopular times as well—very good profs sometimes schedule at these times to weed out the duffers and get good students. Granted 8 a.m. (or, worse yet, 7 a.m.!) sounds like a ridiculous time for a lecture, especially when your hall mates were up until the wee hours singing with their good friend Bud next door, but for the right professor, a pair of earplugs and an early bedtime will be a worthwhile investment. Plus, it's only for a semester (and heck, the rest of the adult world gets up at this time or earlier, so at least you know it isn't deadly).

PROFESSOR TBA

Beware of the class where the professor is undetermined. Since you want to take courses *because* of who is teaching it, signing on for a course where they can't even locate a willing lecturer could be a sign of trouble. That said, the scheduling department could, by happy coincidence, land a wonderful professor. But we recommend holding off on signing up until the professor is named—or sign up with it as your extra course to be potentially dropped later.

ALMOST A PROF?

Beware of the class taught by grad students or staff (especially if you are dropping a lot of dough for tuition). Don't avoid them entirely. (We'd be remiss if we implied that there aren't brilliant college staff out there that *we* would be privileged to hear. For that matter, every great professor started out as a grad student.) Do, however, select these courses cautiously. Likewise, don't take too many classes from visiting profs, not because they won't be worth it—they may be fabulous. Take one or two if you like.

One big danger of taking courses from grad students or visiting professors is that they are harder to track down to write recommendations for you later on. Another danger is that standards for entry into the course are generally lower so the caliber of your colleagues may be lower. It's also tough to evaluate their teaching style before taking the course since no one else may have taken a course from them. That doesn't mean that new profs are bad profs—use your grace window, often called the "drop-add period," during which schools let you change courses easily, so that you can test out if they're right for you.

CONSIDER THE SOURCE

Beware of the course that sounds too good to be true—it probably is. Alex dreaded a particular course requirement, so he took a class because other students told him it was guaranteed to be a breeze. His hopes were confirmed when he saw a substantial contingent of well-known slackers in class the first day. What he didn't bank on was that the professor had also heard her course being called "a breeze." Offended, she set out to regain some respect for herself and the course. It led to an obnoxiously difficult semester. The prof wasn't even that interesting a lecturer. Alex admits that he should have considered the source; if a goof-off swears by the course, do a bit more research to be sure it is worth your time and money.

READ BETWEEN THE LINES

Be sure you know the prof's expectations before signing up. He could expect his students to research topics that he can use in his upcoming book, or require that a different student give a lecture each week while he sits back and grades them. Who knows? It's best to know a little more about what's in store for the semester. This is what the syllabus is for. Read it all the way through and ask the prof about anything that is unclear. Most professors share their vision for the course in the opening lecture. Pay attention to that lecture and that vision, and talk to him about it. It is not a guarantee—the prof's ambition may exceed his reach—but it will give you a sense of what he expects and thus what you can expect.

Aren't "House Courses" a Waste of Time?

"House courses" go by different names depending on the college, but they are basically partial-credit courses that are most often taught by fellow students. Before you mistakenly discount extra-curricular house courses as "fluffy," you may want to reconsider. They can be valuable as a stress relief, for one. They can also keep you fresh by engaging different parts of your brain. There's nothing wrong with breaking up a semester loaded with lots of heavy reading courses by learning American Sign Language (which may not be as easy as you might think).

Some house courses are useful on a professional skill level (such as designing your own home page), others for recreational purposes (such as learning the finer points of rugby). Oftentimes these classes stand ready with valuable life lessons, such as how to begin investing while you are in college so that you have beaucoup bucks in the bank when you retire.

Depending on what's offered, house courses can enhance your transcript narrative. It's not critical, certainly, but a nice touch if you have the extra time. Since the courses aren't graded, they will carry very little weight with your future employer other than to show how you developed a particular interest.

> You don't need to have a good story for why you're taking scuba diving, but you will certainly need a sound explanation for why you took it every semester for four years instead of using that time to pursue an accredited course.

See this as an opportunity to sign up for courses that you'll truly never have a chance to take again, or courses that are worth taking now when they are relatively easy or free.

At the same time, don't be fooled into thinking that house courses are a complete cakewalk. You'll want to check out the strict attendance policy before registering, since a ding on your transcript for one of these is shameful and nearly impossible to explain away. And you don't want to become a house-course addict. There *is* such a thing as taking so many of them that you can't read your transcript with a straight face. You don't need to have a good story for why you're taking scuba diving, but you will certainly need a sound explanation for why you took it every semester for four years instead of using that time to pursue an accredited course.

"I Don't Feel Like I'm Getting the Best Out of College, and I Have No Idea What I'm Doing Wrong"
Introducing . . . Campus Resources

Though it may sound like it, the following story is *not* an exaggerated account—scout's honor. (And, yes, it really was a man.) Edward refused to meet with his advisor to go over his schedule for the spring term even though she had emailed him a reminder early on that he needed to make an appointment with her. Instead, he called the night before registration and requested his access number (which you typically can only get by meeting with your advisor in person). He said he needed it right away. He also told his advisor that he didn't have time to schedule a face-to-face appointment, and he didn't have time to talk on the phone because he was on his way to his hair appointment. True story. He prioritized his coif over multiple thousands of dollars he was paying in tuition for courses he wasn't sure he needed to take. Shocking.

Be sure you are taking full advantage of campus resources, such as the career center (more on that in chapter 8) and especially your advisor. Make a priority of meeting with advisors, profs, or even heads of your major department long before the scheduling rush to be sure you're taking the best courses possible. If, for example, you tell them you're feeling frustrated with your classes, they might be able to find some flaws in your schedule that are leading to your frustration. It could be that you have had really poor luck with professors, or you may discover you have a learning disability that is giving you an unfair disadvantage. Whatever the cause, seek help early—after all, that's part of what you're paying for and thus a big part of getting the best out of college.

Every college offers far more exciting courses than any student is capable of cramming into four years. You are standing at a buffet line of a five-star establishment. Don't settle for beans and weenies. Even if your college seems smaller than most, and thus may not have as many flashy course offerings, don't be discouraged. You may have to search a bit harder, but you will definitely find the WOW courses that will jazz up your personal narrative and make your college experience memorable. Fortunately for you, you have more tools now than most upperclassmen do after years of learning the hard way which courses to take, so you are well on your way.

CHAPTER 4

Alliances, Fellows, and Clubs, Oh My!

Engaging in Extracurriculars

No matter how long four years may seem, you won't be an under-grad forever. Sooner than you think, you will be in the real world, perhaps as a cubicle junkie or some other freeway-shackled member of the global workforce. We know lots of them, and very few play a round of Ultimate Frisbee before their workday starts. Even fewer follow up a good discussion on poetics as influenced by Aristotle with a quick scramble up the campus climbing wall, or regularly join eight other voices harmonizing a cappella in perfect pitch to a dorm of adoring freshmen, or watch anime in their living rooms until the wee hours with five other manga fanatics who should be writers for *Jeopardy*. What is par for the course for college students will soon enough be only a hazy, happy memory.

Let's face it, the world is literally assembled at your dorm doorstep—convenient, funded, and waiting to tickle your slightest whim. Never again will you be in a setting with so rich and convenient a menu of clubs, organizations, and activities beckoning for your time, not to mention interesting people with big ideas at the ready. And, unless you're hoarding some eternally stocked trust fund we don't know about, you'll most likely have a career, a family, or personal responsibilities that prevent you from joining an unlimited number of clubs after you graduate.

> It's almost worth the price of admission just exploring what there is to do outside of class; and at many universities, extracurriculars make your tuition worth every shiny gold piece.

It's almost worth the price of admission just exploring what there is to do outside of class; and at many universities, extracurriculars make your tuition worth every shiny gold piece. Alumni affairs folks know what deans and professors sometimes don't: the good times most alums seem to boast about typically occurred outside of class. So, plan to have fun. It's one thing to challenge your brain, but if you really want to get the best out of college, plan to challenge your *self* too.

Top Two Ways Extracurriculars Go Awry

Campus extracurriculars come with more possibilities than we can describe here, so rather than telling you exactly how to approach them, we'd like to point out two of the most common errors that tend to lead students off track.

THE SPARSE SCHEDULE

Afraid of underestimating the college workload, some freshmen eliminate all extracurriculars from their agendas, determined to use that time to study. Because there will always be time to study later, nearly all freshmen who attempt this strategy end up frittering away their time on . . . *what did I do all semester? I don't remember. I have vague recollections of Xbox,* Bewitched *reruns, and a popcorn fight in the commons . . .*

Were freshmen truly able to make use of their hoarded time for studies, then arguably it would be time well spent. But experience has shown that to be the rare exception. Besides, it's unhealthy to spend all of your time studying.

THE CHOKED SCHEDULE

The second group is just the opposite. They enter the activities fair like a man breaking a fast at an all-you-can-eat buffet, gorging themselves on more clubs than they have time to pursue. Not long afterward, they have more emails about meetings and events than they even have time to read, let alone attend. All too often, these folks discover midway through the first semester (usually right after midterm grades are posted) that the number of extracurriculars that was manageable in high school is ridiculous to attempt in college. Other than one (maybe two?) exceptions, we can think of no—as in zero, none, nada—college student in thirty years of experience who pursued more than three clubs at a time and did it well. More often, those who attempt it fail miserably.

Beyond simply seeking out a happy medium, we actually recommend you set aside less time to study and more time to join a club and play. (Try not to choke on your Coke—it's true, this is one of the few times in life your parents will approve of a book that promotes nonstudying.) The fact is that most first-year students should be involved in slightly more extracurricular activities than they think, but less than they want. A good rule of thumb is that you should be involved in enough activities to make your parents nervous but not so many that they reach for the medicine cabinet. If attending meetings or completing some other club responsibility frequently becomes a hassle or truly gets in the way of your class assignments, your extracurricular life is out of balance.

> A good rule of thumb is that you should be involved in enough activities to make your parents nervous but not so many that they reach for the medicine cabinet.

Somehow, joining an invigorating set of clubs makes what little time is available for study that much more productive. Scarcity of something makes it all the more valuable, and that has never been more true than it is of time. Even during the freshman year, students get more done when they have more to do.

At the very least, try it for one semester. Join some nutty club that's only possible in college (medieval warfare, wilderness survival, or taiko drums are a good start) and tell yourself that you're paying for it, so why not. It will never again be as easy to join as it is now. If nothing else, it will make for entertaining small talk some day while you sit around with colleagues at Friday drinks regaling them with tales of how you managed to survive on pine needles and wild blackberries when you got lost in the woods one weekend with the backpacking club.

How Many Hours Do You Really Have in a Day?
Outlining a Sustainable Work Schedule

Your high-school physics teacher may have told you that there are only twenty-four hours in a day, and that the possibility of expanding on that amount of time was nil. While that may be true in theory, in practice time expands in college and shrinks thereafter. You will never have so much unstructured time as you do in college.

Let's do the math. For the sake of argument, we will assume you spent a solid seven hours in seat time each day of high school. Add to that an hour for lunch, thirty minutes to ride the bus each way, and at least three hours a week spent doing some sort of school activity—let's call it band practice. That brings us to a grand total of forty-eight hours, so far. Now let's add to that two hours of homework a night, at least four hours of homework on the weekends, oh and you had to polish your tuba before the big game Friday night plus your performance that you're going to write about in your application essay, which totals four more hours. Now we're up to sixty-six hours you spent a week on life as a student in high school. You may have worked a part-time job (after all, you had to save for college), and so we may even be pushing eighty or ninety hours. You letter-jackets get to add extra time for athletics. Now, let's compare that with collegiate living.

Time spent in class: three hours a day, plus two hours in a lab once a week. Time spent commuting: zero hours (ah, the beauty of living on campus). Time spent eating: well, since you eat meals where and when you want to (heck, you can often take your mini pizza to class), we won't count it. So far we're up to seventeen hours. Let's assume you spend three hours a day in the library studying your notes and readings (most freshmen take fifteen units their first semester, and most advisors figure an hour a unit in study time). And, now that you've officially "arrived," you don't need to join any filler clubs to boost your application. So, time spent in obligatory extracurriculars: zero hours. Finally, you might want to take on a part-time job. In fact, this may likely be a part of your financial aid package. This type of work is called *work-study* and is part of a government program. Students are not allowed more than 19.9 hours of work-study per week, with most students actually working around ten. Assuming you work the average, that brings us to a grand total of—tuba toot, please—forty-two hours.

Are we kidding? Nope. High school life was roughly sixty-six hours a week and that number is cut by a third once you become a college freshman. Talk about free time! (Great news! Now you can eat your dinner just a little bit slower and actually engage in discussions with your friends about current affairs between mouthfuls.)

High-achieving high schoolers (and you may have been one of the exhausted many) keep more plates spinning than is doable in college. It's not unheard of for a high-school senior—let's call her Maria—to be VP of her class, editor of the school yearbook, and play a varsity sport—but that just isn't done in college. Maria needs to pick just one club or activity and truly invest in it; then a few months later, once she has the hang of it, perhaps she can add another activity that's a little lighter.

It's not that Maria doesn't have the time. After all, we've just shown she has more than twenty more hours a week than she's used to having. The point is that committing all her time to joining Tiptoeing Tap Dancers and being passionate about it (with perhaps an hour a week spent volunteering on trash pickup in her local park) is far better than being superficially involved in four different clubs. Companies that hire freshly minted college graduates are not as impressed by a smattering of shallow interests as they are with a person clearly following one interest and developing it to its fullest extent. Put another way: a top-performing senior in college will have a resume several pages shorter than a top-performing senior in high school. Feel free to let out that voluminous sigh of relief.

While we're on that point of future employers, it's critical to note that the club or organization you choose to join has almost ZERO relevance to your career path. Maria's participation in Tiptoeing Tap Dancers shows little more than how she chooses to spend her time. It does not destine her for a career with the Rockettes any more than joining the Future CEO club would guarantee her a seat in a corporate boardroom.

Joining an organization is valuable more for the experience of becoming part of something larger than yourself than it is for developing a technical skill you will later use on the job. After all, you don't plan on spending 24-7 in your office for the rest of your life, right? Your hiring employer doesn't expect you will either, so outside interests are more than okay. In fact, in one recent graduate's job interview, we'll call her Elizabeth, a critical component of being hired was her proving that she had enough hobbies to help depressurize the intensity her job. Bottom line: they wouldn't hire her unless she could demonstrate she had a means uniquely different from her work to let off some steam. Balance is the sort of thing it's nice to learn early on.

Isaiah is a friend of ours who had a keen interest in law school. However, he preferred singing in an a capella group to joining the Bench and Bar Society (BBS). Because of his passion for singing, his participation in the a capella group actually made him a very strong candidate for law school later on because he excelled in what he enjoyed. In fact, the experience was so influential that he was able to develop it into an impressive narrative in his graduate application and interview. On the flip side, had he joined the BBS out of obligation, he most likely would have been less active in the group since it wasn't as strong an interest, and his boredom would have shown on his resume. And he wouldn't have been able to win his lady's love with such finely tuned vocal cords either.

As always, there are a few exceptions to consider. Students who write for student newspapers or volunteer regularly as a cameraperson on the campus television station do develop marketable skills that may "pay off" in the future. But again, those same students partake because they enjoy it.

Getting involved in extracurriculars is worth the investment of time and pays off with leadership skills—like people and project management—as well as personal development. There are virtually no "adults" involved, as nearly all campus clubs are student run, so this presents a great opportunity to learn how to work with peers.

As you choose a group, consider what strengths it will help you develop and how you would describe them at a job interview. Keep in mind that there are very few clubs that don't pay off with some skill set or another. Even cheerleading, which often gets a bad rap, might be found to teach valid skills like PR, time management, or goal setting. Other than joining a drinking club, you really can't go wrong (and even wine-tasting clubs provide some lifelong benefits). Joining a club is not just a matter of gaining experience or skills; it's an issue of fulfilling responsibilities and proving yourself to be dependable, trustworthy, and recommendable—that last one being especially key.

Maneuvering the Activities Fair

It's electrifying. It's inspiring. It's overwhelming. Long before the first hint of a midterm comes the awe-inducing, schedule-filling possibilities of the annual activities fair.

Despite the hype, it's true that this is one of the most valuable functions you will attend all year. Congregated in one location is a representative from almost all the interest groups, associations, and clubs on campus—and every one of them is vying for your attention. Depending on the size of your institution, it can be truly impressive, not to mention a wee bit flattering.

However, before you start scrawling your email address on every clipboard in sight—a word, or two.

The activities fair is a bazaar where everyone is hawking their wares. While they are selling experiences and not rugs, the same basic rules apply: they are likely to exaggerate how nice their group is, misstate its true cost, and say they like your hairstyle more than they really do. But it's still the best place to shop.

Don't be put off that they are trying to sell you on something. EVERYONE in college proselytizes—and this isn't limited to the religious and political groups at the activities fair. The exuberance of ideas and possibilities runs rampant on the college campus. Profs are doing it on their subject, students on their interests or beliefs, and groups on their mission statements. It's how the world works, and to be honest it isn't that bad a thing. When folks are passionate about something, they typically try to share it with someone else. The activities fair is a rich sampling of college life.

To make the most of the event, consider packing a sack with the following: a water bottle, sunscreen, and an enormous compartment for paraphernalia you will pick up at the tables. (You might want to find out where your dorm's recycle bin is located, for that matter.)

Why bother lugging a bag of fliers around for an afternoon—why not just give a bunch of groups your email address, save a tree, and see what happens? Simple: once you get on a group's list—despite their assurances and good intentions that you can easily unsubscribe—it is very difficult to get off. And then, for the next one to four years, you are spammed on a near weekly basis by people you've never heard of to attend meetings you couldn't care less about.

> Make it clear you don't want to take on any major projects or leadership positions in the first semester as you are still in a courting phase—unless you are certain this is the group for you—and then see if being a part of that group brings out your happy face. Don't worry, these groups are used to being flirted with.

If email is still your preference, a sane alternative is to set up a free email account online expressly for the purpose of the activities fair and give your email out to any table you wish. Then use that account to sift emails for the next couple of weeks and decide which groups you like best. Once you've decided, forward your university address to the groups you like, delete the free account, and take a deep, spam-free breath. Voilà!

While choosing an organization to join is an important decision, don't feel like it's carved in marble. Make it clear you don't want to take on any major projects or leadership positions in the first semester as you are still in a courting phase—unless you are certain this is the group for you—and then see if being a part of that group brings out your happy face. Don't worry, these groups are used to being flirted with.

Of course, narrowing down which group to join may be the toughest part of all. Typically you will see groups that are sports/fitness oriented, production oriented (newspaper, yearbook, movies), arts oriented (music, dance, drama), issue clubs (save the whales), community service groups, demographic clubs (race, gender, religion, political party), and socially oriented clubs (Greeks). Since you only have time for a couple, try to pick what gives you the most levels of stimulation—such as exercise, an intellectual challenge, a chance to build friendships, and developing new skill sets.

Sound like a lot to ask of a group? Try to look at it this way: A student who has only been involved in a socially oriented club probably misses out in college because he never benefits from the exercise, intellectual challenge, or skills development aspects of other extracurriculars. A student who has only joined a sports-oriented club is probably a little better off because the social aspect is coupled with some aerobic exercise, but he may still be missing out. Why? Because sports and social interaction can be found off campus just as easily as on. Students who participate only in these types of extracurriculars don't take full advantage of the unique opportunities they can *only* get as a college student (not to mention the fact they don't engage the mind as fully). As part of a portfolio they're fine, but not as the whole thing.

If you absolutely need a sport, choose team sports over an individual sport because it will help meet your quota for social interaction as well as exercise. Plus, you can always swim laps after you graduate, whereas it will be tough to come up with enough folks to form a decent-sized water-polo team. The goal is to meet as many of your quotients as possible in one group, or perhaps a combination of a few.

The exception to all this is varsity sports—at the college level, it's a whole world unto itself of training, leadership development, mental gymnastics, and social skills. As a result, it is all a student has time to do. For those who weren't drafted to a varsity team, intramural athletics are still nothing to sneeze at. James was a varsity wrestler in high school who didn't make the cut when he attended a major Division I NCAA school, so he decided to follow the "why not" philosophy and went out for intramural wrestling. He ended up facing a state champion who had decided not to try out for varsity.

James says the guy made mincemeat out of him—now *that's* an experience he won't be able to duplicate after he graduates!

One last thought when considering how to while away your time. If you'd like to develop your schmoozing skills for later on in your career, consider signing up for a club such as golf or social dance, which will offer lessons cheaply or even for free. These sorts of lessons tend to be cost prohibitive outside of the campus, and finding the time to develop a new hobby will be easier now than while you are adjusting to a new career.

Why Are There So Many Campus Fellowships and Why Don't They Offer Money?
The Role of Religious Groups on Campus

The term "fellowship" applies most commonly to scholarships, but also pertains to religious groups that meet on campus. In this case, we're referring to the latter—sorry, no cash prizes here.

For those who've never been involved in church or religious groups, college is a great time to test them out, primarily because they are so accessible and interested in new people. Many of the faces in the group will most likely be familiar (and, therefore, perhaps friendlier) since you may have seen them around campus. If nothing else, it's a worthwhile venture and you might be surprised that what you *thought* you knew about a group or a church just isn't the case.

While many religious groups may seem similar at first glance, they usually have a distinctive personality. (You wouldn't be the first person to wonder why there are so many fellowships on campus and why, if so many belong to the same religion, they don't just create one big group.) Some may specialize in inward activities (teaching, developing close friendships with others in the group), others in outward activities (community outreach, missions projects abroad). Some may specialize in the needs of athletes while others focus on international students. Some tend to attract folks that look very much alike; others aim to be as diverse as the college itself. In talking with the leaders of various fellowships, ask them how their focus differs from that of other groups (as well as how their beliefs may differ) so you can match your interests with a group you may want to join long-term.

As much as we'd like to offer specific advice on narrowing down the options, fellowships vary by campus and even by year. What may have been a thriving, engaged organization one year may be in the doldrums five years later, or vice versa. There's no way we can give specific advice (nor even can the alums of the school you are attending, most likely), so getting to know the students and leaders within the fellowships as well as learning more about them at the activities fair is really the best way to get started.

Generally there are three sorts of fellowships (also called college or campus ministries) available to students on campus. One is para-church groups, and they tend to be more active on campus or at least more widely recognized because they are nationwide organizations (such as InterVarsity) that offer a fairly consistent program from campus to campus and are not connected with a local church.

The second type of college ministry is one based in a local church. Though often smaller, these provide a link to the community, which can be nice for getting involved in life outside of campus, getting to know people beyond the college age group, or building networks of friends should you decide to stay in the area after graduation.

The third is more of a free-standing group of campus congregations that have no direct connection with local churches but offer services on campus under the umbrella ministry of their respective denomination—Baptists, Lutherans, Catholics, Episcopalians, and so on. We might even suggest a fourth group of religious traditions (though they tend not to use terms like "fellowship" or "campus ministry" to describe themselves and so may not fit entirely into this category), such as Buddhist, Jewish, Hindu, New Age, and other groups that are active on campus.

If you've been active in your church or one of the para-church organizations in high school (such as Young Life), you may want to get involved in a similar group soon after you arrive on campus. Most religious groups offer retreats or conferences toward the beginning of the school year to help freshmen get to know people quickly, and you can attend without committing to officially join the group. Many anticipate that their retreat is, at a minimum, an initial step in the search process. By attending one of these retreats, you will get to know a bunch of folks on campus at the start of your college career, you'll check out some new scenery off campus, and you'll find out more about a fellowship on campus. There's little to lose. And there's no better time than at the beginning of your freshman year when your workload is at a minimum.

As much as we'd like to guarantee "if it's religious, it's safe," that just isn't always the case. There are certainly groups that appear to be innocuous, friendly, and supportive and instead turn out to be deceptive or even controlling. While that isn't the norm, it's been known to happen. So, as with everything else, ask around and don't check your brain at the door.

Over the long run, it will be nearly impossible to sustain meaningful interaction by joining more than one of these sorts of groups. The time required to attend functions, meetings, conferences, and so on can be fairly substantial, not to mention that you'll probably want to build some deep relationships within the group, and that takes a lot of time as well. Fellowships are the sort of extracurriculars that offer deep involvement on many levels, and as such you should limit yourself to only one as soon as you can make a clear choice.

If you can't pick one from the start, that's okay (few freshmen do). Try to narrow it down to two in the first week or so, and set a goal of choosing one by the end of the first semester. Should you choose to join, consider this your deep engagement and do something totally different (go mariachi band!) for your second extracurricular.

Does Work-Study Count as an Extracurricular?
Does It Require Time Outside of Class?

Absolutely—work-study counts as an extracurricular. While it may not sound as fun as joining a club, if funds are an issue, this is an aspect of college life that could be a great opportunity to develop and enhance your leadership and time management skills while earning some cash.

Work-study programs are federally subsidized, enabling universities and colleges to hire a student at a lower cost to the university. And students' work-study ratings are based on their financial need. To find out your work-study rating, visit your financial aid office. The typical payment split between the college and the government is 50/50, though some students qualify for a 75/25 rating, which makes them very desirable to be hired on campus (because the college is only paying 25 percent of their total earnings.) The bottom line is that your college may be able to offer you a plump hourly wage to shelve books or wipe counters, but it costs them less than hiring someone from off campus. It is, as they say, win-win.

Work-study is an important element of college life for some 30 to 50 percent of students, which is far more than the average undergrad may realize. A lot of students want a job that is confined to a desk and is fairly mundane so they can work on their homework. They think they're getting a two-fer by getting paid to study, such as the sophomore who reads a novel for class while scanning students' meal cards as they pass by her register for dinner. Other students go crazy trying to study in that kind of setting and would prefer more meaningful work or lively interaction, like sparring with the cafeteria chef whose known for his edgy sense of humor while you serve hash at the buffet together, or lifeguarding at the campus pool; they want their senses challenged and don't care about multitasking. For some, work-study jobs can turn into permanent positions if the student performs exceptionally well. More and more students are doing research with professors and that can be a college-defining experience (see chapter 6). The options for work are nearly limitless for those who start their search early enough to get a pick at the best offerings out there.

To be fair, most work-study jobs tend to be fairly routine (which is a nice way of saying monotonous). There is absolutely no shame in being a file clerk or a parking attendant or the student ID photographer, and some students admit that they prefer the assembly-line sort of task after a long day studying theorems or postulates.

These humble jobs aren't without their benefits either, teaching critical office skills and time management and—most importantly—a personal look at how the "other half" lives. Should you choose to become an exec down the road as a result of your expensive education, it will go a long way in earning your employees' respect if you personally know what it is like to walk around in their shoe covers.

Another benefit of pursing a work-study job on campus—even, dare we suggest, if you don't immediately need the money—is that it can free up the budget to allow you to take an impressive (yet no-pay) internship over the summer. Instead of going out for wrestling, Jonathan took a work-study job in the performance arts department spackling holes between exhibits, hanging fliers for upcoming performances, and managing the box office every Friday night. (He was a biology and political science major, so he figured some art exposure might round out his experience a little.) As a result, he could afford to take an unpaid internship on Capitol Hill the following summer because he'd paid for his books the previous semester in spackle.

While no undergraduate believes it, there is ample time to get everything done if time is managed wisely. It is completely doable to have a full course load, a work-study job, and join one campus club. Granted, Jonathan probably didn't catch as many *SportsCenters* or hold the top score in the dorm on his favorite video game, but he was able to manage two majors, a job, and join a campus fellowship—plus a whole host of experiences besides, like courting the girl of his dreams and marrying her after graduation. It's doable.

Your course schedule obviously affects what sorts of jobs you can take. It's not unheard of for some students to sacrifice odd hours for a really unusual job, such as going over to the monkey cages at two in the morning to feed the chimps, or traveling weekends and late nights with the basketball team to be its student manager but getting to sit courtside for every game.

A big question students often ask on this topic is whether or not it makes a difference to switch work-study jobs over the course of four years. This depends on your personality. If doing the same job will drive you nuts, then go for variety. But if you find a good fit early on, there is a real benefit in building up seniority. With seniority comes more responsibility, more interesting assignments, the impression of dependability on your resume, and often better pay. By switching jobs frequently, you return to the bottom of the pay scale with each new position.

Everyone is curious whether there will be enough jobs on campus—to date, we've never heard of there being a shortage. There always seem to be more vacancies than there are available students, since campuses tend to rely very heavily on student labor. Obviously as time goes on, the selection decreases and your idea of a primo job may no longer be available, but a job is always waiting to be filled if the main goal is to make some money to offset tuition.

One semester, Lizzy, for whatever scheduling reason, had to work three jobs because she couldn't get enough hours with one. That meant on Mondays and Thursdays she worked at the computer lab giving out print cards, on Wednesdays she checked IDs of students entering the gym, and on Fridays she shelved books in the library. Her employment obligations were so schedule sensitive that she wasn't able to join any organizations that semester. However, the benefit for her was that each job was totally different and the variety made the time pass easily. (As a side note, you won't get rich with work-study jobs. Federal law allows students to work up to 19.9 hours per week to qualify for work-study pay, and that's it. Hope that didn't burst your bubble.)

If work-study isn't your gig or you're looking for an excuse to get off campus, you can often make more money waitressing (love those tips!), nannying, or working at nearby software companies. The career center is your best resource for connecting with all sorts of off-campus employers who are interested in hiring undergrads. Even if you're looking for an enriching internship off campus (which, by the way, probably won't pay), the career center can help you there as well. For more direction on pursuing valuable internships, be sure you read chapter 10.

Are You a Geek If You Aren't Greek?
How the Greek Alphabet Spells More Than P-A-R-T-I-E-S

We've all seen the movies—brotherhood forever, sisterhood to save the day, cool kids make big bucks—and there is nothing so great as a few Greek letters to get your foot in the door. Sadly, Hollywood hasn't kept up so well with the dramatic changes in the Greek system over the last twenty-five years. It's not as *Animal House* would have you believe—for better or worse, depending on your perspective.

The founding principles of most fraternities and sororities are scholarship, leadership, community service, and brother/sisterhood. Three of those four tend to be ignored on today's campuses. What tutoring or mentoring used to be available within the Greek system has been watered down to something ineffectual at best. There are leadership positions for a few, but not for most. Community service is present largely because it is required by the national organization—and sadly that makes it seem more token than deeply meaningful. There is, however, still brother/sisterhood.

In the past, leadership positions in the Greek community were reserved for the senior or the exceptional junior. The arrangement provided an incentive for students to join early and prove themselves to be "good brothers" or "good sisters" in conduct, discipline, and service. This seems to be changing, and it is not unusual to find sophomores who are taking on most of these positions after being a part of a fraternity or sorority for less than a year. Then, once they reach upperclassman status, they become active in some other organization and remain part of the fraternity or sorority in name only.

As a result, the organization of these groups increasingly appeals to freshmen and sophomores. Many students come to college struggling with leaving home and family and needing to satisfy the strong urge to belong to something. The Greek system meets this need by providing a family atmosphere with a high level of acceptance. However, students seem to outgrow that need halfway through their college career and, consequently, interest dwindles.

In response to this trend, several groups have shifted how they recruit students by trying to appeal to students in all four years. Sigma Phi Epsilon, for example, has taken on a more developmental approach by offering the Balanced Man Program, which makes sure all upperclassmen are provided with career advice and assistance on grad school applications. The program has met with some success, and other fraternities and sororities seem to be taking note.

In the past, Greeks used to offer an opportunity to learn from peers: role modeling reigned. Seniors knew their way around campus and could serve as a resource to help freshmen make connections. When Rick Wagoner, president of GM, was asked if there was anything about his undergrad experience that prepped him for his role at GM, he said it was being president of his fraternity. That leadership opportunity—both difficult and challenging—still exists today. However, today's experience is more short-lived than it was in the past, and much of the valuable networking and role modeling that took place in the past is lost because seniors are absent from the scene.

Understandably this has made a significant impact on the Greek experience. Shekinah told us it was great while she was a sister, and that being president was a wonderful lesson in leadership, but she's exhausted now and doesn't want to lead her sorority anymore. Her reaction seems to be fairly common.

All this might look like we're down on the Greeks, so let us assure you that just isn't the case. What we're saying is this: your time is a commodity and joining the Greek system is a gamble. On the positive side, they can teach group relationships; brother/sisterhood, and accountability to one another. Most Greeks also encourage social service, like holiday food drives, and serving in such activities can forge the kinds of friendships and networks that will last for decades. Many alums will tell you that the Greek system really does build invaluable connections. Clearly there is potential for reward from the system.

On the downside, there are huge costs in terms of relationships and academics as well as finances. Fraternities and sororities alike are known to foster the kinds of activities that fritter away time on unfocused or repetitive events that can destroy GPAs, and sometimes in the extreme can even be medically dangerous. It isn't all hype. To be fair, not all cases of date rape or death by alcohol poisoning on campus can be blamed on the Greeks; we certainly aren't pinning all campus evils on them. But being a member probably increases the likelihood of encountering situations where there are large quantities of alcohol or sexual risks on a regular basis. Those odds may be exactly what you are looking for, but read chapter 5 before you roll those dice.

In most cases, a student must be invited to join a fraternity (as opposed to just wandering into the activities fair and joining any club he likes), and quite frankly that is a really big deal to most. Let's face it; it's a bigger ego boost to be selected than it is just to join something. However, that boost comes at a cost: as much as $500 to $2,000 per year to cover dues, initiation fees, formals, and so on.

A former student shared that the best extracurricular activities he was a part of were those that were centered on a shared theme or purpose. Instead of joining a group built on the us/them theme that is often present in Greek societies, Joshua gained a tremendous feeling of satisfaction by joining a group of students who said, "Let's all get together and build a house with Habitat for Humanity," or "Let's put on this play at the children's hospital," or "Let's host a welcome party for freshmen in our dorm." Rather than the focus being on building an identity as a Greek house and simply hanging out, the goal was a specific end result that produced more rewarding experiences, not to mention tighter friendships with students from all walks of life.

> The fundamental point we're making here is that if students choose to pursue the Greeks, they should do so with their eyes open.

The fundamental point we're making here is that if students choose to pursue the Greeks, they should do so with their eyes open.

Despite the fact that the national Greek organizations prohibit alcohol on campus, not to mention prohibitions by state and school laws, the pledging process (also called "membership education") has still been shown to bring increased medical risks where alcohol is present at functions. Nationwide, roughly 1,700 college-aged students die each year from alcohol-related incidents. Those deaths are not all Greek-related, mind you, but they're still a horrible and totally unnecessary loss.

An unanswered question is whether or not Greeks cause students to drink *more* (that is, if these students were prone to drinking wouldn't they have done so whether in a fraternity or not?). Unfortunately, facts can't be teased out of that sort of speculation. However, what we do know is that fraternities and sororities frequently provide the vehicle for drinking and, were they not taking such liberties, the rates of alcohol abuse on campus would drop drastically.

To be fair, there are definitely students who don't drink and are happy members of their fraternity or sorority. Those who do drink might tell you that they've never been forced to drink and feel quite comfortable drinking up to their limit and then having their wishes respected when they choose to stop. But those members are certainly not the majority. By and large, fraternities and sororities create an environment where alcohol is consumed; drugs are more minimal, and the statistics on date rape are currently unknown.

In the end, should you choose to go Greek, consider being involved in another group outside of your house as well. In other words, be a thin member of the Greeks but a thick member of another organization so that you are less prone to rely on alcohol-related functions for your main social stimulus. The other group will offer an easy alternative should you need one. Not only does this provide healthy choices, it will enrich your friendships and provide a more diverse educational experience.

> There is absolutely no shame—not with professors or employers or colleagues—in saying you joined a club simply because you like it. Don't join because you think it makes you look brilliant—join because it's fun.

Getting the Best May Not Mean Piling on More Course Work

If given a choice between taking a course overload or joining a club, choose the club—unless you have an unusual reason to sign up for an additional course, such as:

- This course is only offered once every three terms.
- A prof is retiring and this is the last chance to study with him.
- You need to save money and get out in three years.
- This is your last chance to fill this grad requirement.

The experience outside of the classroom is such a strong supplement to your academic work, not to mention a stress reliever, that it will be worth the investment of your time. That *was* what you wanted to hear anyway, right?

For those parents reading along who question our recommendation, our answer on this goes back to the notion of balance. All work and no play is not healthy. Being active in a club is a necessary part of a healthy lifestyle because it's playtime. This also ties into our belief that it is critical that students join clubs that are interesting (rather than obligatory). These clubs can provide students with much needed stress relief, a positive energy boost, or a fresh perspective on life when a term paper is returned with a disappointing grade.

However, if a club feels like just one more obligation, it isn't serving its purpose. That's often the tipping point on how students decide whether or not it's worth it. Sure, there will be times in all clubs where work outstrips play and you have to buckle down and do ten more reps, type up that budget spreadsheet, or make a dozen phone calls for donations. We aren't suggesting life will be all cotton-candy sweetness with these groups, just a breath of fresh air.

There is absolutely no shame—not with professors or employers or colleagues—in saying you joined a club simply because you liked it. It's much more disappointing to hear that a student joined a group because she thought she would gain something from it on her resume down the road, simply because that's so rarely the case. Don't join because you think it makes you look brilliant—join because it's fun.

The Best Extracurricular Is You
Healthy Habits Happen Here and Now

Yes, this sounds as cheesy as a Saturday morning special, but it's true.

All too often, it seems as if college students perform the worst of any age group at eating, sleeping, and exercising. The notion of three meals a day at a normal time (or even five small meals at regular intervals), a minimum of eight hours of sleep (many studies show that the undergraduate age group requires ten to twelve hours of sleep), and using exercise as a healthy way to reduce stress and manage weight levels consistently lose out on the priority scale for many undergrads.

The greatest way to achieve balance in your schedule is to tune into three basics.

1. Choose your courses.
2. Schedule three essential life-sustaining activities (sleeping, eating, exercise).
3. Add in your extracurriculars as time allows.

For maximum success, it must be done in that order. Students who ignore this frequently battle illness, don't perform as well as they could either academically or socially, and generally aren't as satisfied with themselves as they could be.

Sleep deprivation is one of the most significant health issues for college students today, one that doctors say affects students' immune systems and enables disease to run amok across campus. Health clinics nationwide are actually quite concerned at the rise of meningitis on college campuses and attribute the cause to students' bodies being so abused (even by simple disuse) that it allows epidemics to spread more rapidly.

It's amazing what happens when Mom isn't around to cook three squares and make you go to bed on time.

Now that you are on your own, begin to develop good habits for a lifetime of mental and physical health. Seriously, it won't get any easier after college when you're working fifty-plus hours a week with many more demands on your time.

Creating and living a healthy lifestyle is one of the most foundational decisions you can make for yourself as an adult, and there is no reason to spend the next four years pushing your body beyond its limits. Build healthy habits that will be easy to maintain once free time dwindles with career and life obligations.

CHAPTER 5

Memories You'll Want to Remember

Maneuvering the Social Scene with Aplomb

One of the best parts of college is the social scene: new friends, a chance to redefine who you are, and many of the freedoms of adulthood with very few of the responsibilities. What's not to love? It's a once-in-a-lifetime, four-year window where your best and most important subject will be you. While some students take this opportunity to an extreme and go wild, we assume (since you're reading this book) you're looking to get more out of college than a four-year kegger.

> We believe students who get a clear view of the social scene—its choices, risks, rewards, and consequences—and then create a strategic plan in response will fare better, make fewer mistakes, and enjoy their college years far more than those who simply walk on campus and follow the herd.

While this chapter will certainly discuss how to maneuver the party scene like a pro, we take the subject to a deeper level than that. This is a chapter about defining who you want to be, how you want to be known, and how your recreational ventures will play into that definition. Rather than stumble onto the college social scene with that deer-in-the-headlights expression of many incoming freshmen, we want to press you to make thoughtful and strategic choices about your future—choices that will have you reaping the rewards from here to retirement, rather than paying the penalties.

We believe students who get a clear view of the social scene—its choices, risks, rewards, and consequences—and then create a strategic plan in response will fare better, make fewer mistakes, and enjoy their college years far more than those who simply walk on campus and follow the herd. That belief has been reinforced repeatedly over the years as we have observed the greatest successes come from students who entered college with five principles in common. Applied to you those principles would be:

- Know who you are.
- Discern what you *want* to do.
- Decide what you *won't* do.
- Envision what types of memories you want to make.
- Identify the personal achievements you want to accomplish.

This is a pivotal time. These five principles—if thoughtfully evaluated and put into practice—will have a greater impact now than they potentially will at any other season in your life.

Ultimately we hope this chapter will provide enough guidance that you are able to enjoy the freedoms of adulthood in a way that makes your undergraduate years some of life's best; that you are able to avoid the pitfalls that trap so many unsuspecting students; that you are able to graduate without regrets and be proud of your accomplishments. Beginning with two sections that highlight creative social alternatives and help you design a strategy for success, this chapter discusses topics that often present the greatest challenges for undergrads—drugs, alcohol, sex—so that you can reshape or solidify your strategy for having fun at college.

Out of fairness to you, we solemnly promise not to do you the disservice of taking the easy way out by citing the overquoted yet popular "everyone does it" and pretending that it won't come back to bite you later. We suspect that rather than watch us bury our heads in the sand, you'd prefer we spell it out like it is so you can make your own best decisions.

This One's on Us

Let us be the first to rave about the thrilling buffet of social offerings before you. While a large university may have a more diverse spread, even small colleges have their own unique subcultures that are waiting to be explored. For example, Stella went to a small women's university and started a group that went rappelling off the clock tower as a stress reliever and organized midnight movie fests projected off the quad walls as an incentive to finish term papers early. At a large public university, Karen was able to persuade her friends (and the administration) to host an open-air French banquet on the chapel roof as a fund-raiser for breast cancer research (though it could just have easily been a fund-raiser). Many campuses have sculpture gardens, primate centers, marine labs, extended field trips in China, and so much more . . . you have before you nearly endless possibilities.

All that to say, aim to do something out of the ordinary at least once a quarter with people who initially may not seem like your type. Should you find yourself needing some inspiration, locate one of dozens of flier poles on campus and pull a couple fliers to take home for consideration; you'd be amazed how many students walk by those fliers expecting they'll see that show or go on that tour "someday," and then life gets busy and "someday" never comes.

Of course, you could be like some students who ignore their campus's social offerings altogether and go the more traditional route of the undergraduate holy trinity for entertainment (drugs, sex, and alcohol). But, why be that predictable? Why limit yourself by engaging in high-risk, low-reward (not to mention illegal) activities when you could be creative about your adventures and have fun—fun that you'll not only be proud of but that you'll also enjoy remembering with friends who are worth having? Really, when you come down to it, that's what everyone wants when they graduate: great friends.

> There are endless exotic possibilities in college that are entertaining to talk about even years afterward, and the memories of those times hold far greater rewards than yet another round of drinking games.

So get slightly crazy as you plan the weekend's festivities. A couple of months after the fact, there's nothing to say about having attended the nth drunken brawl. But parachuting over campus, an all-night soccer tournament, a forty-eight-hour marathon viewing of James Bond movies in chronological order, a social dance class that ends in New York for the weekend—you are limited only by your imagination. There are endless exotic possibilities in college that are entertaining to talk about even years afterward, and the memories of those times hold far greater rewards than yet another round of drinking games.

Why experiment with how many shots you can hold before passing out when, instead, you could explore the world waiting at your doorstep? As long as it doesn't threaten your academic success or put someone at risk, consider your adventures good clean fun.

Before you take a bite out of life, concoct a few capers to keep you and your friends entertained—the kind you don't need to be falling down drunk to imagine, commit, or enjoy. We're talking summer camp sorts of pranks, so let your mind wander . . . hmm, behaviors that are mildly shocking to the mores of polite society but aren't harmful and wouldn't involve a trip to the ER. Hmm.

Drew decorated his dorm to look like a crime scene while everyone was asleep, body outlines included. This was a pretty big step for Drew in developing some playfulness, considering he rarely left the computer cluster. Lonnie was known as being a very serious student, so when she started the rumor that class was canceled next Wednesday just to see how far it would get around campus, folks believed her (plus the free laughs made for a nice stress reliever). Of all the legends we've heard, Jessie's is our favorite. Knowing that the fraternities at her college all had live mascots, this witty lass sent a letter to all the fraternities on the dean of students' stationery directing them to get photo IDs for their creatures, assigning each a particular time and place. Of course, everyone was given the same time and place, which was, of course, the dean of students' office. Several dozen dogs arrived at the appointed hour and pandemonium ensued.

The idea behind encouraging some lighthearted pranks is to use your next four years to experience adrenaline rushes that you won't be able to revel in as much once you have a family in tow. This is a great time to partake of craziness that might scare your mother (and may be irresponsible later if you have a spouse and kids) but you've always wanted to try. Who are we to tell you not to dive off a bridge with only elastic and nylon sparing your life? (Though, the legal training one of us paid for obliges us to recommend that you only do it with trained professionals.) It's these sorts of pursuits that make (and keep) college interesting without developing the rut of the overdone alcohol-induced stupor. So, live it up. Enjoy making memories that will happily last you the rest of your days.

Starting Off Strong
Deciding Who You Want to Be Before You Reach Campus

Chances are you've spent more time your senior year pondering the college party scene than you did its classrooms. No parents to ask embarrassing questions, only a few hours of course work a day, and a lot of time to experiment—isn't that what college is all about?

Not really. We won't even pretend that partying doesn't happen on campus on a weekly basis. But what should remain *at best* (within certain legal confines) an extracurricular activity can become a dangerous distraction that undermines students' opportunities to make the most of their college education. In all honesty, the best party is the one where you know how it ends before you get there.

> The clearer you are with yourself about what goes under the categories of "to do" and "not to do," the more you will be able to enjoy the company you are in because you don't have to second-guess the situation.

What, this book comes with a crystal ball? Okay, you've got us there. We don't expect you'll actually predict the future. What we mean to say is that you can know yourself and your goals well enough to know where, if, when, and how to (or how not to) cross boundaries you have established for yourself. And the clearer you are with yourself about what goes under the categories of "to do" and "not to do," the more you will be able to enjoy the company you are in because you don't have to second-guess the situation.

It may be that the standards you kept in high school will serve you well in college; and, if so, that's great. But even if that's the case, you will need to reevaluate how they apply to the college campus.

(And, if you're reading this after your freshman year, it's not too late. In fact, you now have a solid view of your campus, so it's a great time to block out new goals.) The first step is to make some time (with a notepad in hand and the crowds off yonder) to sketch out some personal boundaries/ standards/goals/values—call 'em what you like, their function is pretty much the same. In a few sections, we'll discuss the most common concerns in more detail to broaden your sketch even further.

> **It is much easier to enter your freshman year with momentum behind goals aiming you in one direction (which you can alter as needed) than it is to try and jump-start the process once you're on campus.**

Granted, if you are reading this as an incoming freshman, it will be much easier to apply your goals once you have a better idea of how the campus works. What we're asking you to do might even seem like a premature exercise in hypotheticals, but we promise it will pay off. It is much easier to enter your freshman year with momentum behind goals aiming you in one direction (which you can alter as needed) than it is to try and jump-start the process once you're on campus.

As you design a short list of guidelines, aim for a holistic view of yourself on the college campus. While this chapter is largely about creative (and not-so-creative) adventures on campus, even nonparty goals will have implications for what sorts of parties you decide to attend.

For example, your choices about the social scene will influence your academics. What do you want "studious you" to look like? Are you naturally inclined toward being bookish so you think you need to focus your study window and set goals to socialize more? Or are you the opposite, and you want to get as much of your work out of the way between 8 a.m. and 5 p.m. so you can spend the evening relaxing with friends? Design your social life intentionally so that the primary reason you came to college (getting an education) doesn't take a backseat to what should remain extracurricular.

A more obvious link in considering how you want to explore the social scene is relationships. Friendships are an easy one—not too many boundaries are required there. Dating, however, is another story. Should you decide to date, how physical do you want to get? Set really specific standards with this one because the fewer gray areas, the easier it will be to honor those standards in the heat of the moment. Chart it out if that helps: how far do you want to go on the first date, once you're officially dating, once you're engaged? What would you prefer to save for the wedding night?

For each of these stages and topics, consider the long-term effect of each choice (as much as you can without that handy crystal ball) and use those potential consequences to help you determine where to put boundaries.

Don't feel obligated to show your final strategy to anyone, though we do suggest you file it safely away for future reference. Here are a few other topics to ponder as you spell out your boundaries and develop an image of who you want to be by the time you graduate. Again, think through these as much as you can before arriving on campus so you have something to work with once you've begun to understand your college's social scene better.

- Health and well-being—goals for exercise, sleep, or a certain diet?
- Studies—scheduled or at random, what about "borrowing" papers, graduating with honors?
- Religion—regular weekly service, spiritual buffet, or none?
- Alcohol use—at what age, in what settings, what about becoming drunk?
- Drugs—if ever, what kind, what setting?
- Sex—activity or virginity, how many bases and when, what setting, under what influences?

If it helps to query peers, parents, or other folks you respect, by all means do so. You can never ask too many questions when it comes to learning from others' successes and mistakes. (Well, the questions might get annoying after a while, but you get what we're saying.)

As you begin to sort through their answers, what you will hopefully find is that setting boundaries for yourself doesn't prevent you from exploring the world; if anything, it frees you to be more adventuresome because you've chosen ways to do so that don't frivolously expose you to risks. To date, we've never heard a graduate say, "I wish I had been more sexually active" or "I wish I had gotten drunk at that frat party," but we sure have heard the opposite. So, be willing to set the bar high for yourself; if necessary, it can always be lowered. (The inverse holds true as well: you can always push the bar higher later, though just as is true of gravity and a bench press, it proves to be a bit trickier.)

> As you sketch out goals and boundaries for yourself, aim to discover the principles that undergird those boundaries rather than simply listing out a block of rules to follow.

In forming your own standards, the best advice we've heard on the subject is "hold principles tightly and policies lightly"—meaning, as you sketch out goals and boundaries for yourself, aim to discover the principles that undergird those boundaries rather than simply listing out a block of rules to follow. Principles allow for flexibility and game-time applications, whereas policies could write you into a corner. "I'm never going to be out after 2 a.m." or some other arbitrary time will be a very difficult policy to sustain and may not apply. Neither will "I'll never be around anyone who's stumbling drunk," since it will be difficult to control someone else's behavior. Instead, a better principle would be "I'll avoid putting myself in situations where my safety is dependent on the sobriety of others," and how that's applied will depend on the event.

It's thrilling, really. From the time your parents drop you off and head for home, you will be presented with a host of new ideas and opportunities. No curfew and no serious course work for a few weeks: that's a lot of time for hanging out, exploring campus, and meeting new friends at orientation events, and it all spells fun.

But large amounts of unstructured time make for other possibilities as well. There is a strong likelihood that you will be approached about alcohol, sex, and even drugs your first week on campus. The key is to anticipate situations that will put you at risk by studying your campus and how your principles apply. Now that you have drawn some bright lines that you have thoughtfully considered from action to end result, it is absolutely possible to color a fascinating array of adventures within them. (And, if you feel like you could use some support or, at the very least, a trustworthy listener, we recommend talking to your RA, someone at the counseling center, a campus minister, or your parents, since the friendships you will have begun at this point won't have had time to be tried and proven.)

Please understand—by asking you to establish boundaries for yourself, we're not suggesting you make up your mind, close it, then lock yourself in your room. While surrounding yourself with like-minded people can help you become the person you want to be, that doesn't mean you should avoid getting to know people who think differently. Every day you are surrounded by people of similar age with similar goals from all different walks of life. A fabulous risk to take would be asking them to treat you to a new perspective of the world from their eyes. Go to an art show your friend likes but you otherwise would never attend; visit a part of town another friend loves but you've never seen; eat white rice with sugar and butter like she does just to see how it tastes; talk about your childhood and what sort of childhood you hope your kids will have someday. Not only will you broaden your friendships, you will broaden your understanding of the world (which, ironically, makes you a deeper person.) And you may surprise yourself by developing new tastes, both for life and for friends.

In that same vein, we recommend that you look for opportunities to intellectually challenge your values. College is a rich smorgasbord of ideas. Use it as a forum to flesh out your worldview by starting some spicy discussions over dinner. Exposure to other viewpoints is a huge part of your personal growth, and one that will hopefully be ongoing throughout your life. So go to that tailgate party. If you've decided not to drink, super (and quite honestly most of your classmates won't care either way). You'll get to relax with new friends and have a blast at the game. Sure, some of the folks might be sloshed so they think they're funnier than they truly are, but that's okay. You've got your lines, they've got theirs; it's entirely possible for everyone to still have a good time.

> **Select your close friends carefully. On almost any campus, you will be able to find others who share your ideas and standards, or, at the very least, people who respect you for them.**

Beyond those general social events, we *do* recommend that you select your close friends carefully. The type of people you spend the majority of your time with—downtime, uptime, or anytime—is quite simply the type of person you will become. Use that to your benefit. Seek out the sorts of people you respect and who will respect you—especially if you feel like your views might put you in the minority. On almost any campus, you will be able to find others who share your ideas and standards or, at the very least, people who respect you for them.

College is not the socially neutral environment that we wish it was. On most campuses, there is prejudice in favor of experimentation, particularly with alcohol and sex. Don't be naive. This is the direction your culture will push, regardless of the school you attend. If you want to push back and stick to your standards, you will need some like-minded friends, or at least friends who support your choice in values. Plus, good friends make college loads more fun.

A final move that will help you live up to your goals will be knowing which parties to join and which to ditch. In the beginning, these distinctions will most likely be blurred and your choices may feel a bit out of control, which should be a yellow flag. Whatever your standards may be (about when or when not to drink, when or when not to have sex, when or when not to do drugs, when or when not to party), focus on placing yourself *only* in situations where you can stay in control of those decisions.

Risks You'd Want Us to Mention

Part of what makes college so exciting is the fairly accurate impression that your opportunities are limitless. Most undergrads see it as a season of boundless exploration and experimentation—and that's largely true. However, it's not a time devoid of consequences. They may be delayed, but folks definitely have to pay up at some point or another.

Some would argue that they are only posing risks to themselves so no one has a right to say otherwise, but their argument is demonstrably untrue. STDs pose risks to future partners, drunk driving is selfishly deadly to society, and hazing is debilitating to fellow students, to name a few. What's hard to appreciate for an early twenty-something (but will become irrefutably obvious later on) is that our poor choices carry scars that will affect us, our loved ones, and potentially even strangers for the rest of our lives.

Perhaps some students make poor decisions because when accountability is low, the risks feel low; because the risks feel low, students feel invincible and behave as though the logical outcomes of their actions will go no further than the campus gate. If suggesting that students might hold such a belief seems condescending, we apologize. We wouldn't mention it had we not seen that belief played out on campus time and time again: students get caught crossing the law and they are shocked to find themselves being held responsible for their actions.

Case in point is one student who recently made a name for herself by committing a ridiculous petty crime. Jordan was in a rush one morning trying to get to class on time, so she parked in the faculty parking lot. Sure, there were signs posted multiple places as well as a mechanical arm at the exit to dissuade anyone but faculty from parking there. But, like she said later, she was late for class so she ignored the signs and parked there anyway.

Her bubble burst when she was caught trying to lift the arm of the parking gate in order to leave. Sometimes students get away with it, sometimes it scrapes up their paint jobs, sometimes it breaks the gate mechanism. Oddly enough, she complained to the judicial affairs officer during the hearing that she shouldn't be held responsible because there was no sign posted stating that lifting the gate would break it. The officer found it a laughable excuse. She was put on probation, lost parking privileges, paid a fine, and now has a permanent mark on her disciplinary record—all to save herself ten minutes.

Will this witless story shadow her future success? Absolutely. Will it ruin her future? Probably not—though it made her look foolish and irresponsible. What is worse, for every grad school and job application from here on out she will have to check "yes" when asked if she's been involved in any disciplinary measures. Depending on the competition for the position, she might have an opportunity to explain herself or it could ding her from the list of hopefuls before she's given a moment to speak. There's no way to know.

> "Everybody does it" turns out to provide no legal protection should you get caught.

Perhaps students are willing to cross the law more on campus than they would otherwise because the lax enforcement of the law has given them a false sense of security. Whether or not we want to admit it, it's true that alcohol restrictions are not as rigorously enforced on college campuses as they are off. However, they are not totally ignored either, by the way, and "everybody does it" turns out to provide no legal protection should you get caught. Even if drinking laws are loose, the rest of the legal paradigm applies, and even more so the principle of sowing and reaping.

True, college may temporarily suspend societal codes or delay the repercussions of illicit behavior. And society may even prove to be tolerant of some campus exceptions, but even that is changing. Underage drinking, for example, has swung from absolute disapproval to approval to society expecting it but not approving. Alcohol-related deaths and date rape continue to press public opinion further into the disapproval camp. But even at that, underage drinking is still not strongly enforced on many campuses.

Over a quarter of the students entering campus each year come with fake IDs. Melinda remembers first becoming aware of their prevalence when a dorm mate begged for her Oregon driver's license because the background was easier to scan and forge. By the time freshmen learn their way around campus, that fraction of fake IDs grows to half of the matriculating class. Don't be misled. Just because that number is enormous and fake IDs are common doesn't mean the sentence will be any lighter should you get caught. Judges aren't impressed by the percentage of students on campus flashing fake birthdates.

So what are the risks we alluded to at the beginning? Simply stated, the risk is that we are all bound by the laws of society and the laws of consequence, whether we're oblivious in our actions or intentional.

The Unforgettable Web

As in "World Wide Regret"

"What do I want to be called for the rest of my adult life? I've always hated 'Leroy.' Should I go by my middle name instead? Should I hide that I like bluegrass and tell people I listen to Latin jazz? What if I stop styling my hair and go natural and refuse to eat all meat products?"

Part of the appeal of college is precisely this opportunity to write a new chapter. You may have been known as "the bookish one," "the cowboy," "the jock," or any number of stereotypes that you might be eager to shed. It's particularly common at highly selective schools to see students go to great lengths to ditch their nerd factor now that it got them into their college of choice. You can almost smell them trying to emanate a bit more coolness (which can be literal for those "discovering" cologne).

The trouble is that in trying to earn extra cool points, some people go overboard. In fact, it's part of the reason why so many big mistakes get made in the first few weeks of college. Included in the consequences of having made those mistakes is the reputation that follows and is difficult to shake. Whatever your moral standards in high school, if you start out as the proverbial good-time-to-be-had-by-all in college, you'll be hard-pressed to convince others that you're no longer that person. Rumors spread across the college campus much like a small town, and tongues tend to wag. So take care with first impressions.

We doubt experimentation was ever risk free, but as our world becomes smaller, the risks become more costly. Nowadays your "worst ever" might not simply live on in your friends' nostalgia: it could live forever on the Internet to the entertainment of your classmates and the wider world (yes, including your parents' friends, future employers, and potential in-laws).

Take a group of young women who enjoyed a well-documented night of revelry when they decided to host a baby oil party and capture it all on film. Ironically enough, some of the women partaking in the shenanigans were leaders in a women's initiative on campus that had recently been demanding greater public recognition and respect for the achievements of women on campus—and they got it. Well, the recognition, that is.

There they were, shown on the Internet in their nothings, laughing it up in a tub of naked friends and grease. Of course, the link for those pictures was some of the fastest spam to make its way around campus, and public response (though flattering from one particularly overly stimulated set) was anything but respect. They were unable to reconcile their behavior with their desire to be treated fairly, and it cost them. No one has the privilege to choose to behave any way at any time and to be respected regardless. What these women were really demanding was the freedom to choose without consequences, and that just doesn't happen.

For good or ill, your choices will follow you even if you switch social scenes, graduate, or move to a different state. That can be fabulous, if you've built a student career to be proud of.

Online displays of adventures don't simply have to go the way of baby oil parties. After growing up as her small town's hokiest dresser (and scaredest scaredy-cat), Betty spent the next four years of college and four more years post graduation determined to broaden her horizons. She braved backpacking trips that began with the dorm and eventually took her as far as Australia. She made a new group of friends at a Japanese church and later moved to Japan to learn the language and culture while teaching English. She traveled from the straw huts of Indonesia's jungles to the beaches of the South Pacific, and with each of her new adventures, her confidence and character grew into the person she'd hoped she would become. (Thankfully the exposure to a world of style improved her wardrobe as well.) Her adventures are posted online and have become a way to meet up with old friends and enjoy new adult friendships with them. Oh, and now she goes by Elizabeth.

Once on the Internet, always on the Internet—somewhere. Here's another one. As a way to earn some extra cash his sophomore year, Paul wrote an article for an online magazine about trends on the college campus. He graduated in 1999 and still gets attaboys from new colleagues who have done Internet searches about him now that they work at the same international firm. And he should. It's a well-written article—now, if only he was still getting royalties. (However, if he decides to run for office someday, he may wish he had tempered his speech.)

On the flip side, that posting Jason listed not so subtly on his blog about the threesome he had on Friday (with one of them being underage and high) is almost guaranteed to rat him out somewhere down the road. Sure, you might be able to pay for a program to scrub your online image if you decide to go the Jason route, but are you willing to risk that it might not catch *everything*? Illegal stuff is especially newsworthy, and once it's reported in the news, the story will be forever searchable on the Internet.

Even less manageable than the Internet is the web of social networks. Should the sister of your best friend be best friends with the guy thinking of hiring you, and should they play the name game of "Oh, you went to that college! Let's see, do you know . . . ," your name just might come up. Are you one quick story away from your dream job being game over, or will the impromptu recommendation be so favorable that you're a clear winner for the position?

We sense the need for a disclaimer: we aren't advocating illegal activity and then instructing you to hide it well. By all means, your best option is to avoid all situations that would injure others or mar your reputation. Our point in this section is to hold up the indefatigable network of wagging tongues as an incentive to keep yourself out of trouble. Somewhere, a wise man along the way said, "Your sins will find you out," and he was right. Should you make a mistake along the way, be as discreet with that information as possible, apologize to those necessary, and refrain from posting it in an email or online to *anyone*.

Let the Good Times Roll

Maneuvering Your Newfound Freedoms Like a Pro

On campuses larger than many small Midwestern towns, how is an unknown freshman expected to thrive his first year without becoming social hamburger?

FIND A TRUSTWORTHY LISTENER

By definition that means someone who is tight-lipped and who puts you at ease. Someone you are in fact so comfortable with that you could have conversations like, "I'm really worried I'm going to try crack when I get on campus, but I don't think I should" or "I lost my virginity and I wish I hadn't." This should be someone you can respect to help you through difficult choices without having to worry about being judged (and preferably someone you have known for years or who is professionally bound to confidentiality). It could be a counselor, a former teacher, a pastor, a parent, or someone you have met on your campus. The point is not to go it alone. Have someone to call anytime for backup—especially that first year while you are still trying to lay the groundwork for trust in your friendships. Remember all those goals you sketched out in the "Starting Off Strong" section? It helps to have someone cheering you on as you excel in them or tossing you a lifeline should you make a mistake.

SAVE BIG DECISIONS FOR DAYLIGHT

Ellie was fortunate to figure this out on her own before becoming a member of the freshman floozies. Here she was a naive minister's kid attending a secular university as big as her hometown, and her first night alone on campus she found herself being led around by the infamous campus band with hundreds of her closest classmates in a whirling frenzy. It was a scene to make Dionysus proud. She tells later that as she stood in the quad that night with drinks pouring and people moshing and gyrating, the sense that anything was possible—and the thrill of those dark possibilities—filled her with simultaneous terror, rapture, and loneliness. Who would know? And worse yet, who would care?

She would. Fortunately the rush wasn't artificially induced (which meant it quickly subsided), and Ellie followed the throng back to her dorm and decided to call it a night before making a life-altering decision in the madness of the moment. She was wise enough to recognize that it wasn't a superb time for reasonable thought. After some pondering the following morning, she decided to head out and make some positive connections with people who seemed to embody attributes of someone she'd like to become. A dozen conversations later, she and her new friends founded a campus Big Sibs program that helps connect incoming freshman with upperclassmen of similar beliefs who can show them the ropes. And, a decade later, it's still going.

The big takeaway from this story is not that you should rush out to start a campus-orientation program. Many campuses may already offer student-run variations. The point is to save life-altering decisions for the daytime, when you have your wits about you.

> Try to connect with upperclassmen in a mentoring sort of relationship. Since they've been on campus for a while, they probably have (or know someone who has) made all the rookie mistakes.

LEARN FROM THE VETERANS

Try to connect with upperclassmen in a mentoring sort of relationship. Since they've been on campus for a while, they probably have (or know someone who has) made all the rookie mistakes. Why repeat them? What could take a year or two to discover on your own about what or what not to do at your particular college is already well known by someone else out there. Plus, then you get the added benefit of stories like, "I once knew a guy in college who . . ." without risking your precious reputation.

Even If You Don't Get Caught . . .
Newton's Third Law Will Find You

Drugs, alcohol, and sex get lumped together for discussion purposes, but they should really be addressed separately. For that matter, they shouldn't be lumped together in any situation.

Alone, they bear a weight that is difficult to manage, but where they become extremely dangerous and where the risks become magnified exponentially is in combination. It's one thing to experiment physically in your relationships within clearly drawn boundaries. It's a completely different beast when you combine it with alcohol and find yourself literally reeling from loss of self-control. At best, you won't stick to your lines; at worst, you could find yourself surviving a real nightmare. Combine that with drugs and you're someplace you may regret for the rest of your days.

The best course of action is to avoid all drinking if you are underage (and becoming drunk even if you are not) and to steer clear of anything with a stronger zap than caffeine. Not only will your liver and brain cells thank you for staying dry, you'll thank yourself when you emerge from college with your health and dignity intact and a happy lineage of creative escapades you can be proud of.

We are tempted to end this topic at that, but it would be negligent of us to do so. Despite the continuing evidence that fewer students are involved in drugs, alcohol, and sex on campus than students actually assume are involved, for those one or two readers out there who plug their ears and plow with abandon into the danger zone, we feel obligated to map out a few escape routes to help them minimize the risks.

So we continue . . .

Alcohol still seems to be the stimulant of choice on college campuses, but drugs cannot be discounted. We treat them differently here because society treats them differently. Illegal drug use is disciplined far more rigidly than the occasional pilsner is, therefore you need to be far more wary about experimenting with drugs.

We're not just talking about the doobie drugs of your parents' generation either. Campus administrations note an increase in prescription drug abuse among students. The average reader of the sports page would generally agree that it isn't fair for athletes to use steroids to boost their games and that steroid use should remain illegal. Yet somehow that same reader, when confronted with the option of "borrowing" a friend's Ritalin to stay up later in prepping for an exam or to have a greater sense of focus when writing a paper under the wire, doesn't see the ethical dilemma. Worse yet, she doesn't see the physical threat.

Were that student found to be taking prescriptions illegally, her integrity would be brought into question. Setting aside the possibility that the judicial affairs office would penalize her were she to get caught, this student runs an even greater risk to her personal future should employers learn that she self-medicated to artificially boost her work capacity. College is all about laying a groundwork for your life as an adult—ask yourself if you really want to make your success drug dependent, and if that's something you will be able to sustain throughout your professional career.

Because of Peter's work for the government, students frequently query him about wanting to get security clearance, often asking how that process is affected by past recreational drug use. His advice is this: admitting to a *single* experimental use of marijuana is not necessarily a deal breaker for getting security clearance, but it's a red flag.

Admitting to drug use? Who would be that dumb? (We actually know of someone who admitted during her interview for the FBI that she tried mushrooms once—that was the end of her never-to-be career with the FBI.)

Actually, dumber still would be lying about it. The security clearance process is looking first for honesty and second for a narrative that demonstrates how you have matured beyond repeating that mistake. As you sit on that splintered park bench or squishy subway cushion reading this, you may not be planning for a future career in defense, so this may seem like a moot point. The trick is, you never quite know where your future will lead you, so why limit yourself? There are a great many careers out there that consider drug use a sensitive issue and require a clear break in your lifestyle choices in order to be hired. The longer that break is, the better. Obviously, the best case is avoiding drugs altogether.

> There are a great many careers out there that consider drug use a sensitive issue and require a clear break in your lifestyle choices in order to be hired. The longer that break, the better. Obviously, the best case is avoiding drugs altogether.

Even if you are absolutely certain that you will never want a security clearance, we still advise against experimental drug use. It's best to approach any sort of experimentation—bungee jumping, eating live baby squid, asking the homecoming queen for a date—this way: watch, learn, then (and only then if your sources come back on it being a worthwhile and relatively risk-free experience) do. Maybe.

It's vastly more dangerous to push your limits on the first night of freshman orientation than it is to play designated driver for a while to get your bearings. The parties won't be going anywhere and this front-row seat will give you a big picture of what the party scene is all about. Once you've seen more than an eyeful, you'll be able to apply your standards that much more accurately, and hopefully you'll decide not to drink. If you feel like the social lame duck, keep in mind that at most schools nearly 10 to 20 percent of students don't drink at all. (Now you can tell your folks you're in the top 10 percent of your class!) With the current trend in thought being "everyone is entitled to their own opinion," no one worth mentioning will think less of you. In all probability, you may become Mr. Popularity for being the dry driver for all your friends.

Since this is a critical section, allow us to recap.

1. Don't drink underage, get drunk, or do drugs. That's a period right there. If you insist on ignoring this invaluable wisdom, consider the next point.

2. Before jumping into an experiment, watch and learn. Measure the consequences as far down the line as you can. There will always be risks, but if they outweigh the rewards, avoid.

3. If you choose to take on these risks and experiment, do not combine the new variable with another control-altering influence.

The bottom line is that for every action there is an equal and . . . well, you know. If it's illegal or poses health risks or other life-polluting consequences, find a better hobby.

"But I Wanna Drink"

What "Drinking Responsibly" Means

In writing this book, we have to be honest: each of us made very different choices as college students. We swung on both sides of the line, two of us by never drinking and one definitely drinking. Despite our personal choices, each of us admits that it was nearly impossible to never be in the presence of alcohol while on campus. It was definitely doable to choose not to drink (in fact, some parties offered alternative beverages that looked like their alcoholic counterparts so no one could tell what we were drinking), but whether it was a drunk roommate stumbling in late one night or a party down the hall, we would've had to go into hiding to avoid it. (On a side note, however, it *is* more doable to avoid exposure to drugs.)

Most students will say they drink either to alleviate stress or as a social lubricant, both of which are an entirely different proposition than drinking with the goal of becoming drunk. (The latter leads to increased damage to major organs as well as the fact you'll no longer be in control of your decisions.) College is a time to explore your world, and we stand by that notion. But challenge the premise that your college experience is lacking if you haven't crossed every line and experienced all.

Exploring issues that conflict with your values doesn't mean you need to test them out on yourself like some supersized guinea pig. It just means you should encounter them fairly by listening to an intelligent voice on the matter. In other words, it's listening to your roommate's spiel about why he thinks it's okay to drink underage, not taking a swig to find out for yourself.

RESPONSIBLE ACTION #1:
PICK A GROUP

For the sake of discussion, let's assume someone around you is drinking. How are you supposed to handle that "responsibly"? To start, let's set up a few safety nets. Assume that you are the only person looking out for your best interests. Should you decide to attend some of the larger parties on campus, go in groups and make sure beforehand that you are going home in those same groups. Where students most often get into trouble is when they go to a party alone, or their group dissolves and no one has their back. It's dismal. As much as we wish it weren't so, the whole notion of trusting people because it's a community of scholars is a farce. One would expect to be safe, but if scholarship made people trustworthy, we wouldn't need bike locks on campus.

RESPONSIBLE ACTION #2:
GET YOUR OWN DRINK

Sometimes the pressure to push boundaries is obvious, and sometimes it is deceptive. Whether you fill your Solo with a nonalcoholic disguise or partake in the punch dipped out of a garbage pail, under no circumstances should you swig a drink handed to you by someone else. Let's face it, unless you've known the person for years, everyone there is a stranger. This is true especially for women. It doesn't matter if the guy handing you the drink has been the nicest guy in the dorm since everyone moved in last week—even if he was the one who helped you lug your heaviest boxes up three flights of stairs. Get your own drink. You need to know exactly what is in your cup, and the easiest way to do that is to fill it yourself.

Date-rape drugs are far more prevalent than most students realize, and it doesn't take many sips to faze a woman—especially if she's slim or new to the party scene. Unfortunately, the amnesia brought on by these cocktails is temporary and over time, via flashbacks or nightmares, the woman who was abused remembers all. It's very real and very disturbing. We hate to be the ones to crush any remaining innocence you may have about the world, but we'd rather crush an illusion than sit back and watch *you* be crushed because you didn't know.

RESPONSIBLE ACTION #3:
GIVE YOURSELF SOME TIME

The most vulnerable time for students is first semester of freshman year, and the risks seem to diminish by senior year as students find more creative ways to entertain themselves and have a better handle on their boundaries. Until then, be wary. Students are vulnerable any time an event involves alcohol. Whatever the cause, the cold numbers remain that victims of date rape tend to be freshmen (male or female) between orientation and Thanksgiving break. At the high end, some groups estimate that one out of four women on college campuses today will be sexually assaulted by a fellow male student.

> The most vulnerable time for students is first semester of freshman year, and the risks seem to diminish by senior year as students find more creative ways to entertain themselves and have a better handle on their boundaries.

Even with our recommendations, you can't bank on the residence hall guaranteeing sanctuary. Not even the group you came with to the party can be depended on to save you. It's delusional to think rape doesn't occur in dorms or that it won't happen the first time you get sloshed. It's one of the big reasons we suggest you wait as long as possible before engaging liberally in the party scene. Get to know what else there is to do on campus. Over time you will learn (via the rumor mill, the campus paper, and observing peers the morning after) which parties are safe and which are not. It could be that in that time you'll discover more fascinating outlets on campus, and the party scene may lose its glittery appeal.

RESPONSIBLE ACTION #4:
ENJOY COLLEGE FOR THE UNIQUE EXPERIENCE THAT IT IS

Despite the advice we have given so far, on her second night on campus Shauna decided to do her own thing and attend an off-campus mixer with some upperclassmen. She was invited by a friend she had known for years who happened to be a senior on campus, and she took her roommate as backup. Before heading out, she and her roommate also secured their own ride home. Smart, on both counts. In that respect, she played the game well. However, what she gave up in attending this ho-hum any-night-of-the-week party was a chance to interact with her new classmates during a campus-sponsored (aka FREE) event. Even assuming for the moment that the event she missed turned out to be the most boring function of the week, for some inane reason the shared misery of those events can bond people faster than the best night on campus.

The good news for Shauna is that no one got hurt. The bad news is that she lost an opportunity to build key relationships with her own classmates. In a year or two, those upperclassmen she met will be gone, and though to the uninitiated it seems like Shauna will have all year to get to know the folks in her dorm, it doesn't work that way.

For whatever reason, there is a brief window of time in the first two or three weeks on campus where memories are made and friendships are forged; unless you don't mind being out of the loop for the rest of the year, you'll have a lot more friends in the dorm if you stick with the group. Plus, those who start out doing the up-perclassman off-campus gig early on rarely return to being in-volved on campus. Ever. It's an isolating experience that—while potentially fun—can be tried out after graduation, whereas the orientation period cannot.

RESPONSIBLE ACTION #5:
SAVE YOUR LIFE (OR SOMEONE ELSE'S)

Should you decide to drink, the single and only absolute point we will sharpen is this: don't attempt to drive. Driving buzzed is driving drunk. And, please oh please, don't take a ride from someone who's been partaking either, no matter how well they hold their liquor. In a split second, you (or they) could kill or maim some-one, be seriously injured, or be killed. Most campuses have some sort of escort service to ensure you get home in one piece. (And they won't be taking names either: colleges prefer students getting home safely over the chance to dole out a reprimand.) Sure, you may have to wait ten minutes for your coach to arrive, but what's ten minutes when compared to a DUI or spending the next six months in traction? Peanuts.

It's Just Sex
Really?

It's not like you're Charlotte Simmons. I mean, really. You've known there were no birds or bees involved for some time now and you don't plan on doing anything stupid. Of course not. But have you decided what you *do* plan on doing (and are you prepared for every possible consequence, not just the ones you think are manageable)?

The major complaint we hear from men and women seeking counseling about sexually related emotional or health issues is that they didn't take their options seriously enough from the beginning. They wish someone had sat them down early on and suggested they put pen to paper and actually spell out their sexual standards— especially while out of a relationship—so they knew ahead of time how far they really wanted to go. Lucky for you, you've already got a head start on that.

Like we said earlier, the grimmest average out there pegs one of every four women potentially being sexually assaulted during college. Yikes. That means that taking cautionary measures up front doesn't make you a conspiracy theorist, it makes you brilliant. What most often happens is that a young woman gets drunk (perhaps faster than she realizes, not being used to hard liquor or an eager supplier of beer) and she arrived at the party wearing something less than modest. Then the guy she's with gets drunk and, well, avalanche. It's not that uncommon nor that hard to imagine.

But state law doesn't side with the booze. The books still state that in order to give consent to sex, both parties must have the capacity to do so—meaning they can't be drunk. And catch this, guys: if both parties are drunk, the burden is most often on the man to put on the brakes. Whether or not you agree, a woman can take legal action even *years* after the incident (depending on the state).

A few movies have stereotyped upperclassman males as piranhas going after unsuspecting freshman females. As much as it's a cliché, it's actually more the case than folks might like to admit. While it's doubtful you'll hear the words "fresh meat" come rolling from the deep voice of a senior, it wouldn't be that unique a thought. And the flattery of being yearned for can be very much intoxicating to a freshman woman, even if she isn't intoxicated. Unfortunately, it rarely leads to favorable outcomes. Let's be fair to the guys though. Some women come to college anxious to win the attention of the BMOC. Which leads us to the next question . . .

But what about sober sex or mutually consensual sex?

In the media, the consequences of sex are often minimized. (I mean, when was the last time you watched a *Friends* rerun where a lead character complained they got hepatitis?) We're in the midst of a great social experiment that is questioning the beliefs society has had for years about the consequences of premarital sex on emotional well-being and physical health (the theory being that those consequences don't merit discouraging the activity).

Before you hook up for a one-nighter, give some thought to the underlying logic of that theory. Is it sound? How will your current relationships affect others in the future? What would you hope your future partner or spouse is doing or not doing? Would you rather your future partner be well adventured in his love-making or have been exposed to fewer STDs? And, depending on your answer, are you hoping for more from that person than you hope from yourself? Are you financially, emotionally, and physically prepared to deal with your own potential STD risks?

The questions about the implications are endless. And for good reason. It's a complicated topic, no matter how featherweight society would like it to seem. Setting aside physical consequences for a moment, does making less of sex actually make it less? Another recent social theory is that the most intimate act we have as human beings can be done casually without long-term effects. How disappointing. Here sex used to be "the ultimate" in an expression of love, hence the term "making love." What seems particularly odd is that our culture elevates the significance of saying "I love you" above the act of sex so that people are willing to make love but not verbalize it. Now *that's* strange, if you think about it.

While we're tossing assumptions at you, here are two more before we wrap it up. Take a stats class sometime and review the odds of STD calculations. Because we figure you've heard them before, we'll keep this simple: it only takes once. And, with every increase in encounters, so go your odds of catching something. Regardless of what you think of the odds (if STDs were exotically rare, do you think drug companies would be running herpes ads on prime-time television?), your maiden voyage could permanently mark you with a disease that will leave you uncomfortable at best. Some lead to sterility and others cancer. And some can be contracted even in the presence of "protection." So run those numbers and weigh your risks. You could play the odds and bet you won't end up a statistic, but is it worth your health?

> **It may seem like everyone is doing it, but really everyone is *talking* about doing it. Students continue to buy into the notion that they haven't lived or had the all-American college experience if they haven't been wasted or hung the proverbial scrunchie on their doorknob.**

The other assumption we want you to reconsider is the one that claims "everyone is doing it." No matter what the graffiti on the stalls may read, the bottom line is that there is much more talk than action. It may seem like everyone is doing it, but really everyone is *talking* about doing it. Students continue to buy into the notion that they haven't lived or had the all-American college experience if they haven't been wasted or hung the proverbial scrunchie on their doorknob—or both. However, national statistics consistently show that far fewer students are doing it than students *think* are doing it—meaning whatever the collegiate average of escapades, it is lower than what people assume.

Okay, well what about those who decide to wait?

Though Hollywood would like to mock virgins as being regretted social outcasts, we actually haven't heard one complain about his conscious choice to abstain as being a waste of time. On the contrary, we've heard a lot of students lament that they gave up their virginity too easily. If you still have yours, guard it. If you don't but wish you did, give yourself a second chance to build relationships without adding the complicated physical dimension of sex.

Oh sure, now we're suggesting the impossible (and we've just exposed how antiquated we really are). Or is it possible (and maybe

> Whatever you decide your standards to be, consider the "first law of sexual dynamics": the physical limit where you and your last girlfriend stopped is where you will get to in a fraction of the time with your next. Or, even if your experience is relatively minor, your new girlfriend's may not be and the same rule will apply for her.

we aren't so antiquated)? Autumn is a recent grad (recent, yes, as in the last decade) who made it to her wedding day with a near-finished degree, her virginity, and the fact that she had never been kissed until the night she became engaged. Her groom had his too (virginity, that is, though he had a college diploma as well). They had known each other four years, and, no, it wasn't an arranged marriage. Anything's possible.

Whatever you decide your standards to be, consider the "first law of sexual dynamics": the physical limit where you and your last girlfriend stopped is where you will get to in a fraction of the time with your next. Or, even if your experience is relatively minor, your new girlfriend's may not be and the same rule will apply for her. If a woman went beyond fondling with her last boyfriend, she sure as heck won't stop at kissing unless you persuade her otherwise (assuming the "you" reading this is her prospective fling and that kissing is where you want to stop). You can thank the law of diminishing returns for that one, which says that it's very, *very* hard to experiment with going one step further and then continue to find the same satisfaction from the previous step.

Against the law of diminishing returns stands the very real possibility of starting a new chapter in your life. Even more so than high school, there is a significant shift that takes place at the beginning of each term. Some students head off to study abroad while others return, some shake off that dreaded lab class that hounded them for months and others begin the agony of aeronautic entropy. So, again, if you're reading this chapter after your college career has begun, it's not too late to make a change. College allows for new beginnings with every season, though it takes a great deal of willpower and accountability with friends to hit the brakes and aim yourself in a new direction.

Does this apply to same-sex relationships too?

Where students have said they feel most sexually unprepared upon entering college is on the topic of homosexuality. The open discussion and presence of homosexuality in your daily life may be the biggest change since high school. You could be rooming with someone coming out of the closet, or it could in fact be you and your closet.

The role of same-sex relationships is a dominant field of inquiry in much of the humanities and social sciences in college. In that sense, where it would rarely be mentioned in the high-school classroom, it is a dependable point of discussion if you take a course in the humanities or ever engage in an academic or cultural forum on campus. At such forums, you may find yourself encountering students who are homosexual, bisexual, or transgender. Or you may even be that person.

The possibilities can make for meaningful conversations with those around you. If you are the one reconsidering your sexual orientation, the same advice we gave earlier about evaluating choices from action to end result applies here. Spend some time on your own thinking through the ramifications of your decisions and how they will affect who you want to become. The heart can be a guide, but so can the mind and the will.

Whether it's your closet or someone else's, and as with all other big topics we've discussed, think through your values about homosexuality away from campus. Get advice from friends, parents, mentors, and peers. If you find yourself needing support thereafter (either because you are experimenting with your sexuality or because you are looking for input about those who are), seek out the friends we mentioned before (the ones whom you respect and who respect you) to ask their advice. Talk with your parents before making a life-altering choice. After all that, we highly recommend visiting the counseling center so you can make your decision with the fullest support possible.

Thanks for Playing

Given the content, this may have been a difficult chapter to read at times, so thanks for sticking with us to the end. For you, we were willing to risk all we've said (knowing you may have heard some of it before) in the hopes that you would find a few gems that will not only help maximize your college experience but also will propel you into a more successful future. Heck, you can't have enough good advice.

And so, we leave you with this parting encouragement: have fun. Your undergrad years only come once. Consider them an animated version of the Choose Your Own Adventure books you may have loved as a kid. Be intentional about choosing the best adventure possible. If need be, go back and reread the first section (This One's on Us) if you need some ideas to get you brainstorming. Graduation probably feels a long way off, but due to some collegiate time warp, it arrives in half the time you expect. So, hurry up and be efficient with your studies so you can get out and have a good time. Consider your standards beforehand with as much a view of the end results as possible. Meet new people. Make new friends. Make memories you will love remembering for the rest of your days. Have fun.

CHAPTER 6

What Professors Wish You Knew

Paying Attention to the Man (or Woman!) behind the Curtain

They are the ones with the power to ruin your vacations with untimely assignments. They are the ones you glorified as your reason for choosing this college in your application essay. They are the ones who may bore you with a monotone that defies caffeine. Or perhaps, if you have chosen wisely, they are the ones who switch on some inner light bulb that makes the world and your place in it suddenly clearer. Professors.

Getting the best out of college means, in part, getting your money's worth out of your relationships with the professors who are paid (largely by you) to provide a product you are buying: an education.

By now you may have heard that every session of class at your standard university tends to be around the price of a front-row seat on Broadway. Unfortunately, few lectures actually live up to that kind of billing. Don't take the Broadway metaphor literally, expecting your professors to be entertainers. They are, after all, only educators. (Hey, if they could do improv they would be making a lot more money working on *Saturday Night Live*). Some star professors manage to be entertaining educators, but more often than not even the good professors are simply adept at conveying the mysteries of their subject—minus the stand-up comic routine.

You don't need your professors to be stand-up comics. You *do* need them to be stand-up academic citizens. And here is a secret. Most of them want the same thing from you. If you can match up these two realistic expectations, you can build relationships with your professors that will make college an incredibly rewarding experience, one worth your time *and* money.

> **Get to know two professors well enough that they are able to write strong, personal recommendations. Even better, seek to establish a close mentoring relationship with at least one professor during your undergraduate career.**

Whether you attend a mammoth state university or an intimate-sized college, your goal should be to know two professors well enough that they are able to write strong, personal recommendations for you. Even better, you should seek to establish a close mentoring relationship with at least one professor during your undergraduate career.

To build these relationships, you must understand the three open secrets about professors.

The first is that profs are human. Not a shocker, though there are some who seem determined to prove otherwise. Look past the quirks and eccentricities and you will discover that professors have fears, foibles, and personality glitches like the rest of us. As we will explain later, if you can keep this simple truth in mind during your interactions, you'll be more successful in getting to know them. (By the way, the reverse is true too. Professors understand that you are human. Okay, so we have established that everyone is human. No one should feel intimidated.)

Second, professors are generally quite good at providing you with quality instruction in their courses, but you can get a lot more from them than a lecture. If you just take what's given to you (that is, the course as it is offered) you won't get as much out of it as you would if you were proactive about interacting with the professor.

The third secret—and professors cannot be persuaded otherwise on this one—is that they believe their time is more valuable than yours. The smart student will strategize around this inconvenient view, finding ways to build relationships without becoming a drain on the professor's time.

As obvious as these points may seem, it's amazing how many students behave as though they do not understand them. Internalize these revelations, act upon them, and watch the doors begin to open.

This Isn't High School, and We're Not Nannies
Understanding a Professor's Role

One of the biggest differences between high school and college is that in college most teachers won't come looking for you if you miss class or fail to turn in assignments. (Okay, if you miss too many classes the prof might turn you over to an academic dean who will come knocking at your door—don't misread our point here.) Perhaps you are counting on this. Perhaps the greater freedom is precisely what you are looking for in college. There is, however, a fine line between being given free rein to roam and being ignored.

Frankly the students who never get noticed by their professors are probably not making the most of their education. But getting noticed (that is, getting the right kind of notice) is difficult because relating to students is only a part of the professor's job—and in many research universities, it is a very small part.

In nearly every college and university in the United States, professors are hired with the understanding that they will divide their time among three baskets: research and publishing, university service, and teaching. Their salaries depend on success in all three areas. The baskets are prioritized differently depending on the institution, but at many schools, research and publishing take precedence. If you are not sure whether or not that is the case at your school, mention the phrase "publish or perish" and see if your professor exhibits a nervous tic.

Beyond that, the urgency of university service often competes all too effectively for the professor's attention. University service refers to a long list of faculty responsibilities such as serving on multiple administrative committees, advising student groups, developing department policies, and reviewing and evaluating the published work of their peers, to name only a few. Most profs have a fairly small appetite for this sort of thing and are force-fed much more than they can stomach.

The third basket, of course, is prepping for and delivering your lecture (or seminar) and grading the polished gems of academic work you and your peers generate by the bushel.

We all know that people have lives beyond their day job, so figure at some time these profs are also going home to raise kids, grow their marriage, care for elderly parents, or often all of the above.

The point is not to make you feel sorry for professors (you shouldn't—they generally enjoy what they do and no one forced them at gunpoint to follow this career), but rather to explain why they may seem distracted when it comes to teaching and relating to undergraduates—why, in other words, they might be harder to approach than the teachers who helped you finish high school so successfully.

A key distinction between college and high-school faculty is their degrees. A bachelor's degree suggests that a graduate has mastered a subject and is capable of passing it along; a master's degree suggests an even deeper command of that knowledge. All of your teachers in high school had bachelor's degrees and some had master's degrees as well.

Most college professors have a doctorate degree (called a PhD, which someone once said stands for "piled higher and deeper"), and that degree confers the expectation that graduates not only have a deep understanding of their subject area but are also expanding the field of knowledge in some way. Their standing in the field and at the university is determined by how much "expanding" they accomplish during their lifetime.

So what is the relevance of this to you? Due to the constraints placed on a professor's time by the university, it is of utmost importance that *you* assume the responsibility of pursuing the professor rather than expecting the professor to discover the genius in you. Make yourself memorable (in positive ways, of course) by showing an interest in the material and class discussion as well as a dedication to learning outside of class. And consider responding as one human being to another when your professor inevitably makes some error either in miscalculating your grade, losing your paper, or mispronouncing your name for the eighth time in a week.

Matt recalled his ordeal attempting to contact a prof in the hopes of networking. In his naïveté, he called the professor once and, finding she was out, left a message assuming the ball was now in her court. Needless to say, the days passed into weeks and still no response. He happened to mention his predicament to a friend, who chided him on his laziness, insisting Matt find some other way to track her down. "Pursue her with the same dedication you would show if you were trying to borrow her car for spring break," he said. "Figure she's too busy to return your call. Understand that you need to see her more than she needs to see you, so you have to want it more. Don't take no—or worse, no answer—for an answer. Find another way to make contact."

We are not recommending that you stalk your professor but that you do the math: several dozen or perhaps several hundred students per lecture times multiple lectures a term plus a few seminars of twenty-five each. Your face is part of the blur. It will most likely require some extra effort to get your prof's attention.

> **We are not recommending that you stalk your professor but that you do the math: several dozen or perhaps several hundred students per lecture times multiple lectures a term plus a few seminars of twenty-five each. Your face is part of the blur.**

Our advice so far has been tailored to students at universities where the student-faculty ratio makes it a bit harder to establish a connection with the professor. If you are at a small college, these tips will apply even more so, since there is a greater expectation among faculty that these relationships will emerge and they are primed to participate.

No Sycophants or Hecklers Allowed
How to Interact with Profs in Class

Professors want students. Real students. Not students who sleep in class—that's frustrating. Not students who hang on their every word—that's embarrassing. (Okay, maybe it *is* flattering, but it gets old quickly). And, not students who put up their verbal dukes

Yes, but Just This Once

If I'm Not Prepared for Class, Should I Still Attend?

Most definitely you should attend class even if you are unprepared, but—we quickly add—depending on what type of class it is, you may need to make a preemptive strike.

If it is the sort of class where you might be called on, such as a seminar or a small lecture, then you should absolutely contact the professor before class to explain the situation. Pull him aside before he steps into class. Don't depend on email for this one. Apologize that you have made a mistake and aren't as prepared for class as you wish you were. There's no need to make excuses, but be clear that you will not be making this a habit and that you promise to be prepared from here on out. Most profs are gracious enough to let you by without damage; however, they might toss you a question in the following class just to be sure you're tracking.

Of course, if the class you are unprepared for is a lecture, then the odds are very much with you that you can sneak by unnoticed. It is still a mistake to be unprepared, but there is no reason to compound the mistake by skipping the class as well. Remember, every class is about as expensive as that front-row Broadway ticket and consistently coming unprepared is like watching the performance from a soundproof booth—you'll understand very little of what's going on. Even if you haven't read the material, you may still get something out of the lecture if you take notes. And those notes will make more sense when you review them after having completed the assignment you originally missed.

at the slightest provocation—that's disrespectful and downright annoying.

Professors want students who interact professionally in both behavior and appearance and who show at least a minimal interest in the topic—a student like you.

Profs are astounded at how often students behave in class as though the professor can't see them. Perhaps it is a weakness of the TV generation, thinking that all life is a plasma screen. Regardless, it

Life is not without its obstacles, and if there is an unforeseen circumstance that has genuinely made it difficult for you to keep up with class (that is, a death in the family, a chronic health issue, a financial burden, and so on), make the effort to speak to the professor about it before the term progresses any further. There tends to be a rash of plagues that mysteriously coincide with due dates each term, making some profs a bit jaded. However, most faculty are human enough to understand that life has an effect on studies, and once you have made it clear that you have a genuine need they should be willing to help (either with extensions or by reworking assignments) if you give them enough advance notice.

Just for the record, the day before a deadline is not "enough advance notice" unless, of course, the trauma occurred just that afternoon. Speak to your prof as soon as you can and be up-front about your improvement as the term progresses so that it doesn't appear you are taking advantage of the situation. If part of the class grade hangs on class participation (something common in small seminars), don't expect that your prof's leniency will head off every grade penalty. We'll cover more tips on how to maneuver emergency needs on campus in chapter 8.

One last word on attendance. There is a nasty rumor going around that since attendance isn't taken in large lectures, students can skip out (perhaps purchase the notes from a classmate), just skim the reading, and show up for exams. Dare we state the obvious that this is not maximizing your college experience but instead is barely eking by? If the lectures weren't worth it, the prof wouldn't bother, so pick a favorite seat and make a date of it.

makes for humorous lunchtime stories in the faculty dining room: students conversing in IM sessions or surfing the Web instead of taking notes, students bringing a pillow and wearing pajamas for a midlecture nap, students engaging in other activities that your father wouldn't like us printing here.

In very small doses, the professor may be amused and might play along. One instructor preempted an incorrigible napper by pulling out a copy of *Goodnight Moon* and reading it to the dozing student (much to the hilarity of the rest of the class). Others like to sneak up on their snoozer and jostle him awake. One in particular—and this is probably an urban legend but it is one professors share wistfully among themselves—wielded a permanent marker like a sword and marked a sleeping student's forehead with a Zorro-like Z. More commonly, some give an instant class-wide quiz or even an extra term paper assignment to punish a student's apparent disregard.

The pendulum can swing both ways when it comes to falling prey to the sandman. One professor made us promise not to include his name with his confession that he fell asleep in his own class during a student presentation. Apparently the student's talk was as dry as crusty toast. Besides, the prof insisted that he had been up late the night before, doubtless with an ill child or some other legitimate excuse.

Another instructor came close to making this same mistake, but she was able to keep her eyes open—just barely. One of her students noticed her drooping and sent her some unwelcome help via a text message chiding her to stay awake. Without missing a pixel, she responded archly that text messaging was inappropriate in class. Lesson of the day: it's better to be a dozing professor than a dozing student.

The larger lesson, of course, is that everyone will be fighting sleep at some time or another, and anyone can lose the fight. But don't be casual about it or you just might lose something more important, such as a grade—or, worse, respect.

Sleeping in class is only the most obvious and infamous classroom mistake. The more common error, and the one we want you to focus on avoiding, is failing to make a positive impression on the professor.

By a positive impression, we don't mean bringing the prof a piping hot pizza after class or tattooing her lectures on your bicep. We mean engaging in class. Practically it would look like this. As you read through packets for Thursday's lecture, make notes to yourself of questions you have in response to the text (yes, you should actually write them down). If one or two of your questions are big enough that they might lead into an actual conversation, or are important enough that the rest of the readings are incomprehensible without an answer, raise them with the prof in advance (preferably during her office hours.)

Either way, come Thursday you are sitting in class (list of questions in hand) with a goal of finding those answers as you listen to the lecture. This will not only help you pay attention (meaning give eye contact and look alive), it will also give you an opportunity to interact with the prof during or after class as you bring up questions that were not addressed.

Chances are that if you are confused about the text, others are too. If the professor is willing to take questions in class, take advantage of that time by picking some tough ones from your list (as long as you remain sensitive to the fact that she needs to finish her lecture.) In high school, this sort of preparedness would have been considered brown-nosing, resulting in ridicule by the entire cafeteria at lunch. But there is more at stake now than your reputation with prepubescents in new tennis shoes: your education, your student loans, and ultimately your career are on the line.

To look at this another way, it may help to consider your title. When you fill in the blank on DMV or doctor's forms, what do you list for occupation? Student. You are a *professional* student. As such, it makes sense that you would approach your relationships with faculty and the administration as a professional.

> When you fill in the blank on DMV or doctor's forms, what do you list for occupation? Student. You are a *professional* student. As such, it makes sense that you would approach your relationships with faculty and the administration as a professional.

Help Me Help You
Getting Profs to Agree to an Independent Study Request

You might be asking why in the world someone would sign up for an independent study. After all, there is no way to hide if the assignment isn't complete and skipping class is nearly impossible.

Don't give in to such reasoning. Many graduates, when asked their most valuable college experience, cite some sort of independent study or research as the pinnacle.

An independent study (IS) is a unique opportunity for a student to craft a semester around a subject that interests her, and then follow through with readings and assignments alongside one of the finest minds in the field on that subject—all at no extra cost!

Unfortunately, at most institutions, there is also no extra pay for the faculty member; so what is a great deal for you is usually worse than a so-so deal for the professor. Before drafting an independent study proposal, find out if the university will be crediting him for his time by asking any department administrator. Even if there is an incentive for the prof, don't assume you are doing him a favor. With all the demands a prof has on his workload, an independent study proposal needs to be attractive to the professor in order to get off the ground.

Above all, remember this: an independent study should be the culmination of a relationship that you already have with a professor, not be the beginning of one.

Practically, this might mean taking an introductory course freshman year and discovering you connect with the prof and his topic during office hours, offering to be a research assistant the following term, perhaps taking another course that is closer to your area of interest sophomore year, and finally finishing up with an independent study as a junior—all the while looking for opportunities to get to know the prof outside of class.

Because of the way course scheduling and publication deadlines work, some semesters may be fuller for professors than others. There is an advantage to seeking out independent study opportunities early on in your college career. The process of finding good faculty mentors can begin in your first year so that you will have time to adjust. If a professor is booked the first time you request an independent study but he invites you to return next year, you have more flexibility to fit it into your course schedule. Not all faculty relationships require this much time, but preparing yourself now for that possibility will give you the most options in the long run.

Should you decide to offer your services as a research assistant for a term, recognize that you may not get paid. If that's the case, consider it an investment in furthering your education and your relationship with this professor. Showing an interest in what a professor is already researching communicates to him that you are dedicated to the subject, willing to give as well as take, and that you are respectful of his time. All three will bode well as points in your favor when it comes time to requesting an independent study (not to mention the fact that being a research assistant can be an incredible learning experience).

Desirable as an independent study opportunity is, we should warn you that it is also rare. Don't agree to being a research assistant if you expect that it will automatically earn you an independent study with this professor. It is probably wise to refrain from mentioning your interest in an independent study until you have proven yourself to be diligent in the work at hand and superb in achieving positive results. (Otherwise it puts the prof in an awkward position where he thinks you think he owes you something, which is irksome and can be damaging to a mentoring relationship.)

As with anything, there are exceptions. Some profs have been known to sponsor a student in an IS after the student has taken only one course with them. It will be up to you to discern the individual prof's various obligations and weigh them against his interests.

A common pitfall on this topic is requesting an independent study as an alternative to taking a regularly scheduled course. Let's say Dr. Rothstein is teaching "Innocence Undressed in Sixteenth-Century Literature" in the fall term. Sonia wants to take the course but thinks she would learn better if it were in a more personal setting. Should she propose taking the course as an IS, she will most likely get an immediate no.

What if Sonia wants to take the course but can't because it interferes with her chem lab? That seems like a valid reason for an independent study, right? Again, Dr. Rothstein is likely to turn her down and suggest she sign up for the course in a later semester. Why? Dr. Rothstein is not an ogre. He simply can't afford to add multiple sections of a course to his already full teaching schedule.

However, if, after taking "Innocence Undressed," Sonia wants to further her own study of sexuality in *The Faerie Queen*, Dr. Rothstein will be more inclined to agree to this independent study request because Sonia has proven herself to be an excellent student in at least one term and is interested in pursuing a subject that he does not teach but that is considered part of his field.

The key here in successfully choosing an independent study topic that is attractive to your prof is to pick one he knows well, one he is also interested in researching, or one he is already actively researching.

An independent study is not essential to getting the best out of college. For most students, it may not even be a realistic option. Despite the size of the college, the student/faculty ratio makes for too many students should every one of them apply for a sustained, individual tutorial with a professor. But it is worth trying. At worst, the work you put into the failed request could rebound to your benefit in other ways in your relationship with the professor, and, at best, you'll be one of the lucky few who get a spot.

We're Never Wrong, Just Mistaken
How to Disagree without Obliterating Your Prof's Respect (Not to Mention Your Grade)

Every subject has its unknowns and unanswerables and no one is above them—not even professors. The first step to intellectual growth is discovering how little you know about a topic. One professor observed that as an undergrad he figured he knew about 60 percent of his topic area; after several years as a grad student, he scaled his estimate back to about 30 percent; now that he is a world authority on several aspects of his field, he figures he knows about 3 to 5 percent of what there is to know.

Nevertheless, in almost every case, the professor will know more than you. That is why you are paying him and not vice versa. However, knowing more about a given topic does not mean that every opinion the professor holds is authoritative and infallible. The trick is to find the distinction between what your professors know and what they think.

To do that, it's important to go to class with two things: an open mind and a sifter. An open mind is required because professors have thought long and hard about their topic and a core part of their job is to convey that knowledge to you. That said, always sift what you hear. All ideas contain some bias, even those that are loudly proclaimed to be fact. Merely calling it a fact makes it *seem* that there is no room for bias—however, don't check your brain at the door.

All professors believe it is their job to challenge you. Expect to be provoked—relish it because it is what sharpens you. Many professors believe it is also their job to convert you, if not to their own ideology then at least to their own view about how to evaluate competitive ideologies. Don't be afraid to push back from a professor's attempts to draw you over to her side of the line on whatever theory she is touting. That being said, some conversions are for the good; don't feel like you must resist every attempt.

A large part of your education will revolve around these conversion conversations, because they will stimulate your thinking and either galvanize your own convictions on a topic or lead to a revelation. The important thing is not to view challenges, nor even the conversion attempt, as an abuse of professorial authority. It isn't. Instead treat it as an opportunity to exercise your brain as well as your backbone.

Should you find a point where you disagree with a professor, keep the fanfare to a minimum. A well-handled disagreement with a prof need not cost you your grade. In fact, it could even help it.

There are two kinds of disagreements you may have with a professor: academic ("I disagree that the world is round," "I think

> Knowing more about a given topic does not mean that every opinion the professor holds is authoritative and infallible. The trick is to find the distinction between what your professors know and what they think.

the argument in this assigned reading has a fatal flaw," and so on) and personal ("I think this seminar reading is boring," "You miscalculated my grade," "You looked at me funny," "You stood me up during office hours," you get the idea). In dealing with both, be professional and speak to your prof before telling the story to anyone else. Too many students have bungled this point and regretted the consequences later.

One such student, after disagreeing with a point in a mythology lecture, called the department chair, the career guidance center, and the administration to complain *before* speaking directly to the prof about the incident. The complaint was a relatively small misunderstanding that could have easily been addressed. However, because Andrea spoke to nearly everyone but the professor, it made for an awkward situation for both her and her professor for the remainder of the term.

Be conscious of your timing in presenting your argument. Some profs are exhausted after a big lecture and are not up to sparring, while others may seem eager to talk while the lecture is still fresh in their minds.

Most profs don't mind a challenge or two during a lecture, and almost all earnestly desire such engagements in smaller seminar classes. But be sensitive to the professor's plans for the course. A brush-off response may be a sign that he has other material to cover, and not necessarily that you have him flummoxed. For sustained challenges, speak to your prof apart from the crowd and offer to come back at a later time if he prefers.

Perhaps even more fundamental than timing and directness in handling conflicts is this: have a sound argument and at all costs articulate it clearly. Merely emoting passionate thoughts only reinforces the professor's original prejudices and makes the next debate with him even harder for you or anyone else.

If the disagreement is not academic but personal—such as you want to question a professor about your grade without appearing to be a grade grubber—approach the professor during what will be an appropriate time where she can fully concentrate on your conversation (such as office hours). Consider the following to be an example of a great opener: "Dr. Lux, I'd like to speak with you about the grade I earned on my last paper. I'm not sure I understand the rubric that led to this grade and I'm hoping you can help me understand what I could have done better so that I can improve in the future." There. You've said it with respect and clarity. There is no accusation, no begging, and no defensiveness. You are showing yourself to be teachable and in want of improvement while finding out what went wrong with your grade. If, after hearing the professor's explanation, you think you deserve a better grade, say so (and be ready to give specific points as to why, the sanctity of your GPA not being among them.) What more could a professor ask?

The question of the hour is how far to take a challenge, and the answer depends on the issue and how much it is personally worth to you. One student told us of a critical moment in her degree program when a disagreement with her professor resulted in a lower grade. Though Wendy approached the professor with proper timing and professionalism—and the professor even recognized her point—it led to one grade lower than she had hoped to earn that semester.

The disagreement was an academic one; Wendy argued that a book on the syllabus was inappropriate for a student discussion group. She invited the professor out to coffee and explained her concerns, asking for his advice on how to approach a book she found clearly offensive and unsuitable. He suggested the importance of reading books that are offensive in the hopes of learning something new; she agreed but asserted that the value of what could be gained from this book was not worth the cost.

In the end, she admitted to him that, out of principle, she would not read that book for the semester, that she would attend class and take notes as usual but would not be a part of the discussion. He understood and chose not to call on her, since it would be a pointless exercise. After the week of discussion for that book, she resumed course work by reading the next novel and became involved in class as before.

Where this plan backfired was on the final exam, when one of the essay questions dealt with that book directly. Did the professor intentionally give a question from a book he knew she hadn't read, or was it mere coincidence? It was probably coincidence, but she didn't consider it worth a fight—after all, taking a stand means taking a risk. The definition of a principled stand is "one for which you are willing to pay a price," and it is critical to evaluate the cost before approaching any potentially risky conversations. But the story doesn't end unhappily. As a result of her integrity and professionalism, she retained a valuable relationship with this professor, who went on to write a recommendation leading to her first postgraduation job. In the long run, she earned the points where they mattered most.

If you're looking for a moral to this story, it would be that pursuing a discussion with a professor may or may not have the immediate expected results, but that it is a privilege to engage with a professor on this level. When done so appropriately, it can lead to a rewarding outcome.

Of course, not all professors will be as congenial as this one. In fact, student naïveté on this could be dangerous. There are certainly incorrigible types who are imperious and vindictive if challenged. If you discover your prof to be of this species, do all you can to avoid confrontation—it can only end in tears (and potentially lower grades).

Contrary to Popular Belief, We Do Have Lives
How to Relate to Profs Outside of Class

Before going much further, let us offer this caveat: each professor is unique. The guidelines we provide are just that—guidelines. The odd professor (and there will be more than a few odd ones in your college career) may well break the mold and have his own style of communication.

That said, there does seem to be a pattern.

Samuel was a young man from a small town in the Midwest who, upon arriving on campus as a freshman, made it his goal to take advantage of unusual social events so that he could get to know faculty and staff. Much to his great surprise, he met another student on campus—Nicholas—who was equally interested in doing the same.

Together these young men took over the campus by attending as many events, panels, and speaker presentations as possible. Through a few stints as research assistants, they got to know faculty well and made it a point to mingle with professors at campuswide gatherings as often as possible. Being a dynamic duo enabled them to stay abreast of happenings around campus, and it nearly always ensured at least one familiar face would be attending the event if they felt entirely out of place.

They were not sycophants or even bookworms; they were genuinely interested in enjoying all their university had to offer. They had active social lives and knew hundreds of students on campus, largely because they hung out at various campus events. They took care of their bodies (which meant no bacchanalias), bedded and woke early, and four years later graduated with top honors—one a Rhodes Scholar heading off to Harvard Med School and the other to Yale Law. The only thing fictional is their names. Even more impressive is that it took place within the last decade.

What is most unusual about Samuel and Nicholas was their perceptive realization that meaningful student-faculty interaction can happen outside the classroom. They were also discreet in their selection of events: gatherings were campus wide, large enough to blend in, and welcomed students.

Consider another radical take on getting to know your prof—a little something we call "dead time." Simply put, "dead time" makes use of mind-numbing tasks a prof might have ahead of her by turning them into opportunities for individual face time. Express to your prof an interest in discussing a few course-related topics and offer to staple packets, file papers, or address envelopes while you chat.

If you happen to be a tireless organizer, you might become the prof's new best friend. Who's to say that sipping coffee is a smarter activity than licking stamps? Throughout history, the greatest leaders in the world cultivated disciples and mentored protégés by inviting them to be a part of everyday tasks, where diamonds are mined in simple conversation.

We aren't suggesting this merely to provide cheap labor to faculty. We're just aware of the many pulls on a professor's time and how few professors are able to find the time they'd like to interact with students. If you happen to have some media savvy, you might offer to help make the professor's notes into a PowerPoint presentation, update his website, or download software that could be a timesaver to his research. (If there is enough of this sort of work, you might offer to become a technology assistant for his research, which might lead to an IS opportunity later on.)

The point is to free up pockets of time for your profs so they are more inclined to find time to meet with you.

As an alternative to "dead time," consider offering to meet where you know your prof is already heading, such as the gym. If you learn that your prof is an avid runner and happen to see her working out at the campus gym, catching up while you both hit the treadmill could work great.

If the gym is not your style, you might offer to take a stroll while you chat or walk your prof to his next appointment if he is short on time. The point is to be creative (while respectful of personal boundaries) in looking for windows of time to meet.

Recognize that any time you spend with a professor outside of class is *not* meant to improve your grade. It will prove a sour experience if that is your goal. If you are genuinely interested in hearing her thoughts on a subject, explain your interest and be sure to follow through by arriving on time. Few things will drown your chance at success faster than being late. To a prof who considers herself busy, waiting for a student to show is a lot like being held underwater—it can only be tolerated for so long.

Of course, being the thoughtful person you are, you are now aware of the pressures placed on professors' time. You also recognize they are not required to make time to meet with you. Any extracurricular conversations should be considered (and treated) as generous.

If you don't go the "dead time" route but prefer to meet in a more traditional manner, be sure to suggest times that are appropriate for the real world. A ten o'clock pizza party might not be the best way to encourage a prof to meet with you if she has been up since six that morning. The best way to find a time that is convenient for her is to offer a selection of two or three times, or to ask outright if she has a suggestion.

One of the rewards of face time with professors is the potential opportunity to see academics applied to the real world. One professor we know regularly goes to Washington, DC, to brief policy makers on his research. An alumnus saw this as a great educational opportunity and offered to foot the bill so a few of that professor's students could tag along and serve as slide flippers and note takers. Over the course of their travels, the professor and students had multiple points of interaction, not to mention that the students had real-time data on how academic research intersects policy making.

The professor was simply modeling the mentoring practice of the political and corporate world. In those settings, the more experienced are often accompanied by their mentorees, using travel time between points A and B for conversations they otherwise could not have scheduled.

While the trip to DC is admittedly unusual, if you are aware of a professor's involvement in an area of research or responsibility that interests you, make it a point to help in whatever capacity he needs and be sure to express your hope of being involved further. You should also check into any research grants a professor might have that would allow for you to become involved on a paying basis.

Just Because We're Busy Doesn't Mean We Don't Care

Office Hours—What They Are and How to Use Them

Before the days of email (gasp!), there were office hours. And despite the presence of email, office hours still exist on campuses nationwide—college is a medieval institution and so it tends to hold on to quaint traditions a long time—though they may not be as popular as they once were.

Were you to poll professors on their biggest frustrations, being stood up for office hours and confirmed appointments would definitely be high up on the list. Being inundated with incoherent, overly familiar, or inconsiderate student emails would also have a prominent showing. Interestingly, these two frustrations are related, and both can be distilled to one issue: personal convenience.

From a student's perspective, it is far more convenient to email a question to a professor than to leave the coziness of a dorm room and walk across campus for office hours (particularly when temperatures are extreme). However, consider the professor's perspective: recall for a moment the number of students packed into her lecture hall, or the multitude of seminars she is offering, and imagine each of those students sending an email to her every week.

Email is a recent enough invention that many professors are still overwhelmed by it, never having progressed past the two-finger typing method. Add that assumption to their three-basket workload we discussed earlier and it's not surprising that it takes some professors days to respond to email, if they respond at all. Tack on that multiple students send emails with variations of the same question and it's easy to imagine why email can drive professors batty. Even more than the quantity, it is the quality that bothers most professors. Properly done, email can be an efficient way for managing large classes. But when students send emails that read like an IM to a high-school buddy—or worse, a foul-mouthed rant on an angry blog—the system breaks down.

Granted, email is a generational skill. Younger professors may actually prefer to answer your question over email rather than in office hours. We are by no means giving an ironclad rule banning emails, just suggesting that you find out the prof's preference and do your best to stick to it.

Whether or not email is acceptable to the prof, it is to your advantage to make use of office hours because they provide more meaningful contact: now your name is finally linked in her mind with your face. It can be a valuable exercise in developing rapport with your prof through genuine face time. It is an opportunity to interact with one of the leading minds in a field—perhaps by asking questions about recent news events or soliciting opinions on a text as they relate to her research. It is also a great opportunity to ask clarifying questions about classwork or lectures, and to get an immediate reaction to the thesis of the paper you plan to write for class next week. Some professors offer individual office hours, while others make the time open to as many as can fit in the room—but there are some general principles that hold in both scenarios.

> **Whether or not email is acceptable to the prof, it is to your advantage to make use of office hours because they provide more meaningful contact: now your name is finally linked in her mind with your face.**

First and foremost, come prepared with something relevant to discuss. Unless you know college basketball is your prof's favorite subject, asking her about the recent playoffs may be a waste of time. You could ask something like, "What is your take on the recent study about X that appeared in the *New York Times*?" or "Could you expand upon the point you made yesterday in class about Y? I'm not sure I fully grasped it." Most profs typically welcome relevant chitchat, done in moderation, toward the beginning of a semester before crunch time hits, and will be happy to clarify yesterday's point (assuming they didn't see you surfing the Web when you should have been taking notes).

If you are looking for conversation starters, you might want to dig up her resume online to learn more about her expertise. Or check out articles or books she has written from the campus library. Don't be fawning about it by dropping hints that you loved what she said on page forty-seven. There is a fine line between stocking up on conversation topics and simply stalking.

Second, and this almost goes without saying: show up. Once you know your course schedule, walk yourself over to the sign-up sheet and pick a time (please, oh please, don't email the prof and ask her to do it for you), make a note of it on your calendar, and be there.

Pretend this is a job interview, where timeliness counts. In a way, it is. You may want to ask this professor to write your recommendation at the end of the term, and the little details of your meetings will play a big role in how professional she believes you to be.

Third, take advantage of off-peak times to cultivate a relationship with your prof, such as the beginning of the term, before grades have become a threat (and when most students are taking it easy). On the flip side, try to avoid busy seasons for relationship-building encounters (such as right before grades come out) unless you have a time-sensitive question to address.

Like we mentioned earlier, profs are human and thus fall shy of perfection. It may be the case that you have done everything right and that, upon arriving for office hours, you find the door locked and the professor nowhere to be found. Try to be understanding—it happens to the best of us—and leave a note or send an email that looks something like this: "I was hoping to meet with you today to discuss Y, but something must have come up, since the door was locked at X:XX. Please let me know when you'll be hosting your next office hours so I can attend." This is not the time to roast the prof. In fact, there is rarely ever a time to roast the prof.

If your professor doesn't even offer office hours, let him know after class that you are interested in coming by and ask to schedule a time. You may need to pursue him a bit on this one, but most profs will kindly agree.

Once you have secured an appointment, come dressed for the occasion. We are not saying "no suit, no tie, no service," but that clothes generate conclusions about character and intelligence whether you want them to or not. Dress professionally for the reputation you are hoping to earn.

You Want Me to Say What?
How to Secure a Glowing Recommendation

We will assume you are a student worthy of an excellent recommendation. Being worthy is a start, but it is only a start.

A fabulous letter of recommendation should not be the highest goal of your academic career, but it is a pretty good sign that you have gotten closer to reaching your goal. (Reality check: the goal of an academic career should be an excellent education that prepares you for a lifetime of growth and learning.)

Earning a glowing recommendation is a process that takes about two to three years. Sadly, many students never get close enough to a professor to even get the filaments warm. Though you may be extraordinarily diligent, realize that you can probably only achieve this sort of relationship with a couple of professors, due to constraints on time as well as personal chemistry.

A glowing recommendation flows out of extended intellectual interaction, much like the progression of working your way up to an independent study proposal. The capstone of your work is a letter where the professor honestly knows you and can speak to your integrity and intellectual development.

What makes this sort of letter so exceptional to graduate schools or potential employers is that it has the unmistakable ring of authenticity. The recommender really knows the recommendee, and so the letter garners more weight.

A good recommendation evolves over time, but that doesn't mean you should wait until the end of your academic career to request one. As soon as you have finished a course in which you did well (and in which the professor got to know you, which may not necessarily be possible in large lecture courses), ask the professor to write you a letter of recommendation. Feel free to wait for grades to come out if you like, though that's not necessary. Email *and* snail mail a letter to your professor saying you really enjoyed the class (add a few specifics here), that you're thinking of following up with more work in this area (add some more specifics), and would he please write a letter of rec *for your file*. Then mention how you intend to return in a year or two to request that that letter be sent to a specific file or location, such as a grad school or a think tank.

> The key is to get the professor to write the letter of recommendation as close in time to the class as possible, rather than close to the due date when you actually need the letter.

Though most professors are willing to store (and perhaps even update) your letter in their computer, if he is a visitor or is likely to leave the school, it would be better to ask that a hard copy be sent to some third party, like your academic dean. (We'll explain why a third party in a moment.) The career center or your academic dean will most likely be prepared to store student recommendation files, which can be updated by depositing new letters as needed.

If you take a subsequent course with the professor (and we hope you will), then ask him to update the letter after you finish that course. The process repeats as often as you complete a "season" (for example, research apprentice, independent study, follow-up course) with that professor. The letter grows in length, but even more importantly, it grows in depth.

The key is to get the professor to write the letter as close in time to the class as possible, rather than close to the due date when you actually need the letter. Every professor has horror stories of barely recognizable students coming back years after taking a course to request that she write a letter. Even if the student was wonderful, chances are the memories will be hazy and the letter will be vague. However, if all she needs to do is change the date, add some final details, and print out the glowing, detailed, personal letter written several years before, you are in great shape.

If you're reading this book for the first time as a college senior and feel like all hope is lost because you didn't ask for recs earlier, some hope remains. With a little apologetic politeness mingled with your request and—at the very least—a month's notice before you need the letter, your prof will most likely be understanding about it.

In these cases, do try to meet with the professor in person so as to help trigger memories. If you have to do it long-distance, send a picture or two (preferably dated to the time you took the course) and include in your letter several of your own recollections to help the professor situate you.

The big question students ask about recs is if they should be requested as open or confidential. We hate to sound brutal, but any recommendation requested as an open letter is virtually useless. Confidential letters are the only kind with credibility. Since profs are human and don't want to hurt an eager student's feelings, open letters tend to be bland. Even if it seems glowing, the people reading the letter will wonder whether the professor was simply avoiding conflict.

University career centers and preprofessional advising offices (such as medicine, law, and business) recognize the need to preserve confidentiality and are willing to maintain student recommendation files upon request. Those letters that are marked confidential can be sent by you via someone in that office to whatever program you wish, but you won't ever be able to see them.

Now the question is whether or not this professor will actually *write* that glowing recommendation you need. After all, if you agree to let him send it confidentially, how can you be sure it will be all you hope?

> Do not ask, "Will you write me a glowing letter?" Do ask, "Do you feel like you know me well enough to write a strong letter?"

You accomplish this simply by asking—but might we suggest using a little artful diplomacy that you probably mastered in the days of asking a crush to a junior high dance. Do not ask, "Will you write me a glowing letter?" Do ask, "Do you feel like you know me well enough to write a strong letter?" That way if the prof (or dean or whomever you are asking) doesn't think she can wax eloquent about your many virtues, it gives her room to respond with, "I don't think I know you well enough" or "I only know you somewhat," which signals that perhaps she would be unable or unwilling to write the recommendation you have in mind. This little song and dance will require that you read between the lines of her response, but at least you'll have a fair chance to find someone else if she seems less than enthusiastic.

Most profs welcome the opportunity to beg off writing letters of recommendation for weak students, those they don't know beyond a name and grade, or those who performed poorly in their class. No matter how desperately you need a letter, you cannot be so desperate that you are willing to ask one from a prof who dreads the idea of writing a letter on your behalf. Trust us, it won't be pretty.

Profs understand that writing recs comes with the job, so don't feel like you need to approach them on bended knee. However, some students have made the fatal error of *not* recognizing the inconvenience of such a request by forgetting to show gratitude—or, worse, by giving very short notice (less than a month). Good profs won't retaliate by slamming you in the letter, but they are human; one might rush a bit, not adding that extra touch of glow to your letter just because you didn't give him enough lead time. So timely, polite requests with follow-up thank-you notes and a final quick note letting the professor know the outcome of the job search or grad school application are not just courtesy—they are self-preservation.

The general rule of recommendations is that you want the best recommendation from the most distinguished people you can get. However, if forced to make a trade-off, go with the recommenders who know you best rather than the famous people who barely know you. Few things are as worthless as the bland letter from some big-wig saying, "Nancy was a wonderful intern in my office for six weeks and I would not recognize her if I ate dinner with her at a table for two."

This is especially true with applications that require personal recommendations as well as academic (such as the Rhodes and Truman scholarships). The more demanding the program, the more closely the recommender must know you to make the letter any good for your purposes. For these sorts of applications, read the instructions weeks or even months before you hope to apply to get an idea of what sort of campus personalities (such as deans, coaches, or advisors) it will expect to see in your fan club.

We Make Awful Wallflowers
Getting Profs to Attend Your Event

"One of the last functions I ever attended for my students was at the invitation of several of them to be a part of a student-faculty mixer at their sorority," a tenured professor at an elite university tells his advisees. "I arrived on time at the hall where the mixer was hosted, and much to my surprise I was the only one there. It was a cavernous room, a well-stocked veggie platter, and me. After a few minutes of getting to know the various tastes of broccoli, a student finally walked in. Not one of my students, it turned out; just the faculty interaction chair for the sorority. She did her best to make me feel comfortable, but it was painfully obvious she knew little about me. My students never even showed, and after a period of desultory conversation which rarely rose to the level of superficial, I gave up. I couldn't wait for class the next day and the chance to single out these students for special recognition."

This particular professor actually doesn't mind chitchat and he enjoys meeting new students, but that was not why he agreed to attend the event. He attended as a courtesy to his students as a way of extending the educational experience beyond the classroom. The prof held up his end of the bargain, but his students failed at theirs (though they didn't fail the course—let's not lose perspective here).

Such student-faculty interaction can be even dodgier if the professor is not the gregarious type. A professor who might be quite animated when discussing Shakespeare in a seminar could become quiet and withdrawn when turned over to small talk at one of these mixers. Add to the batter that most profs are a generation or two older than their students, and you have a recipe for an intimidating venture.

But this is not the end of the matter. There is hope. With a few well-chosen steps, you just might persuade your English professor to read love sonnets to the cafeteria on Valentine's Day or goad your biology prof into playing his trombone for your club fundraiser ($10 for a five-minute serenade, $20 for him to stop after two minutes).

The first well-made step is to play to the prof's strengths—some area of expertise where she will feel comfortable pontificating should the need arise. The second is to be sure the event is something students will be interested in; you may think sonnets over meatloaf is romantic, but if the rest of the student body would rather chatter than listen, it could be a very awkward occasion for both you and the prof. If you're unsure if your event would be professor appropriate, ask yourself two questions: Is the event hosted by a university-sponsored club, and is it something I could invite my roommate's parents to attend? If the answer is yes to one or both, you're off to a great start. The third step is to be sure you (or the person inviting him) actually know the professor.

Once the first three are under way—and this is most critical—invite your professor in person *at least a month* before the proposed event. The personal touch will show your genuine interest in the humanity of your professor as opposed to another faceless email asking for something.

If you're only interested in grabbing coffee with a prof after class, telling him at the beginning of the week is fine and he may be able to work you in before Friday. But when it comes to a specific slot on the calendar, and especially one after normal work hours, nearly a month's notice is needed.

Once the professor has accepted, your work does not end there. You should keep him informed of any important changes in the program (not an hourly ticker of trivial details, but say an every-other-week reminder and update).

Several days in advance of the event, offer to meet your prof a few minutes beforehand so that you can attend the event together. If you happen to have a shy prof on your hands, this will alleviate any fears of being forced to make conversation in a room full of strangers, since you will be there to protect him from boring small talk and general silliness.

An added plus—if you are really trying to make this work—is to invite the prof's spouse or significant other (should there be one) and offer to arrange for babysitting if needed. By doing so, you have turned your event into a kid-free date for the professor.

When inviting faculty members to a function, be sure you are clear about the length of the function and any specific expectations you may have for them during that time. It is not unusual for professors to get invitations to "come speak at our house meeting" with no reference to how long they should speak or what in their vast field of study they should expound upon.

Worse yet, some students try to arrange panels of multiple speakers at once—meaning that all the profs who attend have to sit through each other's mini-lectures. Students love these, especially if they can throw together a couple of faculty who they suspect will disagree with each other about some topic of the day. Smackdown professorial wrestling is great sport for students, but professors are usually less keen to participate. The more profs on the slate, the less likely any of the profs will want to be there. To them, it promises to be nothing more than sitting through a tiresome litany of superficial summaries of points they know all too well.

If the event absolutely needs a range of perspectives, then by all means try for it, but be creative. Realize that if the idea occurred to you, it has probably occurred to other students as well, and yours may be the nth invitation the prof has received. Teaming up with all the other invitations to have one major, well-attended event is probably your best shot, especially if you strategize with those other students about ways to make the event more attractive to your key speakers.

One last note: Be sure to send a thank-you note (snail mail is best, but email is acceptable) within a week of the event, perhaps relaying a favorable student comment or two. You'll want lightning to strike again, if not for you then for the next generation of scholars smart enough to get the best out of college.

That's a Line I Don't Intend to Cross
Gender Etiquette—How to Play Fairly and Why You Should Care

Professor Stevenson tells of a student who approached him during office hours with a genuine conc ern that some psychological issues (for which she was being treated) were interfering with her course work. It was a perfectly appropriate conversation and they were both quite professional about it. Then arrived her apologetic email gushing gratefully about how understanding he had been and expressing concern that she may have told him too much.

Given the context of the situation, her email would seem to be absolutely natural. But since their original conversation wasn't recorded, this email, if read by the wrong person, could incorrectly lead someone to believe that the professor was taking advantage of his student by pursuing an inappropriate relationship.

Dr. Stevenson admitted to us that he is certain the young woman meant no harm in sending the email, but it left him quite limited in how he could respond. University email is university property and may therefore be confiscated at any time: a terrifying thought for most professors.

> As a result of the semipublic nature of email, many profs limit their correspondence to terse replies, and some don't reply to personal emails at all.

As a result of the semipublic nature of email, many profs limit their correspondence to terse replies, and some don't reply to personal emails at all. Email is fabulous for arranging appointments and clarifying class assignments; it is serviceable for follow-up clarification about something said in a lecture; but it is dangerous when used for deep personal revelation. If you are the sort of person who sends emails to colleagues without giving them a quick scrub, be forewarned—your professional reputation and theirs may be at risk. Be willing to invest the time to review the screen before hitting "Send."

STUDENT ETIQUETTE

What goes for the virtual world applies in spades to the world of flesh and blood. Professor Julian asked us to stress this point. Based on the styles of students she has tutored over the years, she believes that professors are far more sensitive to and worried about appearances of impropriety than students.

Whether or not that's true, it is not beyond the scope of reason to see why one professor might choose not to meet with a student for coffee because he's concerned someone might misunderstand why she's wearing tight leather pants. That student may have no intention of flirting with her prof, but should she arrive in provocative clothing, reach over and pat his arm while flashing a bit too much skin and laughing at his jokes—well, it could give a very different impression.

The safest bet is to keep hands off and dress professionally (meaning modest attire and minimal cologne) so that the hassle of defending your intentions will be unnecessary. And, if you're meeting with the prof privately in a classroom or office space, it's a sign of respect to them if you assume they want the door left open for appearance's sake. (If they prefer it closed, they'll let you know.) Sexual overtones apply to both genders, though realistically the responsibility lies most often with female students.

For the male readership who were already planning on leaving their spaghetti strap halter tops at home when they meet with their female profs, here's an added insight. Women professors want to be treated as full authority figures, and many have struggled in a man's world of academia to make it to their place. Be careful not to signal that you are one of those men who disrespect her authority by being either overly familiar or combative—not only is it inappropriate, it could trigger an unfortunate result, such as being singled out for remedial correction.

PROFESSOR ETIQUETTE

But what if you have done your part and it is the professor who is acting inappropriately? It does happen—perhaps less often than Hollywood would suggest but more often than university administrators want to admit.

If a professor is indeed giving you unwanted looks, favors, or flattery, you have every right to put a stop to it. The law is pretty clear on this point. But as it is still a very delicate issue, might we make a few suggestions should you find yourself in that improbable situation?

First, be aware that any accusations you make about a prof will be a *permanent* part of his record. Or her record. These matters are not gender-specific, though Hollywood tends to have the professor role played by a man (usually middle-aged) and the student role played by a woman. (Since you probably have that image in mind, we'll try to keep up with Hollywood on this one.) Were you to visit your academic dean even to ask for advice on how to handle the situation, she would be required to report the prof for inappropriate behavior, whether you were certain he was ogling you or not. Out of deference for his career, be sure the professor's attentions warrant this sort of strong response.

If it is as simple as a misunderstood gesture or comment made by the prof—say he made a crack about "sorority girls" after you made a less-than-brilliant contribution to class discussion—schedule a time during office hours to explain that his comment or actions made you uncomfortable and interfered with your learning experience. Calmly state that you would like it to not happen again. No threats are necessary. That you had the courage to speak to him directly communicates that you will have the courage to expose him should the behavior continue. And, in keeping with the power of paper trails, send *yourself* an email after the meeting explaining the situation and what happened. It will automatically be dated and you can store it for reference should the inappropriate behavior continue.

However, if the prof's attentions have clearly crossed the line into the inappropriate, you should absolutely make a beeline for the office of either an academic dean or a resident advisor and explain the situation. Both will know what to do from there. Fortunately this sort of case is quite rar e, and most professors are more petrified of a misstep than you are; their careers are on the line and very few are willing to risk what they have worked a lifetime to achieve. So breathe a sigh of relief and attend class unconcerned.

My TA Will Be Happy to Help
Learning from Grad Students

Nearly all of the advice on professors in this chapter also applies to your TA in terms of how to manage that relationship. All of your professors started out as graduate students once, so it's not as though TAs are an alien species.

However, they are in some sense a breed apart and that can alter the professor-student dynamic somewhat. You should be sensitive that graduate TAs may have less experience from which to draw and so will probably make more mistakes or be slower to adjust to awkward situations than your professor would be. On the other hand, graduate students will likely be better able to read the latest cultural cues and may therefore have a better intuitive feel for the work.

If you have grad students as your TAs, you should treat them in essentially the same professional manner that you would treat a professor—and you have a right to expect essentially the same professional treatment in return. What should drive the relationship is the professionalism behind your roles (teacher and student), not the age difference.

> If you have grad students as your TAs, you should treat them in essentially the same professional manner that you would treat a professor. What should drive the relationship is the professionalism behind your roles (teacher and student), not the age difference.

In large classes and especially lab courses, students often work more closely with a graduate TA than with the actual professor. In those cases, you should not hesitate to get a letter of recommendation from the graduate student. The rule of thumb that personal authenticity trumps distinguished signature still applies. Of course, best of all would be if the graduate student could write a couple paragraphs of personalized evaluation that would be inserted in a larger letter written by the professor. It is worth asking whether or not both are willing to do this.

Let's Not Relive That Nightmare
Profs' Top Pet Peeves and How to Avoid Them

Throughout this chapter we have given a variety of tips on how to cultivate meaningful relationships within the academy. On the flip side, here is a series of professorial pet peeves that reinforce the basic point.

▶ *Being stood up.* One professor claims that in his many years of teaching he has never hosted a meeting involving more than three or four students outside of class where at least one student didn't stand him up. What an awful record!

▶ *Unprepared and unmotivated students.* There are few things as disheartening as devoting your life to a topic only to find that someone who, after paying thousands of dollars to study with you, considers it so worthless that he doesn't even review the notes you labored to provide.

▶ *Techno addicts.* You may think you're being discreet as you type a quick message into your cell phone or catch up on your favorite team's final score, but your facial expressions give you away. That glazed expression or that odd look of glee that doesn't relate to anything your prof just said are clear ringers that your body may be in class but your brain is elsewhere. Be aware that you are being watched, and come exam time your prof may be less than sympathetic if you can't recall large chunks of the course material because even though your face was in class your mind clearly was not for most of the course.

▶ *No-search research.* After a full day of lectures and meetings, it is not uncommon for profs to return to their inbox and find students asking them to do their homework for them. "It drives me nuts that students email me asking me to help track down a book as if I was their personal librarian, while others want me to decide their research topic for them," said one professor expressing a common complaint. Unfortunately, modern search engines seem to make the average student even more dependent on the professor for cues than he was a generation ago. "I have no problem offering suggestions for summer reading if a student is looking for extra material on a subject, and I'll help students puzzle out a research topic if they come in for office hours to ask. But for students who are just plain lazy and ask me over email, no way."

▶ *Late rec requests.* With scores of students flooding through a professor's life each term, it's no wonder she gets a bit stressed when one from the masses requests a recommendation months to even years after taking the course.

▶ *Scantily clad office hours.* There's nothing quite like trying to keep eye contact with a student who insists on baring all, or attempting to breathe through the fog of cologne without keeling over from the fumes.

▶ *Email dumping.* One student went so far as to generate the following email correspondence with her prof:

Student: Do you have office hours this week?

Prof: Yes, the sign-up sheet is posted outside my door.

Student: What days?

Prof: Wednesday and Friday, the sign-up sheet is posted outside my door.

Student: Do you have any openings on Friday?

Prof: Yes, see the sign-up sheet posted outside my door.

Student: When are they?

Prof: From 12 to 1 and 3 to 4. The sign-up sheet is still posted outside my door.

Student: Would you mind signing me up for 3 on Friday?

Prof: I would most certainly mind.

Though this student thought she was being polite, ten emails prove that she was clearly more interested in saving herself the hassle of walking over to the prof's office to sign up than respecting her professor's time. Do your own grunt work.

▶ *Time sappers.* No matter how hard they try, some profs feel as if student demands are insatiable. Even the most accessible professor will get complaints on end-of-term evaluations about how she could have done more to help students enjoy the learning process (such as come to the library to help with research or attend a cram session to help students prep for her final). The students who make these complaints have no idea about the pulls on a professor's time and have clearly not read this chapter. We're glad you aren't one of them.

Wrapping Up

This chapter wins the prize for being the longest in the book. (What can we say, we had a lot on our minds!) So if you're a little overwhelmed by the professor-student relationship, don't be. The baseline for nearly everything we've said here is to behave professionally and with genuine respect. Of all the areas in your undergrad experience where time invested is directly proportional to maximum value, your relationships with your profs is at the top.

CHAPTER 7

Getting What You Came For

Studying Smarter
(and Why It Shouldn't
Be All That Hard)

If you're like most students, you've made it to college with a few
academic tricks up your sleeve. The cram session over a bowl of
cereal before your first period French test; the cram session over a
pizza slice before your fifth period chemistry test; the cram session
walking between sixth period and seventh period mumbling Medi-
tation XVII before reciting it in English class—they may have
worked then (though even that is questionable)—but they are unlikely to work now.

Most freshmen figure out too late that very few of those habits
are suited to the unique and intensive challenges of collegiate
course work. Too often those students opt for the easy way out like
they did in high school. Then they either find themselves settling
for mediocrity and hoping that future employers won't ask about
their undergraduate GPA (sorry, almost all employers check) or,
even worse, they risk their reputation and college career by handing in work that isn't theirs.

The good news is that a college admissions board tends only to
admit students who are capable of making the grade. If you are
smart enough to get into the college, you are smart enough to
thrive there. So reserve the panic attack for prenuptial butterflies.

The Easy Way In
Confessions of a Cheater

But what if the whole reason you performed well in high school (and thus got admitted to college in the first place) is because you *did* cheat? Don't you need to cheat to keep up the performance? And since college is often so much larger, isn't it true it's less likely you'll get caught? Well, no and yes.

No, you don't need to cheat to get the grade you want. Regardless of what stunts you may have pulled for the last four years, you—and every other freshman—will be changing your habits. You are *all* back at square one in terms of learning how to study, how to take effective notes, and how to learn (and it may be the last time in your college career that you get such a fresh start, so take advantage of it).

> There is little to no grace if you are caught cheating. It's sayonara and so long to your academic record: every job and grad school application will see that pockmark on your transcript from here until your teeth fall out.

Yes, it is true—the likelihood of getting caught is lower in college than it was in high school, but in that same breath let us add that the consequences are far, *far* greater. There is little to no grace if you are caught cheating. It's sayonara and so long to your academic record: every job and grad school application will see that pockmark on your transcript from here until your teeth fall out. That's no exaggeration. Learn to be master of (rather than be mastered by) your course load.

"Toto, We're Definitely Not in Kansas"
How College Differs from High School

The most significant difference between college and high school is that you aren't required to be here. So if school isn't for you right now, you might talk with your parents about some creative ways to take time off. Seriously—we aren't saying that in jest. College is an expensive proposition, and it will be here when you are ready.

THE SYLLABUS

Assuming you decide to stay, one of the biggest differences in course work is that from the first day of class your college courses will be governed by a syllabus. With the exception of a few slacker profs (oh yes, they do exist), every professor will hand you a syllabus on the first day that maps out what you will read, discuss, and examine for the whole semester. Every significant deadline and every major reading will be listed there. Cool, no? Overwhelming too.

It can be daunting to see an entire semester's worth of work listed on a few (or—horrors—many) pages. But think of how much easier it will be to plan your social life and weekend getaways now that you know what to expect. It will be rare that your weekend plans are soured (as probably happened more than once in high school) by a professor giving you a surprise massive assignment on Friday that is due Monday. (You can start thanking your lucky stars now.) In this scenario, if your weekend is ruined, it will most likely be because you failed to plan (and work) ahead.

Because of the syllabus, you will have more power than ever before to plan your academic life, as opposed to just reacting to it. We recommend the following strategy to help you get the best out of it. Start off by buying a month-at-a-glance calendar and fill in all the major reading and writing deadlines, as well as any labs or course meetings listed on your syllabus. (Or do it on your computer or PDA. Trust us, the technology doesn't matter as long as you can see the full month at once.) Next, backtrack from each of those deadlines and figure how long it will take you to prepare for and complete them, and build a couple of your own milestones for each. For example, if you have a fifteen-page paper due halfway through the course, fill in a date by which you'll have all of your research finished and another to have your annotated outline completed. If you really want to crush it, plan to have your paper finished a couple days *early*.

Whoa! We know that sounds like nerddom and insanity talking, but if you have never experienced the "done early" high, you shouldn't knock it. It's a fabulous feeling to look at a beastly deadline and know that you were finished long before the midnight hour, especially when you see your colleagues slaving away at all hours in a state of panic, drinking sleep-depriving concoctions to keep their eyelids open while you head out for a game of Ultimate Frisbee instead. Plus, in case something goes wrong—"Ack! It's harder to write a fifteen-page paper than I realized and my laptop just died!"—you have a little breathing room. By allowing for a couple of extra days, the worst-case scenario is that you finish on time—the best case is that you get to gloat and take yourself out for ice cream.

ACCOUNTABILITY

The second huge difference between high school and college is that no one will be checking up on you (unless you commit some sort of heinous crime). Whatever support props you used in high school are gone now, and though assignments might be daily, they won't be monitored on a daily basis, if at all. Profs rarely even check if you attend class unless you're at a smaller school or in a smaller class, so you need to set up some sort of artificial monitoring to alert you if/when you're falling behind.

For example, if you are expected to read a novel a week, it might help to create a reading schedule for a while until you've learned to bring your reading pace up to the college level. Remember, if you don't have the desire to challenge yourself and learn, you may as well spend your time elsewhere and save college for later.

It is also worth probing the professor's expectations about readings listed on the syllabus. For many courses, especially in the social sciences and humanities, there may be some readings that are required and others that are only recommended. Few (if any) students do all of the recommended reading, but the very best students *will* do the recommended reading for particular weeks or topics that seem especially interesting. Supplemental readings are designed to reward the student whose curiosity has been piqued.

Every syllabus, no matter how vast, really just skims the surface of the topic. Some profs underscore this with a lengthy list of recommended readings just so you don't get smug thinking you have mastered the material prematurely. At some point, nearly all of us have promised ourselves, "No pressure, I'll just read the recommended readings this summer," but we don't believe we have ever met someone who actually did that. So, if you think it's worth the read, carve out the time now while the subject's fresh in your mind. Beyond just passing a class, getting the best means educating yourself well.

One more point on accountability before we risk beating a dying behemoth. Alongside writing up a monthly chart of deadlines, create some sort of grid that maps out a typical week's schedule. List the whole week from wake to sleep and fill in blocks of time for immovable obligations you will have consistently, like courses, labs, or a work-study job. Now, look at all that blank space. It feels like Christmas, doesn't it? Before you get carried away and start decking the dorm hall, it's time to fill in a couple other necessities.

What may have been peak study time in high school (7 to 10 p.m.) is peak social time in college, so now would be a good time to adjust your study hours to a better part of the day. The best time to hit the books is often in the morning, when others are asleep and the campus is quiet. Now before you start groaning about how tired you are, remember that virtually everyone in high school was able to function from 7 a.m. on and that most working stiffs have to as well. You may as well keep your body in peak performance by training it to work by the day-means-work-and-night-means-play philosophy. Not only will you be the life of the party (because your course work is done and you can play with a light conscience), but you'll be a rock star in your classes as well. It's really the best of both worlds, and all it costs you is a little self-discipline.

ANALYSIS

The third major difference between college life and high school will be that you are expected to analyze more. (This is why your rote memorization strategies from high school won't work.) By and large, the expectation is that students begin to internalize and synthesize what they're learning as opposed to just regurgitating facts. You will be expected to go deeper with the facts and to make meaning of them. A good way to test whether or not you are really analyzing the material as you learn it is to try to interact with what you're reading—ask yourself questions at the end of each section to see if you were actually paying attention. The ultimate test after you finish reading is not only your comprehension of the material but your ability to communicate what you learned. If you don't know it well enough to teach it to someone else, you don't know it well enough.

> **The ultimate test after you finish reading is not only your comprehension of the material but your ability to communicate what you learned. If you don't know it well enough to teach it to someone else, you don't know it well enough.**

Upper-level courses take analysis a step further in the direction of critique. Master's students go even deeper and are expected to master, synthesize, and thoroughly critique whole subfields. PhD students dig down to bedrock by making original contributions to knowledge in the field. The very best profs at the very best schools in the very best courses will try to expose students to all of these levels—analyze, critique, contribute—and you should enroll in a class like that before you graduate, but maybe not in your first semester.

In keeping with this, students will definitely be expected to analyze resources more. A quick Internet search will no longer be sufficient. See this as a great opportunity to develop a more astute grasp of the Web. Just as you wouldn't use the "journals" by the grocery checkout as sources for a science paper (tempting as the two-headed pig story may be), you can't use everything your search engine lands upon either. Real research involves reading a lot of sources and evaluating their credibility, seeking to understand whatever biases may lead that source to its point. Ultimately you will learn which sources can be trusted and which require some skepticism.

To help plow through the avalanche of hits you may discover on any given topic on the Web, it would be wise to talk with your TA or professor about respected sources in the field and start there as a point of comparison. The point is not to bad-mouth search engines but rather to say that they are a very sophisticated instrument that most students mishandle. By itself, searching doesn't lead to good analysis. Entire books could be written on how to weigh the value of sources, so we can't delve into it here as much as we would like. If you assume that the sources listed on the syllabus or in books on the syllabus are reputable, then build your own web of sources from those references and you'll be off to a good start.

Beyond that, see your college librarian. Reference librarians are the secret weapons of successful research, and far too few students use them. Some colleges have sought to remedy that oversight by offering workshops on navigating library databases and websites. Still, there's nothing quite like talking to a warm body when you're at a loss for information, so we recommend you stop on by for a chat.

Success in college depends first and foremost on you. Unlike high school, college is voluntary, lacks lots of reinforcing reminders (like Mom and Dad) to keep you on the straight and narrow, and requires that you master material to the point where you can analyze (rather than merely verbalize) information. Fret not. You'll be able to make the adjustment if you plan ahead and develop successful routines.

He Who Procrastinates Is Lost
Studying Smartly

We danced around this topic earlier by encouraging you to create some sort of study schedule that will build a consistent and sustainable routine for your college career. However, let us emphasize that we are NOT suggesting you study all the time.

(We'll even make a paragraph break just to emphasize that point.) In fact, it's just the opposite. If you are studying smartly, you should feel like you are studying just a few hours each day, as opposed to frequently feeling crushed by your books in the wee hours of the night when you are too tired to think clearly. So have no fear: we aren't killing your social life, we're strengthening it.

Busyness Is Not a Virtue
Going Easy on the Extracurriculars

Most freshmen study well for the first few weeks but distractions frequently take over and—when they realize there are no immediate penalties—they fall behind. The first week is not wasted, but the first month often is; and, no matter how extreme your efforts to salvage the semester, you cannot make up in December what should have been done in September. We're hoping to counteract the irretrievable (and costly) loss of an entire semester by giving you some significant tips early on.

For the first two to four weeks, it's possible that you won't have any assignments due (particularly if you're not taking any math or science courses). Even more exciting, in many classes you won't have anything due for a good long while. As a result, a couple things tend to happen: as a freshman, you enjoy doing zero work and build an unrealistic mind-set about college life, or you begin to fill your time with other activities.

Some students go crazy on that second one. Because they were involved in a zillion clubs in high school or did dozens of hours of community service each week, they continue in that habit. Then, once the semester gets rolling, they find themselves either having missed the boat in what they were supposed to have learned in class or on a ride going faster than they can handle because they are overcommitted. (We devote a whole chapter to the topic of extracurriculars, so be sure to check that out.)

The key here is to get involved early on but not at the expense of not getting your work done later on. Take your current free time as a very brief gift, and enjoy it as such.

DO WHAT WORKS

The best way to do this is to establish a realistic yet "stretching" routine you can follow from week to week (meaning, don't just pick a routine that is comfortable—challenge yourself to get up a little earlier than you'd like or be diligent about getting to bed on time) and stick to it. One possibility is to start your workweek on Sundays and use that as your primary study day to lighten your load for the remainder of the week. Another experiment is to study only during the typical workweek of 8 a.m. to 5 p.m., Monday through Friday (but to use *all* the empty spaces between classes in that time window for study alone), and then the rest of the time outside that window is gravy. The point is to know your learning style and try out some creative solutions to getting your studying done so that you don't feel constantly hounded by work.

MAKE USE OF SMALL POCKETS OF TIME

As you consider how early you need to wake up to go to the library, take a look at the nuggets of time hiding between your classes. The most successful students take advantage of that hour here and there by reading, studying, meeting with a tutor or professor, or exercising to invigorate their brain cells with a new supply of oxygen. Those measly one or two hours between classes can turn out to be a gold mine that adds up to a lot of free time later if you use them to get your work finished.

Something else to consider as you manage this study schedule is that most readings are paced with the lectures so that they make the most sense to read when the prof suggests. (This is one good reason never to fall more than a week behind in your reading.) If possible, read the assigned material as close to the day (if not on the day) of the lecture as possible so it is fresh in your mind. You may find this strategy affecting how you schedule courses as well. If all of your classes are on the same day, keeping the reading timely and fresh will be nearly impossible! (Yet another reason we don't recommend scheduling all your classes for the same day. Review chapter 3 for more reminders on how to balance your course load.)

Some people are auditory learners who need to hear it to get it; if that's you, attend the lecture first and then read immediately afterward. On the other hand, if you tend to be a visual learner, read before you attend class. No matter when you read, the point is to have the reading finished before the next lecture. Later on (what seems like eons away), when it comes time to prep for the final, it will truly be review since you learned the material at the pace it was taught.

STUDY WHERE YOU CAN BE STUDIOUS

Most important of all—and this one you shouldn't ignore . . . please . . . of all our advice in this chapter, heed this—don't make your room your primary place to study. Go to the library or discover some special study location the rest of campus has overlooked (tip: it probably isn't at the table near your friendly neighborhood barista), but don't study in your room.

> Despite your best intentions, your room is nothing but a small area packed with distractions and people dropping by who aren't interested in watching you read. It may have worked at home, but this balance shifts now that you are living with your friends.

Despite your best intentions, your room is nothing but a small area packed with distractions and people dropping by who aren't interested in watching you read. It may have worked at home, but this balance shifts now that you are living with your friends. You need to go somewhere else in order to focus, and it's good to make that distinction early on. We are all creatures of habit. If you train your mind that the bed means sleep, it will be very hard to study well and stay awake in bed. Also, be very wary of "contaminating" a dedicated workspace with frivolous activity no matter how innocent, since you may be undermining a habit you worked hard to establish. Most campuses have quiet zones or creative study sites if you aren't the library sort of person, and that's fine. The idea is that most students will experience more quality study time if that time is not spent in their room.

DEVELOP YOUR OWN STUDY GUIDE

So now that it's your designated time slot for studying and you are in your designated space for studying, how do you study? A basic tool we find to be highly valuable is the outline. It sounds bland, we know, but give it a chance.

The idea is to limit yourself to one sheet of paper and after reading your material for class for the week to construct some sort of outline or logic chart that concisely summarizes what you read.

Tempting as that extra ream sitting near your elbow may be, keeping it to a page will not only force you to test whether or not you understand the information well enough to simplify it, it will also provide you with a handy study guide. Believe us, it is *much* easier to review than to go back through all of the handouts, class notes, and highlighted text in your textbook only hours before a final exam.

This can be applied even further afield. In studying for the bar exam, Sue made only one page of notes for each of the nine areas of study. So, regardless of what she was asked, she at least had something to talk about. Depending on your study habits, this sheet is also quite portable, which means you can review on the go.

You can take this one step further and distill your weekly pages onto single index cards, and then at the end of the term summarize all of your weekly cards onto one or two pages—this may be some of the most intense analysis you will do all semester, but as a result it will make your exams that much easier (and, hopefully, successful).

The bottom line is that if you have studied the material properly throughout, there will be no need to cram at the end of the term. We all remember new material better if it is systematic, linked, and logical. Memory devices involve constructing narratives so that the facts aren't cold but instead are part of a story. And in weaving this story, the organization of details and facts is key since that outline imposes a certain order to the information. Even if the information doesn't seem connected naturally, there *is* a connection of some sort since your prof saw fit to link it all together in one course. Sitting down to search out the course theme with the TA or professor at office hours partway through the semester (so you don't have to fight the frantic crammers at the end of the term) may prove to be an invaluable exercise.

> Since most courses are cumulative, with later material building on earlier material, the better you learn the early stuff, the easier it will be to master the later stuff.

Most material can only be mastered over several weeks of sustained study, so start early and keep it up. Since most courses are cumulative, with later material building on earlier material, the better you learn the early stuff, the easier it will be to master the later stuff.

One Is the Loneliest Number
Using Peers to Your Advantage

Boy, they got that right. When it comes to getting the best out of your education, why go it alone when there are tutors, comrades, profs, and campus resources ready to come to your aid?

TUTORS

The most common mistake we have seen in this regard is with students who assume that only dummies need tutors. They wait too long to admit their confusion and when they finally do, the tutor sign-ups are full. There is a sort of stigma or humiliation that goes with needing a tutor, especially for those who are used to *being* the tutor. The best advice we can offer is—get over it. What most students don't realize is that tutors are in high demand campus-wide and to get one, they need to sign up early. LOTS of people need and use tutors. In fact, most big league universities frequently run out of tutors because they are so popular. By the last three weeks in the semester (when the lost folks are truly panicking), all the tutors are gone. So should you find yourself needing a tutor, you can assuage your pride by reminding yourself you aren't the only one.

The point of tutors is to supplement your education. They are the life buoy that's there to rescue you when you've fallen off the yacht. As soon as you don't understand a concept—that is, when you're in over your head—you can grab on to that buoy and be pulled to safety. If you allow yourself to flail about in the water for a few weeks, it will be nearly impossible to survive. That, and your brain will look like a big raisin. Wait, it kinda does already . . . You get the point. A little help early on is better than cranial CPR at the end.

Nearly all tutors get paid, but you should check whether you are the one who has to pay for their services or if the honor belongs to someone else. Most schools provide at least some tutoring for some students for free (sometimes athletes) or the equivalent of a generic help desk at a study center. Depending on the department, some tutoring may even be offered free to students within that major—it depends upon the school. However, for more extensive and tailored assistance, you may have to pay out of your own pocket.

Most tutors are subject specific—that is, they tutor English lit, writing, biology, computer science, and so on. Sometimes they are organized by department, so upperclassmen majoring in the field or grad students can tutor underclassmen. Checking with the main office of the department in the subject for which you want a tutor is a good place to start your search. Or you can ask a prof for help locating a tutor, though chances are he may not know. Academic deans may know where to find them, as well as RAs—and just because these people haven't heard of a tutor in your field doesn't mean one doesn't exist. Most colleges have many tutors, but unfortunately they are not always well advertised, so it will take some tenacity and a lot of asking around. Should you be unwilling to be tutored by someone who might recognize you at the next fiesta, your parents might be willing to hire a tutor from outside the campus, especially if they think it will help your grades.

STUDY GROUPS

If tutors aren't your gig or you would like to get help beyond a tutoring service, study groups can be a great way to go. Depending on the subject, three to six seems to be the ideal number of people, with four to five people being preferred to maximize learning. Dividing work among you can be an effective means of getting more accomplished, but be aware that input/output is a critical element of learning. That means you need to be handling all of the information yourself at some point in order for it to sink in.

Most people learn better with peers in an interactive setting because—let's face it—it's fun. Heck, most anything is fun in a group. And it's been proven time and time again that the best way to learn a topic is to try to teach it to someone else because you reinforce what you already know and quickly figure out what you don't. It is a paradox: study groups can be a good place to learn if you go there prepared to teach other people.

Where a study group tends to go wrong is when its members rely on it too heavily, such as a student attending her group expecting to take more than give. The most effective groups are those that require some sort of advance preparation from each of the members so that coming together is an opportunity to resolve, clarify, or synthesize what each has found. The group can also be effective for brainstorming questions that may be on the test or drilling each other on certain concepts.

Of course, sometimes groups can be less than helpful, being more pooled ignorance than shared wisdom. Most students get in trouble with their study groups by not spotting difficulties early on. A healthy means of evaluating the productivity of your group is to meet week by week and to frequently check in with each member to determine if time is being well spent. By arranging the meetings from week to week (as opposed to promising to meet for the entire semester), there is more freedom to change or leave the group if you or others are unhappy with it. Just remind yourself that the study group isn't some twisted popularity contest and that everyone needs to pull their own load if they want to stay—which includes you as well as the guy everyone thinks is so funny but always has a convenient excuse for not doing his fair share.

FACULTY

Let's not forget the profs. While we covered the topic of getting help from them extensively in chapter 6, there is one final point we can add here. If you are lost, before seeking out a tutor or even your study group, the first person you should consider speaking with is your professor. (We promise he won't bite.) As fun as those other resources can be (because, quite honestly, someone your age will rarely be as intimidating as a professor), a simple visit to office hours to say, "I don't get this" and a few minutes of help will illuminate whether your problem will be easy to solve or if a tutor will be necessary. Your professor should be able to help you assess whether you need a tutor or if reading some other book should clarify the concept for you. Ultimately you know yourself best and should go with whatever resource—professor, study group, tutor, or all of the above—that enables you to *learn* the best.

UNDERUTILIZED RESOURCES

Our final tip is to ask campus resources for training on time management and study skills—it may be that there is an afternoon course or weekly session you could join "free" (aka, part of your tuition). Because studying is so individualized, it's doubtful that your professors will spend any time on either of these topics; that doesn't make them any less important. Your best bet is to seek out an academic resource center or counseling center. Libraries are also rich resources—the reference libraries especially. Most staff are knowledgeable and eager to help (particularly for research papers or projects) and are not well utilized. It isn't against the rules to ask a librarian for help searching out sources or recommending materials, and she may be particularly helpful if you visit during nonpeak library hours. Some campuses also offer writing studios where peers or instructors can help you with writing a specific paper or even writing in general. After your meeting, they'll write your professor just to let him know how they were able to help you, but that's more as a gesture to show that you were receiving official help and therefore not running afoul of honor codes or otherwise seeking an unethical advantage in your studies than to bad-mouth you to your prof. If anything, your prof should respect your assertiveness in getting help.

Every college offers a host of resources to help you learn better. It may take some sweat and a few tears—okay, not really tears—to sort through the offerings to find the one that best suits your needs. Do so. And once you've found it, be proud of your efforts in getting help, provided the help is legitimate.

ILLEGITIMATE HELP

Everything we've described in this section is legitimate help. But we don't have to tell you that there is equally illegitimate help out there. Instead of getting a tutor, you could get someone to write your paper for you. Or, instead of brainstorming with your study group about possible test questions, you could beat down the doors of upperclassmen in the hopes of finding copies of old tests you can use to study. Neither of these is new to the world of academia, but that doesn't make them any less corrupt.

While cheating may be monitored less than it was in high school, the consequences of being caught are far greater. As a way of protecting yourself, if you decide to get help from a tutor or another student, let your prof know the scope of the help you are getting and that it is within the academic integrity guidelines of the school so that your record is never brought into question. Even better, *leave an email trail* with the prof on this subject so that you have it for future reference should it be needed.

"Did I Do That?"
Cheating, Whether You Meant to or Not

"I regret to say that we have seen more plagiarism in recent years than we ever wanted to imagine," said an ethics board member at a prominent university. "Without question, there are two causes of plagiarism that dominate. The first is the act of desperation. This is the student who waited until the last minute to write her paper or lab and now has to throw something together. It's 2 a.m. and the class meets in six hours—she simply just panics. She cuts and pastes from the Internet and it's destined for doom.

"The second type is the truly ignorant act. This is where a student doesn't fully understand what the college expects in terms of citations when writing a research paper. In many schools, improper citations equal plagiarism. The intent is irrelevant! The student who commits plagiarism out of ignorance is as guilty as the one pasting from the Internet. This second student probably has limited experience in writing a research paper and really doesn't know what is expected, but it still appears as though he is trying to get away with something. Ignorance is no excuse.

"Both students then face not only a failing grade but also major sanctioning or a period of separation from the school. Tuition is not refunded for the time of their absences (depending on the school and the situation). The good news is that if a student doesn't know how to cite a paper, most schools offer writing clinics they can take in advance. They can ask their professor for information on citing as well, but few do this because they are either afraid of appearing stupid or they are just lazy; then they wait until the end and don't have the time they need and we're back at the beginning with student number one."

Most students don't bother to read their university's guidelines on plagiarism—seriously, it feels a lot like reading the manual to your parents' dishwasher—but you should. Those same students who didn't set out to plagiarize but did (more out of ignorance than deviousness) were convicted because they erred on the side of inadequate sources. Enough students fail to read their school's definition of plagiarism that a growing number of universities are now posting it as required reading before students can register for courses. Take it from the ethics board member above: "It is much better to have a prof say to you that you footnoted too many times rather than not enough. The first is annoying, the second is a major violation that could get you thrown out of school."

Most cases of cheating begin with the research paper, when a professor reviews the bibliography and finds the sources to be either inadequate or imaginary. It should be obvious that every source you use must be genuine. Beyond documentation, where most students inadvertently trip up is in researching information on the Web and then cutting and pasting more than they should. Clark got carried away and actually cut and pasted his entire paper, thinking the professor wouldn't notice the one set of open quotes at the beginning of the paper and the closing quotes at the end. She noticed. Fortunately for him, she thought he had a few screws loose and after a good chuckle sent him to the dean for tightening down, but it could have been much worse.

Like we mentioned earlier, the best investment you can make in covering your hide is spending the time to develop a paper trail. Mistakes happen, and you never know when you'll need some backup. A friend of ours—Bob—was accused of cheating in organic chemistry when he had only been following the instructions of the TA. The problem came when the course rotated TAs a couple times. By the time they got to the third TA for the course, she thought he was academically out of line and sent him to the ethics committee to be reviewed. Fortunately for Bob, he had a paper trail of notes from the original TA advising him how to proceed with his course work, so his name was cleared. Phew. That was a close one.

> While you won't want to seem like an insensitive conspiracy theorist assuming every course assistant is out to get you, you *will* want to highlight upon the critical conversations and follow up with appropriate emails.

While you won't want to seem like an insensitive conspiracy theorist assuming every course assistant is out to get you (meaning, don't send an email after every conversation saying, "You said this and then I said that"), you *will* want to highlight upon the critical conversations and follow up with appropriate emails. Possible ways to follow up would be to say, "Thanks for your time after class yesterday. Just to review, so I'm sure I understood your instructions, you suggested I review this and then talk to so-and-so and then use his suggestions as one of my sources," or whatever the conversation may be, so it sounds like you are being grateful rather than preparing for a witch hunt.

Some profs make past tests available, and even though it seems like cheating to read them, it isn't. In law school, some profs encourage their students to go to the reserves in the library and use old tests to study. The prof may not ask the exact questions, but the format is the same. Just knowing how the test will be structured can be comforting. The bottom line is that it's always best to ask—if the prof doesn't mention his policy on consulting previous tests, be sure to ask permission. Don't rely on explicit instructions and then look for a loophole. The judicial defense process is painful, so permission (and a paper trail) is critical.

The coaches of well-respected collegiate sports teams tell their players that it is better to take a lower grade—even an F—than to plagiarize. The risks just aren't worth it. Professors are darn smart, and there are a number of clues that tip them off to a paper being a fake. (We'd love to list those here, but we might have to go into hiding as a result.) It may not seem like they catch many students, but figure that every student taking a course is writing in her professor's area of expertise, so he will be able to sniff out inaccuracies or misappropriations faster than she realizes because he will be familiar with the material. Profs didn't get their degrees—or their posts—for naught. Some of them know their field so well they can even tell you in which chapter of what book a "borrowed" quote was published. Borrower, beware.

Even if your professor isn't as smart as some, many universities now have different forms of software that detect cheating. All a prof needs to do is have his assistant send the stack of papers through a scanner and an hour later—voilà!—a printout of any papers that appear on the Internet.

One student made a blunder by turning in a paper answering a question using literary terms that had not yet been covered in the course. This sent up a yellow flag. When her professor dialed her up and asked her for a candid explanation of what she meant when she said X (reading the quote from the paper), the student was speechless. And caught. And flunked. It's not that you must write a paper that matches the vocabulary of the day, but rather that you have to know your material and that the material has to be yours.

If you can't get the paper done and need more time, ask for an extension. If you don't get it, take your lumps. But don't cheat—

it's a quick ticket out of school for a while, if not permanently. Some schools show on transcripts an X rather than an F to indicate when a student has been suspended or failed a course due to discipline. And that means your future employer will have some hefty concerns when it comes time for your interview.

It is better to flunk a course than to pass a course by cheating. To future employers and graduate schools, flunking often looks like immaturity that one can grow out of—or, at worst, skill limitations for which a person will need to compensate. Cheating looks like—and is—a sign of something far more serious: a deep character flaw that may make you far too risky to hire.

"Wait, I Thought You Were Going to Teach Me How to Cram"

Ninety-nine percent of the time there is no reason to cram. If learning is managed properly, students should not find themselves needing to cram and pull all-nighters—which is why we devoted so much time at the beginning of this chapter to setting up structures for studying properly. Occasionally there are exceptions—where the prof will throw something in that you didn't realize you needed to know or a minor emergency arises and your carefully crafted schedule doesn't work as planned: accidents happen. But for the most part, if you establish priorities and stick to a schedule, there is no need to cram.

> An hour spent reviewing organized notes is worth four hours of looking at information for the first time and trying to shove it into your long-term memory.

An hour spent reviewing organized notes is worth four hours of looking at information for the first time and trying to shove it into your long-term memory. We would even add that an hour of studying in the first month of the semester is worth two in the second, three in the third, and so on because you are laying a foundation in a very time-sensitive manner.

Certainly there will be times when you need to focus only on an upcoming exam and it looks like cramming. But what it will really be is just focused review. There is a tiny fraction of students who can successfully cram in college, to be sure. Brent is a friend who would skip a third of his classes, reserve all of his reading for the last week of the semester, then lock himself in his room and read nonstop. And more often than he deserved, he was able to make that strategy work. But many who tried to follow his example failed miserably. What they didn't realize was that Brent was gifted with a certain and very unusual genius that enabled him to store large quantities of information quickly and temporarily—it's rare, and a risk we don't recommend you take.

There are certainly times in real life when cramming becomes necessary, especially in the business world when project dead-lines hit. Prior to the deadline, team members do all that is required, which may mean getting very little sleep. The ability to perform at a high level on little sleep is a valued skill and exercised in countless careers to be sure, but it is an emergency plan and not a daily survival skill. Don't plan on making a career of it. Companies are far more interested in you learning how to learn first and, second, in you having good time management skills so as to avoid unnecessary emergencies. Then, as a third bonus quality, they may want you to have the ability to fly into emergency mode if necessary.

Should you find yourself in desperate straits with an impending deadline, here are a few tips (what kind of help would we be if we didn't at least throw you a rope?):

▶ *Look for course themes.* Start with the syllabus and look at the texts that have been assigned with a view of the course as a whole. Is there some sort of theme or big-picture argument the prof is trying to get you to understand? What is the perspective of each assigned reading and how do they differ? Your familiarity with the thematic structure of the course will be helpful should you need to write any essays on the exam, and your ability to cite some of the assigned readings will go a long way—even if you haven't read them in their entirety.

▶ *Recharge your brain.* Consider taking power naps to help recharge yourself. A twenty-minute nap can go a long way in helping you push yourself an hour or two longer. You may want to experiment first to see if this strategy works before depending on it at crunch time, but most folks find that a short snooze helps.

▶ *Reorganize the workload.* Break an unmanageable amount of work into chunks to make it more manageable—it's hard to memorize a chart of diagrams when your adrenaline is pumping and your brain is in fight-or-flight mode because you're superstressed. Breaking the job down, saying, "I'll work on this half of the page for the first hour, the second-half of the page for the second hour," and so on can be calming because the project feels more manageable. The end result: you are able to focus.

▶ *Refuel your body.* Eat snacks—the healthier and more nourishing, the better. Think protein. Think carbs. Your brain needs all the help it can get, so go for nuts and cheese and fruit and skip the pound of jelly beans. The refined sugar may give you a temporary high, but if you are pushing yourself without sleep you may crash to an unrecoverable low.

▶ *Avoid artificial highs.* The latest craze is to borrow prescription drugs, especially attention-related drugs, to help get that extra edge to focus. They allow students to work through the night, and some perform fine, so they see these drugs as an effective way to get their work done. Of course, whatever works becomes a habit and popping an occasional "emergency pill" becomes more routine. There are huge long-term implications for this sort of drug abuse that are dangerous and, frankly, frightening. A primary goal of college is to prepare yourself for the professional world. Do you plan on popping pills to help get by for the rest of your life? There is always something new and different, some caffeinated concoction or way to hype up your oxygen levels. Rather than abusing drugs in college, use the time to develop healthy lifelong habits that don't rely on artificial means to get the job done.

▶ *Get some fresh air.* Take a hike. Really. If you've got a lot of work to do, next to a nap and a snack, a quick stroll around the building can do a lot of good—especially if it's cold outside. But even if it's late summer and positively sweltering, getting out of your chair and allowing the blood to pump and circulate a little faster will have your synapses cheering. Just don't overdo it. If you strain yourself beyond your usual workout, you may do more harm than good, but a quick fifteen or twenty minutes of cardio should do the trick.

▶ *Make time for creative study breaks.* Paint your toenails. Or if painting your toenails isn't your style, find some other means to relax if you find yourself anxious and sweating through your shirt. The more relaxed you are, the more successful your brain will be in transferring short-term knowledge into long-term memory. (Brief) hourly study breaks are critical to maintaining focus. Plus, your feet will look pretty.

▶ *Take it easy.* Don't expect much of yourself the day after (and for some people, two days after) a major cram session. Meaning, don't schedule two all-nighters back to back. It takes the human body a fair bit of time to recover after this sort of trauma (and that's exactly what sleep deprivation is), so be nice to yourself.

You're capable. You're smart. You've gotten this far. Now you've got some tools to help get you started as you crack the books. If after following through with all our suggestions in this chapter you still feel lost, be sure to check out the next chapter on campus resources for another dose of help. Consider every minute of desk time an investment in your future (even if you don't know how the life of Genghis Khan relates to your aspiring dreams), and tell yourself that no matter how long the educational road in getting here, in a matter of quarters or semesters it will all be over and you will be glad you got the best out of it.

CHAPTER 8

"I've Never Needed Help Before..."

Navigating Campus Resources

The question of the hour is not "Do I need help?" but "What kind of help do I need and where can I get it?" The typical freshman arrives on campus having managed high school well and largely without professional help, and as a result assumes it's time to assert his independence by relying only on himself for the next four years. Then stress begins to pound away—deadline after deadline, decision after decision—until the pulls of campus life are enough to unhinge him. The result is all too often seen in sleeping disorders, eating disorders, roommate conflicts, relationship issues, substance abuse, and personality dysfunctions.

Don't panic. You don't need to place your therapist on speed dial just yet. What we're saying is that it is not uncommon for students to be unaware of the scale of the challenges confronting them in college, and many fail to take advantage of the extensive professional help that is available.

> It is not uncommon for students to be unaware of the scale of the challenges confronting them in college, and many fail to take advantage of the extensive professional help that is available. Everyone in college needs help.

Everyone in college needs help. In many cases, that help can be provided informally by the wise peer, the sympathetic prof, or the alert RA. Help could be as easy as getting some advice on how to balance a tough course load, how to use search engines properly for research, or what not to wear to the Bare-All Ball at Halloween.

Then again, you could land an unforgettable weekend course on study tactics that changes your college career. Or you may find you need some more structured help, such as personality or interest tests at the career center, or a session with a counselor to suggest strategies for managing stress or to provide a listening ear while you watch your parents work through a rough patch. Heck, getting outside help could be less about you and more about you learning how to support your roommate who may be having a tough time.

It comes back to getting the most out of the resources available to you. This sort of help comes once in a lifetime—for free, anyway—and it comes at a critical moment in your personal development. Actually it's not really "free." One of the reasons college tuition continues to soar is that the campus increasingly resembles a sort of socialist utopia where there are A-to-Z services available to all students. Back in the real world, these services cost extra. Since they're part of the cover charge for the next four years, you should get your money's worth here as well.

Better Late Than Never?
When Help Is No Longer Helpful

Though it may be true that any help is better than no help, we've found that all too often people who get help get it too late. The dreaded F (or worse, dropping out) can usually be traced to an earlier denial of timely help. Students who get help early rarely see their situation get worse. In fact, it's so rare that after nearly thirty years in the biz, we could probably name from memory the times that has happened. When in doubt, get help sooner rather than later. Crossing your fingers and hoping things will pan out just doesn't work.

Needing help takes a lot of different forms. Certainly we could start off with flashier topics like depression or eating disorders, but those are fairly easy to spot. If you are in the midst of one of those scenarios, you probably know it and should get help immediately. What is harder to get a handle on is why you can't seem to pass stats class even though you aced it in high school and you're working your tail off. So let's start with that one: feeling clueless.

INTERNAL STRESSORS

What typically happens in the first week is a student will feel a little confused and may not understand the material. The second week she is a little more distracted and confused, but she has a lot on her plate, so she doesn't want to talk to the prof just yet. After all, the F-wave on the normal curve—which right now sounds like a lot of gibberish—might just start to make sense come Friday. Cassie doesn't want to look like an idiot having needlessly gone running to the prof for help. This is college. It is supposed to be challenging. The third week comes, the fourth week goes, and Cassie decides she may as well hold out to see how the midterm pans out. Who knows, it could be that she's being too hard on herself and that everyone feels just as lost and so she will beat the curve (see, she *is* understanding *some* statistics). Of course, it takes two weeks to get grades back since the class size is over a hundred students, so by the time Cassie gets her grade the semester is half over.

And it isn't pretty. The midterm confirms that she Doesn't Know What She's Doing with a big D+. Strangely enough, even at this point a remarkable number of students don't ask for help. Cassie figures she'll make it up on the next midterm, or eat a magic mushroom and somehow manage to ace the final. Of course, by this time she is fully engaged in the rest of collegiate life so she has a whole lot of other pulls on her time. The futility of this exercise becomes apparent when she sits down to study a few days before her final and doesn't even know where to begin. Desperate emails to the prof and TA ensue. We'll spare you the crash ending, save to say that there is very little the prof can do at this point to bail her out. She's in too far over her head. Had Cassie approached her prof during the second week of class, when she started feeling like she'd eaten some bad tofu, she could have arranged for a tutoring session or met with the TA or gotten some solutions with the prof during office hours. At least she would have been able to demonstrate to the prof that she cared and that she was trying diligently to improve her performance.

This same story can be retold for group projects that go awry or research papers that write themselves into a brick wall five pages away from the minimum requirement.

Most of the problems you are likely to face in college are easier to solve the sooner they are confronted. The earlier you seek help, the sooner you can go back to not needing it. We could come up with some cutesy mnemonic to help you remember to Get Help Early, Einstein, While Help Is eaZy, but we'll spare you.

> Most of the problems you are likely to face in college are easier to solve the sooner they are confronted. The earlier you seek help, the sooner you can go back to not needing it.

Whether or not you have proof that you're flunking the class or flailing helplessly, if you are feeling stressed about the course, always approach the professor first. Sometimes he is part of the problem. We have known enough professors in our time to know that some have unrealistic expectations of how much their students can either manage or comprehend, so it's best to provide at least one data point on his radar that says, "Hey, this isn't working for me." With enough data points, the prof might hopefully get the message. (We did know of one ogre who insisted on teaching grad-level stats to his first-year undergraduate statistics class. The fact that his office hours were bursting at the lintels with scads of confused and panicky students delighted him. He was one of those unusual sorts of academics who take a perverse pleasure in making others squirm in their ignorance—but this type is a rarity.) Of course, the shoe fits on the other foot too. We're assuming you're keeping up your end of the bargain and at least cracking the book nightly before attempting to tell the professor that his expectations are unreasonable.

As a general rule, professors are in the business to educate, so they won't be surprised if somewhere along the way to becoming smarter someone gets confused. That's a natural part of learning. As a result, they won't lose respect for the student who approaches them early feeling lost. Sometimes profs will suggest that the student come back in a week or two to see how she is managing the material. Despite what it may feel like, it isn't a brush-off. The prof is most likely tracking the student's progress and wants to give another week for the information to seep in.

Where a student is guaranteed a professorial brush-off is when the professor recommends she do A, B, and C and she doesn't—and then comes back a week to six weeks later wanting the prof to spend one-on-one time explaining more.

In the unlikely case the student has done all that the professor asked but he still ignores her requests for help, she should pursue other options. Out of frustration, she may want to focus all her energies on red flagging this prof to some academic council. While that would leave her with a feeling of satisfaction come the end of the semester, the time-sensitive prioritization is for her to focus on learning the material first and organize a picket line later.

EXTERNAL STRESSORS

We know we mentioned this earlier in chapter 7, but it bears repeating: academic challenges can be exacerbated by personal challenges. If you have a personal emergency on your hands that will most likely last the semester and cause significant distraction, the time to tell the prof about it is now when she can help—not two days before the exam (unless, of course, the emergency occurs two days before the exam). Sample stressors could be your father losing his job and not having enough to cover your bills, your brother getting diagnosed with a terminal illness, your best friend becoming a victim of date rape, you entering the hospital to undergo major surgery, and so on.

It's true that profs can sometimes seem jaded about personal emergencies, so be prepared to overlook some rolling of the eyes or a huffed sigh or two if you begin the conversation with "I can't turn in my paper because . . ." It's a standard but true joke among profs that there is a rash of plagues that seem to strike students right around exam time. We knew one professor who had a student tell him that he was in the midst of a crisis and couldn't focus on his work because his high-school girlfriend had just dumped him. Fortunately for him, his prof felt empathy for the poor guy since at one point ages earlier he too had been dumped by a girlfriend and remembered it feeling like a cataclysmic disaster. Still, there were real limits to what he was going to do for the guy given the nature of the situation. The professor was able to work with him and his group-project colleagues (this was the real problem—it turns out the student was totally leeching off his group) to develop workarounds, so this became only a romantic disaster and not a romantic and an academic disaster. So, don't waive the possibility of getting help just because you think the prof won't understand. He was young once too.

It is an increasing phenomenon that students enroll with medical problems that warrant some special treatment within the classroom. It is so common, in fact, that there is an official procedure for getting a letter from the dean to the professors explaining the need and parameters for getting help. If you think your illness qualifies, be sure to get the letter at the start of the semester so your professors can alter assignments or exams; it doesn't work so well as a "get out of jail free" card if you hide it until finals week.

Most profs will honor this sort of alteration, but there will be a range of opinions on the matter. Some profs will say that they refuse to level the playing field 100 percent but are willing to give 80 percent more help than the student otherwise would have had. In the last few decades, many more students have been diagnosed with learning disabilities of all forms, and while there is debate about how much help students should receive, most professors tend to agree that some help is warranted.

It is critical to have this understanding settled as early in the semester as possible. If the prof is not amenable to assisting you and you don't think you can make the class work without it, take another class. It's also important to note that you should not use the letter to enroll in a class where your point of weakness is one that most students will be required to employ as their greatest strength. For example, if you are dyslexic, you may want to avoid taking "Shake-speare: Every Play He Ever Wrote, in One Semester" since the prof will be less likely to cut you a break after being up-front about the unique requirements of her course.

There's a big difference between obsessing about your prog-ress (or lack thereof) and ignoring it, and finding a balance can be tricky. If at all possible, try to be conscious of your progress with-out getting panicky. If you tend toward the panicky side of things, limit the frequency with which you dwell on the topic; of course, if you lean toward denial, you might want to post a few fluorescent notes around your room to remind you that you are, in fact, en-rolled in some courses that require steady work.

Either way, a good yardstick is to track your progress closely up until the second or third week of the course and then to speak with the professor if all is not well. Most minor kinks will have worked themselves out by that time, and if they haven't, then there is good reason to look into it. Depending on your conversation, you can either proceed as you were or develop a strategy to work your way out of trouble.

Questions to ask yourself may be simple, such as "How should I study?" and "Should I be approaching my fields of study differ-ently?" TAs may even have suggestions on how studying for chemistry is different from, say, studying Russian.

Everyone needs help sometime, and you are no exception. Sign-ing up for tutors, taking study-prep classes, learning how to manage stress—these sorts of activities are the norm; they just don't seem like it because they are typically done in private. So what are you waiting for? Get off your futon and go grab a tutor.

It's Hard to Find Good Help These Days
Knowing Where and How to Look

No man is an island, but some people sure try to fake it. Don't be one of them. Admitting your shortcomings and seeking a solution are some of the surest signs of maturity out there. Like we mentioned

You Know You're in Too Deep When . . .

- You've stopped attending class because you "don't get it anyway."
- You treat every decision on campus as your most important decision.
- You believe every prof who tells you that his class is the most important one.
- You notice that you're failing, but you keep doing what you were already doing (with a bit more persistence, perhaps) and actually expect a different result. This is a pretty good definition of insanity.
- You can't find a clean pair of pants to wear, and don't really care. (Okay, maybe that isn't a sign you're in too deep. But you are definitely in too deep if you can't find *any* pants to wear and you don't really care.)
- You insist you don't need help, even though it's clear to those around you that you do. There's no shame in getting help for *any* need if it enables you to succeed.
- You drink large quantities of alcohol on a regular basis, but you know you can quit anytime because you have quit lots of times.
- Whenever you are blue or stressed, you go home for the weekend to see Mom and Dad (as opposed to just visiting to say hi).

earlier, campuses these days offer assistance covering every problem from A to Z, and chances are you aren't the first person with this need, illness, or issue. There is someone sitting at her desk right now waiting to help. You couldn't give yourself (or her) a greater gift than to knock on her door.

The question is, how to find that door. It may seem a little like hunting for the White Rabbit at times, but here are a few guides you can query for suggestions (no, one of them isn't the Eat-Me box of doughnuts—sorry).

PROFESSORS

It might seem that professors would have the pulse of campus resources and that they would know which services are available and where to find them. But unless the problem is an academic one (and even then . . .), don't crawl into the fetal position if they don't know where to send you. By all means, feel free to ask your professor for help if you think she might be able to point you in the right direction; just don't give up if she grins goofily like the Cheshire Cat. A good professor may turn out to have great life advice, but she was hired to be an expert in her subject matter only, and thus was given very little formal training on being a campus guide.

RESIDENTIAL STAFF

A better guide is your residential advisor (you know him or her as your RA) or even the dean of students. If your challenge is big enough that it requires help across two or three offices on campus (such as mediation with your professor and counseling), the dean will be the person to coordinate that. If your challenge requires more guidance than it does administration (such as needing some ideas on how to improve study habits), your academic advisor (AA) should have some connections. In fact, it might be helpful to ask your AA and RA for a mini-explanation of their roles at the beginning of the year if you think you could use some clarification on who does what. Their roles differ slightly from campus to campus.

COUNSELING CENTER

Virtually every college has some level of counseling available to students, whether it be for something serious like having hallucinations and suicidal thoughts or something less serious but still critical like managing stress or the blues. RAs are specifically trained to know where to make a referral, whether it is a personal issue or an academic one. The most important thing for you to know—next to the point that this counseling is almost always free—is that anything you say under the guise of professional counseling is confidential. It's so hush-hush that not even the faculty or the dean can find anything out. Unless you sign a waiver that you are willing to release your records, the counseling center can neither confirm nor deny whether you are *even being seen* by them. So please don't let pride keep you from getting help.

ADMINISTRATION

In most cases, you can even speak with an administrator and invoke this level of confidentiality, though be forewarned that if you speak with an administrator about issues involving harassment by anyone on the faculty, he is required to act upon that information. You are welcome to discuss as many hypothetical situations as you like, but he is legally bound to involve the appropriate people should he learn of any alleged misbehavior going on in the faculty or the administration. So, should you or someone you know need to discuss this sort of situation without automatically launching it into a legal issue, you may want to set up an appointment with the counseling center since they will still be able to fall back on client-counselor privilege.

While it's better to use the confidentiality as a crutch if you aren't willing to seek help otherwise, the best scenario is to find help and to free those professionals to talk with other key people in your life. Confidentiality, though well intended, can sometimes keep information from the people who are best positioned to help—like professors—or who could at least keep from exacerbating the situation.

Shock of all shocks, one freshly minted freshman began the fall of her college career by learning she had a heart condition that required immediate surgery. Becky had otherwise been a healthy, active individual, so this came as quite the surprise. Not knowing there were campus services available to help, she spent the remainder of the semester in a pharmaceutically induced fog (required to keep her heart rate down) that made walking across campus difficult, let alone late-night studying. What she *should* have done was talk to her AA, RA, professors, or dean about her health situation, but she was one of those independent sorts who figured she could just take care of it herself. At least she had the common sense to notify her professors in January that she would be undergoing heart surgery and would be missing a few days of class.

What came as an almost greater shock to Becky than her diagnosis was when one of her professors claimed that her surgery was an inappropriate reason to falter in class and that it was in her best interest to return to class within the next week. Out came the tears. Becky was appalled, exhausted, and frustrated, so she went to her RA to explain the situation, more out of need for a listening ear than looking for a solution. (She still didn't see the need to ask for help.) He connected the dots for her, and in less than a day Becky met with a dean who provided support for the remainder of her recuperation, handling whatever communications with professors were necessary to keep them abreast of her recovery and to ease her back into her course work.

Now, it would have been a whole lot simpler if she had gone to the RA in the first place back when she noticed she was falling behind in class. This is not to condemn Becky—she's a good friend of ours and this is nothing she wouldn't say herself. In fact, she's kicking herself right now that her self-reliance cost her as much as it did in her GPA since she didn't ask for any extensions or leeway that first semester. (We're not sure why the RA didn't step in sooner either, but Becky says ultimately she was responsible and we agree.) You don't need to be diagnosed with a congenital heart condition to ask for help; any genuine challenge that may affect your college career is worth asking about. Take Becky's word for it.

CAREER CENTER

Since it bears repeating, let us say it again: you don't need to be ill to get help. The writing center might have a Saturday session that takes you to the next level in your writing. The career center offers various tests (Myers-Briggs, for example) that may help you understand yourself and your vocational interests better. Then there's a whole range of help available for goal setting. Going to law school? Talk to a law-school dean. It is a sign of mental fortitude and an indication that you are working through the system appropriately to ask for this kind of help. Anne was startled to discover one of the smartest students in her class at Stanford was actually taking a speed-reading course so he could work through literature faster than he already did. His forethought is a sign of just how smart he was.

On this note, one graduate bemoans, "I didn't know there were courses on writing research papers or study skills at my university until the end of my freshman year. I'm sure it had been advertised on one of the DOZENS of colored fliers I received during orientation—it was just too much to process in the beginning and I forgot about it. Woulda, coulda, shoulda. I wish I had sat down with my RA as well as my advisor during the first couple weeks of college life and asked for the lowdown on all the extras so I could have taken advantage of them."

PEERS

The final word on getting help is that if you are going to rely on the informal network of friends (as most students do), be sure you are getting help from people you trust. The most challenging or heart-wrenching of trials can cause a person to lack judgment or become desperate, so think through the consequences of whom you choose as your loyal listener.

Early on, students look solely to their peers for help—and some of the best support comes from them—but it's often difficult for peers to handle delicate information properly. It's not that their judgment won't be sound, though that should also be a consideration, but that they may not know how to handle the information confidentially. It only takes one misspoken word and your secret is out.

If the stressor is one you'd like to keep secret, your safest bet is to be discreet on a peer level until you know a person well (say, a couple of years) and you've had a chance to hear how well they handle *other* people's private information. There's a hierarchy of help waiting for you on campus for this very reason; don't feel like you must rely on peers for a compassionate ear. Campus counselors only know you as your adult self; they've also been around the block a few more times than your roommate.

"Won't It Hurt My Chances for a Good Rec If I Tell My Prof I Got Help?"

We mentioned earlier that profs aren't professional counselors, but that's not to say that you shouldn't tell a prof about what's going on behind the scenes. Admittedly it does change the way she thinks about the student, but that is a welcome improvement over her perception of a student who clearly needs help but seems too proud or lazy to seek it out. Of course, this is also much better than believing a student is simply an academic slacker when there really is an underlying problem. You sacrifice something when you acknowledge a problem, but you sacrifice far more if you try to hide it and hide it poorly.

A possible way to salvage your pride is to include a success plan in the conversation. When sitting down privately with your professor to discuss whatever entanglements have you tied up in knots, show him you are doing your best to work free of the issue by mentioning some personal boundaries or deadlines or goals you are working toward.

To be more specific, if you admit that you are too involved with alcohol on the weekends, tell him that you have appointments to see a counselor every Friday and have made alternative weekend plans to prevent you from getting wasted (and, thus, behind in his class) yet again. Or if you were date-raped and you are in an emotional wasteland, show that you have backed out of a course to ease your load or are seeking counseling or are being monitored by a physician.

It's not that you have to bring all skeletons out of the closet. To be honest, neither you nor your professors want to discuss the details. They will (and should be) happy to lend support, but the relationship is still a professional one, so be cautious about revealing too much information or too intimate of details.

"Okay, So How Do I Prevent Myself from Needing Help?"

Truth be told, we all need help. It's just a question of whether it's a need that has us on the defensive or the offensive. Your best bet is to catch a need when it is still small—that is, when you get that first inkling that this could affect you later. Here are a few sanity-check questions to ask yourself.

DO YOU HAVE A HISTORY OF TROUBLE WITH ____?

Most problems that show up in college have their roots in experiences (or at least could be anticipated) before college. If you had a problem in some area before college, chances are the stressors of college will only magnify it. Things that were manageable in high school and weren't technically a problem, especially if you had a supportive family, might become one in college because you don't have the same kind of support network. As we've shown in this chapter, support of some kind is certainly present in college; it just requires more initiative on your part to get it. Your mom would have knocked on your bedroom door if she noticed you skipped dinner because you were upset—the dorm RA will not nor will your professors, so it's your job to hunt down some help.

HAVE YOU HAD AN ANNUAL CHECKUP IN THE LAST YEAR?

On a preventative health note, many student health services across the country include an annual physical exam for men and women as part of their campus health-service fee. It's a pretty great service, and taking advantage of it will be the start of a great habit. You may also want to take advantage of various health-education classes offered on campus—don't worry, they will probably be much more practical than the ones you took in high school. These classes show how health today will impact your quality of life down the road with topics on nutrition, sexual lifestyle, exercise, stress reduction, and supporting family members with chronic conditions.

HAVE YOU STARTED YOUR PORTFOLIO?

Another service students often ignore but shouldn't is the opportunity to build a portfolio at the career center or in the prelaw, premed, or prebusiness advisor's office. The sooner you are able to visit the center in your academic career, the better. Once established, most colleges will keep records of this portfolio until you request otherwise. Copies of relevant test scores, letters of recommendation, and career searches will all be stashed on file for you. Whether you plan on being employed immediately after college or not, it's best to beat the rush and get your file started early.

DO YOU HAVE A TUTOR?

As we mentioned in chapter 7, by a certain point in the year it is not uncommon for a college to completely run out of tutors. That means you're on your own if you wait until it's too late. It's a bit difficult to step over the ego and ask for help, but we've found that once students find out how helpful campus resources are, they generally use them often and get their friends to sign up as well.

DO YOU HAVE A MENTOR?

A final (and quite successful, we might add) measure of help would be to find a mentor on campus who can point out potential pitfalls before you trip into them. A mentor doesn't need to be a hero, so it's not as though by choosing this person you're saying you want to *become* them. At the same time, try to choose someone you can identify with and respect, someone you click with personality-wise who can provide some support or help. It may be a professor, a coach, an administrator, or someone on staff. You just need to feel comfortable approaching that person to ask about bouncing a few ideas around.

Everyone is busy and not everyone will be willing to be a mentor. The best thing to do is to ask the person up front to mentor you in a specific area, whatever that

> A mentor doesn't need to be a hero, so it's not as though by choosing this person you're saying you want to *become* them. At the same time, try to choose someone you can identify with and respect, someone you click with personality-wise who can provide some support or help.

may be—carving a path through your major, providing some accountability in the party scene, helping guide you in some career and relationship decisions—that way the person knows what's required of them and whether or not they can accept your offer.

Even if the sun is shining, life is smooth, and you are happy and confident, the best thing you can do to ensure the happy days will continue is to schedule an appointment in a campus resource center of some kind at least a few times each semester. We get our teeth cleaned, our tires rotated, and take vitamins on a regular basis—why not add campus help to that list?

Cheer Up
Where to Find Your Happy Face, in Case You Lost It

You aren't alone. Just because you don't understand everything on the first day doesn't mean that the admissions office has made a terrible mistake. In case someone hasn't already told you, that's a standard fear of being a college student. In fact, it's nearly universal, much like the dream about having to give a class presentation in eighth grade on the day you forgot to wear your pants. Just because everything isn't crystal clear on the first day or even in the first week doesn't mean you shouldn't be here. Have confidence in the nearly ironclad fact that the admissions office rarely makes a mistake.

> You aren't alone. Just because you don't understand everything on the first day doesn't mean that the admissions office has made a terrible mistake. That's a standard fear of being a college student. In fact, it's nearly universal.

Admissions boards send out their thrilling acceptance letters based on the assumption that if students take advantage of the help provided on campus, they have the capability to thrive. So if you were planning on thriving all by your lonesome without any outside help, you may want to reconsider.

But college life isn't all about academics, now is it? If you're feeling lonely or homesick, give yourself a break. Anyone who says they haven't been homesick is lying. Not all students leave a home that is supportive or nurturing, and most students actually come to college looking forward to leaving something behind. Even *those* students are homesick for something. The longing tends to wear off after the first semester once you've got some routines in place and feel more settled. If you find this isn't the case and you are weeping in your egg nog about having to return to campus after Christmas break, you may want to look into extra support on campus. Tut-tut—it's what it's there for, remember?

College is a long series of distractions. You thought you knew what you were coming to get done and accomplish, but along the way there were bright lights and enticing music and you may have wandered off the trail. The point is to keep your eyes on the big picture. Have fun and enjoy this ever-so-brief season as a college student. The whole notion of discovering your preferences, managing your time, and sticking to whatever schedule works best for you is a big part of your diploma. *You* are one of the greatest subjects you will ever study, and some students clearly flunk it: "Wait, there wasn't a textbook on *me* in the bookstore, so how am I supposed to study? Oh, wait . . . I got it . . . campus resources . . ."

No matter how much wisdom we may chuck your way, and no matter how much of it you actually swallow, some days in college are just bad days. It's pouring rain, you have no umbrella, you miss the bus or your car breaks down, you lose an assignment on your computer, you run out of money and can't buy lunch, and the girl said no. The key is to remain calm. DON'T FREAK OUT. Tomorrow will get better—and if it doesn't, deep breathing is underrated as a cure-all, so you may want to give that a go. Just because you hit a rough patch of a few hours, days, or even a few weeks doesn't mean it will continue for the rest of your (what seems to be miserable) existence. For whatever reason, college can intensify the good as well as the bad. Since your dad isn't here to say it, let us be the ones to hand you a mug of steaming sunshine and remind you to take one day at a time.

CHAPTER 9

So What Do You Want to Be When You Grow Up?

Choosing Your Major vs. Your Career

There is a great misconception among students (and especially their parents) that a student's major determines her career. Rarely is this true.

What determines your career—and what employers look to see in college graduates—are the qualities that a college education hones: the capacity to think critically, the ability and desire to problem solve by learning new things, excellent communications skills (both oral and written), and a commitment to success. Did you see economics major listed anywhere in there?

Of course, there are some jobs where a specific major is all but required: it is hard to be a civil engineer if you didn't major in civil engineering. But increasingly in the information age, the line from major to career is a dotted one, with lots of curves thrown in for good measure. Even graduate schools will accept promising students from outside the "traditional field." So, the title of this chapter may be catchy (it caught your attention, right?) but it is deliberately misleading. Repeat this mantra: a major rarely makes a career.

In selecting a major, the best approach is for a student to pursue her passion and then to perform passionately well, thus demonstrating her desire and ability to succeed. If that is clear enough for you, skip to the next chapter. Chances are, however, you might still have a question or two—we are certain your parents will—so keep reading.

Why Do They Call It a BS?

How a Liberal Arts Degree Prepares You for the Work World

The theory behind a liberal arts education is that exposing a young-adult mind to a variety of fields and asking it to synthesize and analyze that information helps develop the character and intellect of that person. If a liberal education were about getting a degree that would immediately, directly, and narrowly translate into a career, you'd be attending a vocational college. There's nothing wrong with vocational schools; in fact, the modern world depends on them. But their goal is different from a more traditional university, and it's critical you recognize that going in.

The rapid pace of change in the information age puts a premium on learning, relearning, and retooling. Think of how many variations of computers or cell phones you have used in the last decade, and how they continue to get smaller, thinner, lighter, and more complex. You had to learn anew each time you upgraded. Properly done, a college degree is supposed to certify that you know how to "learn anew." The certification of survival skills for the twenty-first century has an exotic name: Bachelor of Science or Bachelor of Arts. You may think the premise is nutty, but it has helped make U.S. higher education the envy of the world.

You will need these skills because you are very likely to engage in multiple (maybe more than a dozen) career shifts in a lifetime. You would either need more than a dozen separate qualifying degrees, or you need one (with maybe a graduate degree thrown on top) that demonstrates you can learn, relearn, and retool.

If you are still skeptical, don't take our word for it. If you have a particular career path in mind, it's wise to do some research and see if it requires any specific undergraduate major. The betting money—and given tuition rates, you are betting a lot of money—says there are many majors that might end up on that same career path.

Hopefully this will come as a breath of fresh, minty-clean air. Bluntly, what we are saying is that students are freer to pursue fields of interest than they (and their parents) may have realized. True, it may require a bit more from the art major than the econ major to get an interview at the bank. However, once he has that degree and if that art major has a stellar narrative (that is, a transcript of well-chosen courses plus complementary extracurricular activities), his profile will stand out in a uniquely positive way. It might even garner more attractive job offers than a more pedestrian profile would.

A student should major in a topic that excites him rather than the topic that looks like it might lead to the highest starting salary. A student who picks a major merely because it implies a job will be less motivated and may end up doing poorly—ironically, making himself less employable than if he had picked a different major in which he would have excelled.

> A student should major in a topic that excites him rather than the topic that looks like it might lead to the highest starting salary. A student who picks a major merely because it implies a job will be less motivated and may end up doing poorly.

"I've Always Wanted to Be a . . . So I Shouldn't Major in . . ."

Most of the advice in this book is premised on the idea that students are by nature inclined to be too casual about their college experience. This chapter assumes the opposite. For some reason, choosing a major is the one activity that arouses all sorts of extra and undue anxiety—even for slackers.

One meta-theme of this book is that students should spend less time worrying about what college they get into and more time working to get the best out of the college they have picked. By now, we're hoping you have caught that. It also applies to majors: spend less time worrying about the job at the end of your major or the major you need to get that job, and more time enjoying and developing the major you have picked.

The bottom line is to pursue your passion studiously even if it cuts against the well-trod career path. We tend to be most successful in areas that intrigue or fascinate us. If the activities are not fascinating, human beings reduce to human "doings." So as you choose a major, choose something that makes you look forward—for at least three years—to going to class, reading your texts, and, dare we suggest, even writing your papers. You want to want to write your papers, hang out with profs, join discussion groups, and do your work. Sure, some days it will be plain old work, but we hope—and we're sure you do too—that those days will be the exception and the thrill of learning will be the rule.

Let's get practical. If Kelly is interested in a career in international economics but prefers to major in psychology because it fascinates her, then she should choose the psychology major. However, being a psych major doesn't prevent Kelly from taking classes in other fields. The wise student who is willing to take a risk in her major for the sake of pursing a passion will hedge her bets with a well-chosen minor or a well-crafted set of auxiliary courses that weave a narrative of breadth and potential. In Kelly's case, a few courses in economics and international affairs are a prudent complement to her psych major.

As long as you excel in whatever major you pursue, and as long as the major is respected as one in which you truly worked for your grades as opposed to merely warming a seat each week, you should be in good shape. In fact, it's almost better to stand out with the odd major as long as when you stand out, your academic record truly shines. We know of an internist who was accepted to medical school having majored in home economics. He loved the field (yes, it was a he, we aren't making that up; no, we don't know if he makes a mean chocolate-chip cookie), and he fulfilled his other medical school requirements well enough to be accepted to the University of Illinois Medical School. Not bad.

> If you *haven't* done well in the major, and by lacking excellence your major is merely odd, that could significantly slow or deter your progress on winning the career of your dreams. We won't lie to you: a so-so economics major has more options than a so-so art history major.

Of course, if you *haven't* done well in the major, and by lacking excellence your major is merely odd, that could significantly slow or deter your progress on winning the career of your dreams. We won't lie to you: a so-so economics major has more options than a so-so art history major. Whether or not that is as it should be, it is what it is. However, a stellar art history major probably has at least as many options as a so-so economics major. Okay, we admit it. The stellar economics major may have even a few more options. But how many people do you know who can actually stay awake through four years of economics courses well enough to succeed in them if their principal motivation is simply to get a better job? Plus, whom would you rather take to Italy?

If you have always wanted to be a poet or a pastor or a politician, how do you know which major is "the one"? Here are a few questions to help guide your thinking:

- What section do you turn to first in the newspaper? (Okay, *after* the sports section, what section? If it is sports and more sports, there are even good careers in that: sportswriting is a noble profession, not to mention sports medicine, coaching, teaching adaptive physical education, or—well, you get the idea.)

- Where do you go first when you have twenty minutes to kill in a bookstore? (If you spend the whole twenty minutes deciding which scone to buy, you've got more important worries than your major and we probably can't help you.)

- What subjects excite you most frequently into discussion or even debate?

- Other than fantasy football, what gets you reading articles online or talking around midnight pizza in your dorm?

- What makes you eager and willing to attend class multiple times a week for multiple weeks a year for multiple years, and where you walk away from class actually feeling like you got something out of it?

If you get stuck on your own, don't hesitate to get professional help. Most colleges offer two resources to help you find a major. The first is the formal premajor advisory system. It is called by many different names, but it functions basically the same: it assigns students to an advisor who—in theory—is knowledgeable about the array of majors and so can help students plot their way. (Once students pick a major, they get another advisor who—in theory—is knowledgeable about the array of opportunities *within* that major and can advise accordingly). In practice, it is a mixed bag. No one can truly understand all a modern college curriculum has to offer, and so advisors tend to specialize. If you know the area in which you are interested, you can get an advisor who knows that area and how the system works. If not, it is hit-or-miss.

Which brings us to the second resource (da-da-da-dum!)—the career center. Appearing this evening in resplendent sequined bulletin boards, the career center offers testing to help students narrow down skill sets and fields of interest; with abundant staff who are eager to help and sure to impress your next dinner party, this picture says, "I can do it" (if only selecting a major was as glamorous as *The Price Is Right*). At the very least, the career center might help you knock a few options off the list based on your personality type and whether or not you see yourself plugging away in the dungeons of the library for the next eight years (which is what some majors require if you intend to pursue the degree to its intended end in a PhD). So you might consider starting your journey there.

Please don't misunderstand. We are not suggesting you major in scuba art just because you know you can get an easy A. There are some fields that are more respected than others—and we'd be flogged if we listed them here, so do your own research. Don't be fooled—grad schools and employers *do* consider GPA, but they couple it with the rigor of the major in sifting through applications. While we wouldn't dare hint that you should choose a major just to build your resume, you don't want to be naïve to the fact that there are a few majors out there that have not yet garnered the respect of the professional world. If you really must take classes in scuba art and your life will forever be marred by regret if you don't, then consider it as a minor (at most) or immerse yourself in as many supplemental courses as your schedule will allow.

Once you've narrowed down a couple options as a starting point, research carefully to take the "best" course each major has to offer.

(And, now that you've read chapter 3, you know how to do that.) If you like it, take a second course with a *different* prof the following term to test your interest as the subject expands. Don't dismiss the course as not being "real learning" just because it comes to you easily.

In fact, Sydney did just that. She thought she was a psych major who was taking some English classes for fun. Each semester she found herself battling it out barely making Bs and Cs in her psych courses all while the English As and Bs came easily. Why did it take her until her junior year to realize that she should be majoring in English instead of psychology? She admits that she doesn't have a good answer. She just thought that because English came easy, it must not be valuable; she didn't realize it was easy because she was naturally talented in that field.

Oh So Many Majors
Factors to Consider in Narrowing Down Your Options

In our experience, most students do not know from birth what is the "right" major for them. In fact, for most there may not be a single right answer. As you narrow your search, here are a few questions to consider.

WHAT IS THE STRENGTH OF THE DEPARTMENT?

You could be one of the lucky few who has already narrowed your major options to two or three possibilities. If that is the case, and one department is stronger than the rest, go with the stronger one. You'll get a better education. After all, that is what you're paying for. The best professors can make a field come alive, even if the subject didn't get a second glance from you in high school. College is about expanding horizons. And, should you have time in your academic schedule, you can continue to take classes in the other major for the sake of personal interest. (As a general rule, we would shy away from majoring in both, as attractive as that may seem. We'll explain why toward the end of this chapter.)

Departmental strengths (and thus the desirability of certain majors) differ from school to school. Find out the best departments at your school and consider majoring in them. Sample at least a course or two before you commit to a specific major, because even within departments the quality of the experience can vary widely with the courses or professors you take.

DO YOU NEED TO GO TO GRAD SCHOOL?

Are you looking to take your major further, or are you content to get your undergraduate degree and call it quits? If you want to go further, there are two tracks of grad programs: professional and academic. Professional graduate programs (such as law, medicine, and business) rarely require an exact major for entry. A lot of great majors provide an entry into law school (especially if you perform well on the LSAT), and virtually any major can work in applying to business school if a student can prove some knowledge of economics. Most business schools, in fact, care more about your work experience than your major. Medicine is fairly flexible as well, though there are many more course requirements in math, biology, chemistry, and physics. Medical schools love students who have majored in nonscience areas (like our home ec friend). A career counselor or perhaps even your academic advisor can advise you more specifically.

The academic grad schools, on the other hand, are a bit more demanding in that they expect students to have a strong background in the field (or a close cognate of that field) as their major. While it isn't entirely unheard of to see students jump majors into grad school (such as having a BA in history and applying to a graduate sociology program), they would need a compelling narrative—such as having taken courses in that area beyond their major track, having worked closely with a professor in research, or having participated in multiple internships—to explain why they are still a good match for this particular program given their major. It can be a bit difficult to choose a grad program before even having declared a major, but if you find your interest piqued by architecture and are curious what a grad program would look like, go online and take a look at the requirements out of curiosity. There is really a lot more flexibility in transitioning to grad programs than most students realize. While this is a caveat that should be saved for another book, we can't help but mention it here to complete the thought: don't attend grad school in a subject you know doesn't interest you just because you would like to pursue a career in that field later. Grad courses are difficult enough, and having a lagging interest in the field will only make the work distasteful. As we pointed out at the beginning, most careers aren't picky about your major. If they are (and if it's a field of study you know is not your best), you might strongly consider altering your plan.

HAVE YOU SAMPLED A DIVERSE SET OF CLASSES WITHIN THE DEPARTMENT?

You never know what classes you'll find absolutely wonderful until you try them out. And two classes in the same department might look similar but turn out to be vastly different. Much of your experience in a class will be determined by the professor. However, in testing out a department, try to hold off on declaring your major until you've taken courses from at least two or maybe even three different professors within that department. One professor is not always a good representation of what to expect. You may have accidentally discovered the most fascinating professor and topic in the entire department. Or the opposite may be true. You could have had a devastating experience in a subject you thought you would love. Do a reality check and sample a different prof next semester. Not only will this give you a good idea of the strength of the faculty, it will also give you a flavor of the work required and types of classes available in that major before you declare.

It may not be realistic to take multiple courses yourself, so at a minimum take them "virtually." Talk with upperclassmen who have had the professors you have had and who have had others in the department, and ask them to compare. But ask several and, if possible, ask a diverse range of students, since individual opinions will vary widely.

Don't dismay if you take some courses you dislike. Part of the selection process is weeding things out, and it may be that by taking a course that combines statistics, engineering, and science you realize that all three stop your brain waves cold. Consider it a valuable part of the narrowing process, not a mistake. It fits well into your narrative too in showing not only your willingness to embark upon new fields but also showing the weight of your certainty once you discover your true passion for learning.

DOES YOUR PERFECT MAJOR EVEN EXIST?

If not, then designing your own major is another option to consider. However, it is not done frequently, and for good reason. Designing a major (and all of the courses it will entail) is not as easy as it may sound. Not only does it require heightened scrutiny by the faculty (because there is the assumption that students designing their own majors are trying to avoid something already being offered that they very well might need), it requires an unusual degree of clarity from the student in purpose, imagination, and explanation of how courses might fit together. Coupled with this is the significant time investment needed to plot a course and alter it (with permission from the board) as professors or classes come and go. Tack onto those reasons the possibility that you'll spend the rest of your employment interviews explaining exactly what majoring in "symbolic structures" (or whatever you decide to name your course of study) means and you'll see why few students choose to go this route. Still, for some it is the right way to go.

A thumbnail sketch of the process begins with a student who proposes a major as well as its specific course work. A faculty committee reviews that proposal and provides feedback and suggestions or criticism. The student then makes adjustments to the proposal and resubmits it. Some schools may limit the number of times a proposal can be reviewed, but even if not, such reviews can still take weeks or months, and most students are restricted by the college's deadline to declare. What students often find is that, by the end of the process, the major has morphed into an unattractive structure because it no longer reflects their original intent. Don't be discouraged. You have an entire lifetime to study random topics of interest to you; you don't need to be registered in a college to visit your local library or purchase copies of lectures online.

Of course, there are students who have designed their own majors and gone on to be incredibly successful in them. We know of one student named Dean who was bored by the usual premed major of biochemistry. He designed a special major in medical ethics and health policy that blended political science, philosophy, and public policy, as well as the more traditional science courses. He went on to do postgraduate study at Oxford and then entered medical school. Designing your course work can be a way to turbocharge your college career (it was for Dean), but it's tough to pull off and, except in rare circumstances, probably not worth the effort. A similar effort invested instead into a more traditional major tends to yield a higher dividend.

"Just Because They Used to Change My Diapers..."
Your Parents' Role in Choosing Your Major

In *most* cases, any parental pressure you may receive in declaring your major is well intended. We are fairly confident in saying your parents do love you and have probably sacrificed greatly just to get you to this point. Money gets to talk too.

However, just because your parents think you should major in what they want doesn't mean you should. After all, you are the one who will be studying and writing papers on the topic for the next four years. Their suggestions aren't mandates; and if they are, perhaps you should have a conversation about how to have a mature relationship with a certain young adult (you) before you tackle the majors question.

We aren't suggesting you ignore their advice entirely. After all, they probably know you better than many others you will consult. But we suggest treating their insight as counsel, not gospel. This is an issue on which there are ample opportunities to compromise by altering how you design a schedule with extra courses, include a supplemental minor, or even register for well-chosen summer activities or internships.

The conversation could look something like this: "No, Dad, I'm not going to be an econ major, but I *am* going to be an officeholder in the young businessman's club on campus as well as doing an internship this summer at a corporation so I can give the field a fair try; I still think I really want to be a philosophy major." Of course, be prepared for your dad's counterproposal: "Why don't you be an officeholder in the philosopher's club and major in economics?" Look for creative compromises before the battles ensue. Your folks probably have enough gray hair already.

Arguably, the top two majors that give parents cause for concern are music and art history. Parents who hear the dreaded news that their son wants to be a music major (why did they spend all that money sending him to math camps every year?) picture their little drummer boy being forever consigned to a garage band—and worse, it might be *their* garage. It's not that their concerns are irrational. As we mentioned earlier, the more exotic the major, the more will be required of you to make it work in the professional arena once you graduate.

In holding up your end of the conversation, be sure to communicate to your folks that a major that enables you to thrive while challenged (even if it *is* religious studies) will serve you better in the long run than scraping by on a major traditionally thought of as sound (which really means "diploma comes with a high-paying job"). You may also want to add that college offers you a fleeting opportunity to study a subject you most likely won't have the opportunity to revisit so intensely at any other point in your life—and you may even be learning from some of the leading minds in the field.

We recognize that the following tip may only work at small colleges, but it's worth a try: encourage your folks to speak with a professor in your proposed department. Regardless of school size, your parents can probably connect with a few alums who chose a risky major and then succeeded professionally years later. If you can't connect in person, you can connect virtually; invite your parents to access the career center websites of some of their favorite colleges and universities.

In all of this back-and-forth on who is right about your future, do talk with a few other adults from your parents' generation about what they majored in and how it mattered to their careers. We're guessing you'll be a little surprised to see how loose the connection is. But even if you see an airtight connection, be sure to interview people between your parents' generation and your own— people who have entered the marketplace in the last fifteen years. The economy is changing its opinion of what criteria are used to hire and fire, so for the immediate future, the major might actually matter. What you'll most likely find is that the longer folks have been out of school, the less significant their major will have been to their career.

It's rare, but not unheard of, for parents to insist on a particular major. If you *do* find yourself in that unfortunate position, it is time for a gut check: how badly do you want to major in art history versus fulfilling your parents' hope for biology? Enough to foot the bill? Should your parents prove to be more unmovable than Rushmore on the topic (even after you have had the reasonable conversations prescribed above), our inclination is to give in to their demands. If you are strategic in how you organize your schedule and major requirements, you may be able to satisfy your art itch by taking as many courses outside the premed track that you can. Then, once you've graduated and are footing the bills, apply to the best art history grad programs you can find. It's not exactly having your cake and eating it too, but at least you won't go hungry.

The End Is Coming
Common Worries Before Choosing a Major

What will I do when I leave college with this major? Because we don't want to overwork this topic, we'll leave it at this: we have known philosophy majors who have gone on to be investment bankers on Wall Street, and deans of big-name universities who majored in math. It matters very little what department you choose as long as you do well.

What painful course requirements must I endure to complete this major? In the event we have misled you in our talk of pursuing passions, allow us to make an important clarification. It is worth both doing well in your passion and pursing a passion where you *will* do well. Please note, however, that it is also worth being stretched by ideas that you might not find easy to master. Fulfilling your passion doesn't mean simply taking courses you find simple. That your major takes you beyond your comfort zone is a good thing, and it's especially valuable when it comes time to explain your narrative in a job search. Employers want to see you perform well, but they also want to see how you've succeeded in the face of obstacles and opposition. Taking theoretical physics might make you uncomfortable all semester, but your diligence could prove to be a valuable experience—and hopefully one you can brag about.

I'm halfway through my freshman year and don't know what I'm doing with the rest of my life! Relax. Most adults are halfway through their *lives* and say the same thing. One big mistake college undergrads repeat is getting paralyzed by fear when they can't answer the third question in that annoying scholastic trio: "What's your name, where are you from, and what's your major?" If you still know the answer to the first two questions by the end of your first week at college, you're doing fine. Not knowing your major even after the first year is okay, provided you have been strategically choosing courses and getting exposure to a range of possible majors in a reasonable fashion. Students who are not at this point by the end of their second year *are* in trouble, and at most colleges they won't be surprised to hear this since they will have been getting pressure from administrative watchdogs.

I aced biology in high school and loved it, but it seems so different in college and I'm not sure why it's not coming as naturally. I thought I'd be a bio major, but now I'm having second thoughts! Virtually every subject on the college campus is approached differently from the way it was handled in high school. There are lots of students who like high school [fill in the blank] but not college [fill in the blank]. Rather than memorizing equations or anatomical structures or historical dates, you will be asked to analyze them and produce new ideas or conclusions based on your analysis. It requires a new level of confidence and passion for the material that goes beyond the superficial introduction you may have experienced in high school. Obviously, subjects that you excelled in or enjoyed during high school are a good place to begin the quest for a major, but don't despair if you find that the college version is not for you. One of the best things about college is that there are many more fascinating pockets of knowledge to explore than you ever dreamed of as you filled out your application. So why not give, say, anthropology a try?

To Those Who Know Exactly What They Want to Major In, and Have Known It since They Were Five . . .

Lucky you. While a rare breed, this will be the case for some. Political science may have fascinated you since your prepubescent years. The fact that a prof in this field may have been a close friend of the family didn't hurt matters much either, and you can't imagine doing anything else. Great! You've found your major. But don't stop there. While starting your major early opens the possibility for you to delve deep into this field (and we encourage you to take a few grad courses by the end of your undergraduate term), take as broad a range of courses *outside* your major as you can. Don't be ashamed if poli sci is your dream world, but test it regularly with a broad range of other courses that will make you appear less narrow than if you are only versed in one subject.

Be careful of being overconfident that your major is encoded in your DNA. We know of one successful professional who thought she was meant to be a doctor. Frances did well in all her classes and fulfilled her requirements for premed in record time. What she couldn't figure out was why so many medical schools kept rejecting her applications. Then she spent some time interning in a hospital. It quickly became clear that she had no idea what the profession of a doctor was like, and she was both ill prepared and ill suited. Somehow the med schools had seen through her interests better than she did, and nowadays she can look back and admit she is grateful she got turned down cold. It's good to have an interest in a field, but be looking for yellow flags that say perhaps this is more an avocation than a vocation. Oh, and Frances is now running a college campus somewhere and doing marvelously, so don't feel too bad for her.

For Those Who Have No Idea What to Major In . . .

If you feel clueless about what to major in, join the club (with a membership of thousands)—and consider attending a majors fair. These fairs are offered at most universities. One student we know chose her major based on her interactions with the faculty at her university's fair. Sure, Susie had an idea of five or six subject areas she was considering going into the fair, but it left the possibilities wide open. She moved from booth to booth and had a series of questions she wanted to ask the faculty in each academic discipline as a way of getting to know them. She tried to pick an area where she felt the faculty had the greatest amount of enthusiasm or energy around their subject, and she was looking for people who inspired her and who cared about her as an individual. In the end, she found herself avoiding large departments where she would be another faceless student ID number, except when she felt there was a particular faculty member she could use as an advisor.

After perusing the fair, she talked with students who had majored in her top three potential departments to test the accuracy of what she was deducing about faculty. Were their professors helpful, available, interesting? Susie has since graduated and highly recommends this as a means of adding clarity to the majors search, saying she considered it a remarkable experience just to spend an hour getting to know the caliber of faculty at her institution.

While potentially helpful, we recommend weighting the major fair less than other sources of information about the quality and accessibility of the faculty. There is bound to be a large margin of error in your experience at a fair like this. Perhaps a great department is staffed by a bum professor who got stuck manning the booth because he missed the wrong faculty meeting, or perhaps a cagey department sends its sole "normal" representative in a desperate attempt to lure unsuspecting buyers. Some research beyond first impressions will go a long way.

Before You Sign on the Dotted Line
Knowing Your Major's Requirements

One mistake we see too often is students who've taken a course from a single fabulous professor in a department and, because of his class, decide to major in that field without researching what else is involved. A year into her major, one student discovered that she had to take advanced Arabic in order to complete her degree, which she wasn't willing to do. Due diligence is critical.

Entire departments thrive on students who arrive premed and then meet (and fail) organic chemistry. They also attract students who remain too long in a major they chose in error, either because the end-result career looked sexy on TV or because it's what their parents wanted them to choose. After a rickety semester, they disregard the signs (that is, failing grades, panic attacks, dread of attending class, unalterable confusion) and pursue the major for two or even three more semesters and then find themselves with a transcript full of classes they wish they could hide. They may try to apply it to a major that is a distant cousin just to graduate on time, or they may have to extend their stay at the university another year to earn a degree in a major they truly love. To the tune of thousands of dollars, those are some expensive little yellow flags to ignore. The bottom line is pay attention to any and all flag waving

> There is an overwhelming notion in the student body that two majors are better than one. Sometimes yes, but often no. The time required to fulfill both majors will cost depth and potentially unique study opportunities.

that signals this may not be the right major for you. While you shouldn't jump ship at the first sign of a bad grade, continued poor performance deserves at least some reevaluation.

Finally, we land upon this oh-so-worthy point. There is an overwhelming notion in the student body that two majors are better than one. Sometimes yes, but often no. The primary reason we resist so strenuously the suggestion to double major is that the time required to fulfill both majors will cost both depth and potentially unique study opportunities—there are only so many hours in the semester. It sounds impressive to brag about holding your own in two majors to your peers, but unless it is something you absolutely must do for your career path (like economics and Russian so you can work overseas as an economic advisor neck deep in snow) or because you are trying to indulge an exotic passion (since your parents insist that you graduate with a sociology degree but you really want to major in engineering), you may find it just as rewarding to focus on developing one major with a host of skill sets and unique course work surrounding it. Plus, a year or two after you graduate no one but your interviewer will ask what you majored in, and should you try to insert said boast into cocktail conversations, be prepared to be verbally backstabbed after the party.

Two majors are not always better than one. You want your transcript to show depth in at least one topic (meaning you have gone well beyond the introductory level and are engaging the material at a sophisticated level) and breadth beyond that topic (meaning you are not limited to baby-step intellectual excursions out of your comfort zone). And, sure, sometimes a double major will do just that. But what is more likely is that the double major will force your schedule into little more than checking off requirements instead of choosing courses.

At the End of the Day

Just as it matters less what college you attended when compared to how you performed in college, it matters less what major you chose when contrasted with how you conducted yourself within that major. If financial considerations have forced you into a college that isn't your first pick, you can still excel. And if a parent ultimatum has forced you into a major that you wouldn't have chosen for yourself, you can still build a narrative in your transcript that will enable you to be successful in your chosen career later on. Take heart. College will be over someday soon and no one but the freshman from the alumni office hitting you up for donations will ever ask about it.

Be prepared to answer the question "Was it worth getting your degree?" should you pursue a career that doesn't show a direct correlation. Your diploma is more than a plaque on your wall that collects dust. Your diploma is knowledge. It's confidence. It's a new perspective on the world that influences how you think and analyze. Whether or not what you study connects directly to your future career is not important, because in the long run, the skill sets you learned while maximizing your college experience will challenge and augment your performance in your career.

CHAPTER 10

It'll Be Over Before You Know It

Preparing for Life after College

Alas, even something as wonderful as college cannot last forever. Before you know it, you will join the ranks of alumni dodging solicitations from your alma mater. It is a mistake to be so completely preoccupied with life after college that you miss opportunities you'll only have as a student. But it is also a mistake to ignore planning for the future (or to put it off until after spring break of your senior year).

Students determined to get the best out of college can take steps even as early as their freshman year to position themselves for maximum success as college graduates. The key is to develop a plan that not only flexes with natural growth but has planted enough beacons along the way to form a discernible path.

It's the Journey, Not the Destination— and Other Fuzzy Clichés

Planning your life after college while you are still in college is relatively easy since it's all about theory. Theoretically you are willing to live on less than your colleagues to teach in the inner city because it's something you're passionate about. Theoretically, you don't mind postponing marriage and kids until you're done with grad school.

These choices work in theory, but not always in practice. We have seen people show uncanny foresight and map out a plan they actually follow. We have seen others get ambushed by surprises—some happy, some not so.

The wise student will find a way to strike a balance between preparing for potential careers early on and recognizing that those careers are not the irrevocable fate of a Greek tragedy. You are not doomed to one and only one future. Our priorities change as we age, and for most there are many job changes and interludes between "passing go" and "game over."

It's the old cliché from the strategic planning business: it is not the plan, it is the planning. The real value in thinking ahead is not in developing some detailed and rigid blueprint that actually charts your course. Rather it is that in developing that plan (or plans!) you go through a series of steps—self-inventory, self-discovery, exploration—that stand you in good stead whatever happens.

This sort of planning is a classic case of "do unto it before it is done unto you." For better or worse, college will end someday, and when it does you will be free-floating in possibilities. Procrastinators will hear in those words an excuse for waiting until then. Students who get the best out of college will hear a reason for letting the future cast a wee shadow over the present so they can start building momentum now.

Check Your Reality for Defects
A Second Look at Past Choices
Now That Your Future Is in Sight

College offers a brief season to test out new ideas and adventures. It's not that college is four years of risk-free anonymity where consequences are minimal, but four years of intense focus on building your future.

In this season of exploration and risk, we encourage you to weigh some reasonable life choices, and once you have landed on a couple, test and countertest them. Are you interested in becoming a lawyer? Sign on to be a paralegal for the summer. Spend the following summer as a construction worker to see if you prefer working outdoors. Over time, the back-and-forth between possibilities should help you file down your choices.

> College offers a brief season to test out new ideas and adventures. It's not that college is four years of risk-free anonymity where consequences are minimal, but four years of intense focus on building your future.

In terms of social choices, be wary of taking on too many risks since they will influence the rest of your diligent plan. Once the consequences start rolling in, some students find that they have experimented too vigorously in sex, drugs, or alcohol, which constrains their options postcollege. This four-year interlude doesn't suspend the law of reaping and sowing. Even activities that are totally innocuous in one setting could be problematic for some jobs. For instance, some positions in the intelligence community are supposed to be so apolitical that membership in any politically oriented clubs as an undergrad will raise yellow flags on your application. And yes, joining the Make Weed Legal Club is going to make for a rough interview should you apply to the FBI.

One alum named Brad recently told us about how he had never completely bought into the precept of "your past will find you" until the day he went before a judge to be admitted to the bar in New York. As Brad's name was called, the judge listed off many of his inane escapades during college that had resulted in fairly minor disciplinary action. Brad was at first stunned by the retelling of his glory days, which then turned into horror when the judge asked him to wait outside the courtroom until the other candidates for the bar had been considered. At the end of the review, he was called back into the courtroom, where the judge said, "Don't worry, you passed—I just wanted to scare you a little bit." It worked. Brad told us he reeled with panic while he waited in the foyer, wondering if all his hopes for his career and future would be terminated. He realized then just how stupid his entertainment choices in college had been.

If you have erred by experimenting where you should not have, the game isn't over. All hope is not lost. While you won't be able to shrug off the outcome entirely, now's the time to begin to write the next chapter of the story that shows *a strong response* to those mistakes in your narrative. You are not rewriting the past; you are writing an alternative future, one that puts the past in a more favorable light. How has your character improved as a result, and what measures have you taken to ensure you don't repeat those errors?

Making mistakes during your freshman year (which is largely preventable, especially if you've read this book) is more "acceptable" than making those same mistakes as an upperclassman. Should you find you have an evil to explain away, your story will hopefully be "I goofed around the first semester of my freshman year and then realized I was ruining my college career so I reformed. During my junior year, I got interested in working for the CIA and that summer interned for a think tank in DC." It's not that you should give yourself carte blanche as an underclassman to do what you will in the hopes you can apologize and reform later. Success may not feel in the mood to be merciful when she calls your number. But everyone makes mistakes, and the mark of those who succeed is that they have learned from their mistakes.

Even harder than being saved from the first scenario is being saved from one like this: "After I studied with Professor So-and-So my freshman year, I was convinced that I wanted to work for the CIA. That professor then helped me get an internship on Capitol Hill the summer after my sophomore year. The summer of my junior year I worked as a beach lifeguard and that is when I got into drugs pretty heavily."

Where students find poor choices especially hard to disown is when episodes occur during spring break of their senior year. All that proves to the big world outside is that in four years they haven't grown up at all.

How rigid will your future career be in its demands? That's hard to say, especially if you haven't drawn some boundaries and narrowed down your choices. Far better to be narrowing your choices for yourself than to have them narrowed for you *because of* your choices.

"Yoda, You Need"
The Value of a Mentor

On a personal note, Dean Sue admits that her expectations would have been different had she done this sort of introspective planning as an undergraduate. Would college-Sue have been able to

Know Thyself—Or at Least Make a Formal Introduction
Looking Ahead to Potential Careers

When it comes time to consider a career, oddly enough, the career center can be a helpful resource. Here are some questions that counselors generally ask, which you can consider even now:

- Do you expect to make a lot of money?
- How important is your standard of living, and what would that look like?
- Where do you expect to live—a large city, on the East or West coast, another country?
- What level of commitment do you plan to make in terms of having a family?
- What kind of work schedule do you prefer—one with flexibility or dependability?
- Have you thought about working various shifts, and could you be nocturnal if your job required it?
- In what sort of schooling are you willing to invest?
- What does it mean to you to sacrifice one of these priorities for another?

The value of the various tests at the career center is not necessarily in what the computer spits out as the single "correct" answer for your future. (One of us actually took a test that recommended becoming an assembly-line worker. After deleting and inserting commas on a couple hundred pages during the last round of edits of this book, maybe that test actually detected a skill she didn't know she had.) The value of career-center testing lies in what the results teach you about yourself and what they make you consider as you go through the process.

fully understand the costs of her career path, financially and especially personally? Hard to say. Going through the exercise of imagining and planning out various hypothetical scenarios certainly couldn't have hurt.

In Sue's case, a mentor played a key role in helping her sort through many of the initial demands and opportunities of her career. To this day, how she prioritizes work or responds to professional relationships has been profoundly influenced by that former mentor, both for good and bad. She credits a lot of her great work tactics (such as time management and organization) to him as well as some of her misconceptions about the balance between professional and personal life. Because her mentor seemed to be at work all the time, Sue thought she needed to do the same thing to be successful. In spite of the fact that Sue loved her work (and still does), it was not healthy to spend as much time at work as she did. She reached a point where she was not able to distinguish between work and play since everything in her life seemed to be related to her work. And, although being passionate about one's work is a good thing, there needs to be some balance. Unfortunately, this sense of balance was not something that Sue's mentor was able to model for her (and even today, Sue warns her younger colleagues NOT to look to her as a role model for establishing balance between work and play). In that respect, Sue (with seconds from coauthors Peter and Anne) encourages you to choose your mentors carefully. While mentors may not mentor you in your personal life, still note how their career has influenced their home life and weigh their words on that topic carefully.

Counselors and mentors aren't your only resources. The library has shelves of wisdom in the form of biographies, memoirs, and even self-help guides on how folks have balanced the art of survival, leisure, and home. And while most professors or administrators won't come out and offer to trade ideas over lunch, it wouldn't hurt to ask them some advice in your brief interactions. Most successful adults have more advice to give than they have time to give it—but they also have more advice to give than they have people asking for it. Should you find yourself in a conversation with them—and you should, if you have been following the advice in this book—and if your listener seems amiable to it, work your way up from a discussion of the weather to questions like "What personal sacrifices are required of a woman who wants to be a professional?" or "How is it possible to be an international leader and yet raise a family?" or "How does one go about rebuilding a department and yet not be engulfed by its demands?" Most people enjoy telling their stories or giving advice, as long as the questions aren't too intimate.

This can be valuable on a number of fronts. First, it makes you an interesting conversationalist—most people like to talk about themselves and may consider you witty just for prompting such soliloquies. Second, the more you engage them in meaningful conversation, the more you will see the wisdom of the "many roads up the mountain" aphorism—that is, that there are many different ways to reach your goal. Regardless of the career, there is rarely just one way to pursue it. Third, so many of life's lessons are age-and-stage-related, so talking with people at different ages and stages will give you insights that your peers simply don't yet have. It doesn't matter how smart your roommate is, chances are she does not have deep personal insight into the "biological clock versus promotion clock" problem.

On another personal note, Peter remembers how one of the most perceptive and piercing things anyone has ever said to him came from a retired Cabinet secretary who talked to him for less than five minutes at a cocktail party. In that brief time, the gentleman sized him up and pointed out some weaknesses that Peter admits he has guarded against ever since. People who are deeply wise may be able to say deeply wise things, even in a brief encounter.

So talk to lots of people, and then winnow down their ideas. It's probably better not to start the conversation with "Will you be my mentor and teach me how to find success?" Jumping in too quickly can be a little embarrassing—for both of you. Simply enjoy the good conversation and you never know—a mentor might emerge or, if not, perhaps at least an invaluable insight about yourself.

Racing the Clock
Deciding on Life's Trade-Offs Before
They're Decided for You

College-age folks tend to have trouble correctly anticipating the challenge of balancing work and family, and for good reason. It's not the sort of conundrum those in the midst of it can figure out easily, let alone someone on the periphery. Shelves of books have been written on the topic of home life versus advancing career, and it is a matter of an ongoing, painful debate.

No gender has it easy, but the ever-ticking clock seems to hit female graduates the hardest. Many women want to establish themselves in a career before starting a family, and so they postpone having children until their mid- to late thirties, when they will have more time. (Or when they think they'll have more time. Is there really such a thing?) However, women who adopt that strategy must confront the reality that the risks of complications or birth defects rise significantly once the mother is in her mid-thirties. In casual conversation, we have overheard doctors admit their surprise at how many highly educated women walk into their clinics expecting some miracle fertility treatment to work. Miracles can happen and certainly have, but there are many sad cases where they haven't. Medicine has yet to outsmart the clock completely.

This dilemma then transfers to the men, who on the whole also expect to marry later, in their thirties, once their career is under way, but somehow also hope to travel and enjoy the "five-year plan" with the new wife before they start a family. Unless the woman is ten years younger, these expectations aren't very realistic. Then once the kiddos *do* arrive, today's dad is expected to do far more hands-on parenting than dads of yore, and when he's nearing fifty and driving a car of kids to soccer practice he wonders if he's too old to have kids this young. There may even be biological risks associated with conceptions from older dads—medical science is discovering more on this front every day.

We aren't trying to scare you. Each of us—Peter, Sue, and Anne—has made our own choices on the matter, and they are different. Plus, it's not like you can schedule meeting your soul mate. The point is to think about and—to what extent you can—prioritize your value of family and career. Consider your options while you are twenty, twenty-one, twenty-two and still able to make decisions that will aim you more accurately in the direction that your self-identified values and priorities ought to take you.

Singles as well as married folks need to measure the trade-offs between personal well-being and work. Decide what in life is most important to you and then cling to those priorities. You may be surprised to find that what was important to your parents is not necessarily what you hold most dear. And, as you experience more of life, you might find that your priorities change (hopefully while you still have the option of making the necessary course corrections).

"What If I'm Not Ready to Go to Grad School?"

Imagine your toughest seminar, then imagine taking only those kinds of seminars for all your courses every semester; think of the smartest peers that left you a bit intimidated in class discussions, then imagine taking a class where most if not all of the students are just like them. Welcome to grad school.

Unless you have a beefy trust fund that can only be spent on schooling, it is probably a mistake to view graduate school as "the thing you do when you don't know what to do after college." Graduate school would be better thought of as a strategic investment. Well chosen and well timed, it has huge payoffs. Poorly chosen or poorly timed, it's a waste of money and, even more precious, time.

Grad school probably warrants a whole other book. Here all we can say is this: imagine your toughest seminar, then imagine taking only those kinds of seminars for all your courses every semester; think of the smartest peers that left you a bit intimidated in class discussions, then imagine taking a class where most if not all of the students are just like them. Welcome to grad school.

Yes, grad school still has the perks of an academic calendar (though summers involve far more work, usually). And yes, grad school does give you access to many of the social amenities of college. But you will have less time—and less willingness to risk time and probably even less money to indulge those risks—in grad school. Another senior year it ain't.

What we are seeing more frequently is that those students who are considering grad school for the right reasons usually plan to do something else before going to grad school. Some students apply in the hopes of deferring enrollment, and in many cases that is permitted. Should you decide to consider this an option, get your test scores in place (while your brain is still toned) and your recommendations written (while your name still summons a face) and then perhaps delay applying as long as your scores will permit.

During that time off you might consider joining Teach for America, teaching English overseas, joining the Peace Corps, or serving in some nonprofit with minimal pay. Outsiders will see this as a valid experience that perhaps has strengthened you because many of these adventures challenge your survival skills in ways college— with its fairly elaborate safety net—does not, or has given you more compassion because of the diverse population you served. You may even walk away with a new foreign language. If nothing else, consider it an opportunity to give to others, hone a new set of skills, and experience life outside your comfort zone. It will give your graduate experience a fresh perspective and make late nights at the library *almost* a welcome retreat.

Those who have come back from such adventures and gone on to grad school have told us they are much better students as a result. It's not so much that they study better or earn better grades, but that they have a deeper appreciation for what they are learning, having had a greater taste of the world.

I Know What You Should Have Done Last Summer

The three summers in between your undergraduate years are some of the richest pockets of time you will have as a college student. Spend that time wisely. Too many students fail at this in one of two ways: either they waste the time by treating it as three solid months of recuperation via TV reruns, or they panic and try to secure an internship at The Company I Will Work at for the Rest of My Life. The former is a clear waste of time, but the error in the second is that by trying to start their professional life too soon, they miss the chance to try something they otherwise would not have had time to explore, such as study abroad, an outdoor job with the forest service, a short-term mission overseas, or an internship that gives back to the community.

For some companies, it's true that a summer internship is an extended interview, particularly in the business sector. You'll find your summer to be a delicate balancing act between using the time to test out a few career options and laying the necessary groundwork for whatever that career will be. It's worth investigating by speaking with the advisor in your major as well as folks in that industry. And the career center may be particularly helpful in connecting you with other alums in that field.

If you can afford to work for free during the summer, you have even more options available to you (and many of them admittedly cooler than the paying jobs—it's a trade-off). A time-honored path for college students is working as interns in DC for any one of countless think tanks. While this sort of job typically isn't paid and may not necessarily lead to a career on the Hill, it adds sparkle to your narrative and creates a small professional network to draw from later.

Should you decide to go a more traditional employment route, summer is not so much a testing ground for a specific company as it is for an industry in general, as well as an opportunity to socialize and meet people in your potential field. It is rare to find a quality internship as a freshman, though it's been known to happen. Don't stress too much about the wow factor of the job you take the summer after your freshman year. If possible, develop a financial plan that will allow for an impressive (aka unpaid) internship the summer before your senior year.

If you can't afford to work for free *ever*, there are still some incredible paying summer jobs out there, but they're few in number so apply NOW. Even if it's a year or two away, you'll rarely apply too early. If you find you've already missed the deadline for applying to work at Disneyland, there is no shame or limitation in taking any job that pays. For example, waiting tables of needy patrons can be a wonderful training ground for learning how to deal with demanding clients.

Clocking in at an average sort of job has its own perks as you develop the reputation of a trustworthy and responsible employee and learn how "the rest of America" works. Sue—yes, the dean who wrote this book—was a waitress for two summers. To this day, she tidies up her own table at restaurants because she knows how hard the job can be. There's a lot to be said for the value of empathy derived from the everyday experience, and it can make for a compelling interview when you recount how you spent your summer.

In fact, sometimes those stories can prove to be just as compelling as a flashy summer job. Josiah spent a summer working at Wal-Mart when he couldn't find another way to cover his tuition bills. What started out as a job stocking shelves resulted in a deep respect for people who keep the world running by working mundane or dirty jobs we'd rather not do ourselves. That lesson had a permanent impact on Josiah. Though he's now an executive in an internationally renowned consulting firm, he still gets to know his building's parking attendants and greets them every day by name. Does it earn him any sticky stars with his firm? No one even knows about it. He does it because he learned early on to have a bigger picture than himself, and it's made his work that much more fulfilling. If you know you're bound for the corporate world, this is a great time to gain credibility with future employees by choosing a "real world" summer job that will give you a better understanding of their position and thus make you a better manager.

Or, as an alternative to employment, study abroad or summer school might be an option. We tend not to recommend the latter unless you're in an academic pinch since you need some time to decompress from campus life (and many of your top professors will be

> Study abroad is a tempting possibility—after all, how often can you earn credit for traveling the world? It's like being paid to eat dessert.

on vacation anyway). Study abroad is a much more tempting possibility—after all, how often can you earn credit for traveling the world? It's like being paid to eat dessert. An entire book of its own could be written on that topic, so we won't attempt to say much here—other than this: make sure before you register for the excursion or send a deposit that your college is prepared to accept all the credits you will earn while you are away.

Developing Your Own Year-by-Year Plan

Okay, so we've sold you on the benefits of planning. How about a list of what to do when? If you're coming into this chapter after your freshman year, it would be worth your time to read through all the headings in case there is something earlier on that you missed. However, if you're reading this as a newly minted freshman, we recommend that you read your section below as well as the other three while you're at it. Then at the end of each school year review the upcoming section once more and revisit during the year as necessary.

FRESHMEN

The biggest advantage freshmen have is more lead time for engaging in academic experiments and for considering a wider range of future careers.

▶ *Develop a working strategy.* Jot the plan down, but don't write it with a permanent marker. A fair amount of maturation occurs in college, and what excites you socially or academically as a freshman may not get your wheels spinning as a senior. Included in this strategy is revisiting the boundaries and goals you established for yourself in chapter 5 (charting an academic sketch of what you'd like to accomplish and identifying people you'd like to know better). Figure out a way that all these goals can flow seamlessly together.

▶ *Explore with some distant goal in mind.* For now, your job is to keep in mind the notion that you will graduate someday soon, and to take steps toward that end without letting it consume you. Take a rich romp through a variety of courses, disciplines, and jobs; be leisurely about it if you like. But have some end in mind to provide your exploration with structure so that you have a sturdy narrative when you are through instead of your resume shouting, "I had no clue and was purposeless in my decisions at all times."

▶ *Begin scouting professors.* You may want to reread chapter 6 on professors and take some notes on how to start grooming—or at least, start thinking about grooming—some relationships that can generate strong letters of recommendation. Look for either a deep appreciation for how a prof handles the subject matter or some sort of personal chemistry as you begin your search for professors you'd like to know better.

▶ *Research sophomore perks.* Some colleges offer unique seminars or programs available only to sophomores that you need to register for as a freshman. Since this is largely dependent on your college, we must remain vague. Stop by your advisor's office or career center to see if there's anything more you should be taking advantage of this year.

SOPHOMORES

You know you're a sophomore when you begin to recognize a whole new set of acronyms.

▶ *Study for the GMAT, MCAT, LSAT, or GRE.* These tests tend to be taken later on, but it is not too early to squirrel away some time now and begin your test prep. The standard procedure for preparing for these exams is to take workshops specific to your test to help you prepare not only for the knowledge base but for the unique test structure you will encounter with your sweaty #2 pencil (or mouse) in hand. It's not abnormal to attend a session two to three times a week in the evening, even as early as your sophomore year, especially if you plan to take a course or social overload or study abroad your junior year. By planning ahead, you will have more chances to retake the test should your initial scores not be as high as you hoped.

▶ *Explore MFA, MBA, or MDIV programs.* If you are interested in pursuing a graduate degree, make an appointment with a professor in that field whom you already know. With his help, sketch out what you need to know and what your future may require of you should you pursue a further education in this field. You might consider getting to know a few grad students in this field as well since they will have recently finished one or more of those whopping entrance tests and will know the process of getting accepted to grad school. They will have a wealth of information to give you. You'll also want to check in with your career center at this point to see what exactly will be required of you as an undergrad (in terms of courses, tests, and internships) to apply to this field for future study.

Grad school isn't for everyone, especially if you don't think your future career will be able to shovel you out of debt very quickly.

▶ *End with a BS or BA?* What if you aren't considering grad school as a postgraduation option? Should you be? Not necessarily. Grad school isn't for everyone, especially if you don't think your future career will be able to shovel you out of debt very quickly (such as if you become a public high school teacher). If you are fairly certain that grad school is not for you, breathe a huge sigh of relief.

▶ *Apply for SI.* No, not *Sports Illustrated*—student intern. Use your summers to discern what careers might be of interest to you by interning in similar areas. Or perhaps you already know what you want to do—that's even better. Definitely intern for a summer in that line of work (as well as a summer or two in something *completely* different) to be sure it's actually what you had in mind. Remember Frances and her med-school mistake we mentioned earlier? Had she spent a summer volunteering in a hospital as an undergrad, she might have discovered her true preferences earlier on. The career center will be able to give you some internship suggestions as well as make other connections you may have missed (such as seminars, workshops, or upcoming guest lecturers) in teasing out potential careers.

▶ *Tabulate GR1, GR2, GR3, GR4, and GR5.* Graduation requirements tend to vary in name from college to college, but the shudder feels about the same. Now would be a good time to take a gander at what you have left to cover in your general and departmental graduation requirements in the next couple years so you aren't caught off guard. Don't panic or feel obligated to complete them all by Christmas, but do begin to look for ways to knock a couple out in the next year.

▶ *See the world.* No acronyms needed for that one. If you've always wanted to see the world, junior year is a great time to do that (which most often means you have to apply as a sophomore). Many majors offer programs to study abroad, but even if they don't, there are often national programs available that offer courses with credits, which can transfer to your college. Some may even cover a few of your graduation requirements, but double-check this BEFORE you go abroad. Every college has preprinted "We are sorry you chose not to read the rules before going to the [fill in the blank foreign school here], but we can't accept outside credits and are not going to change the rules for you now" stationery that will come your way if you don't do due diligence before you leave.

JUNIORS

Some say this is the hardest academic year (assuming you don't continue on to grad school) that you'll ever face, but if you've been following along with us since day one as a freshman and have your ducks in a row, it may turn out just, well, ducky.

▶ *Wrap it up.* Junior year is a great time to finish up any standardized test preparation and take your GRE, LSAT, MCAT, or whatever your test of choice may be. Once you feel well prepared, take the test as soon as you can. Not only will your mind be sharper, but you will also have a larger window of time to retake the test in the event your scores aren't beefy.

▶ *Revisit those reqs.* Now it is well past time to review those graduation and major requirements and to make sure you are on-track for completing them. It's not necessary that you know exactly which term you will take what, but by the beginning of your junior year, you'd better have more than a general idea of how much is ahead of you (and whether or not you can get a two-fer by overlapping some reqs).

▶ *Research your future.* If you haven't been to the career center yet, shame, shame. Take some time and invest in your future. Trust us. At worst, you'll waste forty-five minutes of a rainy afternoon; at best, you'll save yourself from some catastrophic career move that otherwise would have pummeled you.

▶ *Challenge your course load.* If at all possible, schedule an intensive seminar or tutorial with a professor early in your junior year. Not only is it a memorable learning experience, it is also good timing for requesting a letter of recommendation that reflects, as a mature student, your ability to maintain a focused engagement with a faculty member. This is especially important if you are planning to apply to graduate school your senior year. Applications are due in late fall and it's a risk waiting to harvest a good letter from your fall senior classes.

▶ *Start planning for next summer now.* The summer between your junior and senior years will be the most critical for your next career move. If you can manage to secure a solid internship or job, or some other notable experience, it will give you plenty of rich material for conversations in your job interviews. We can almost guarantee they'll ask what you did last summer. Many of the desirable or impressive internships have big lead times in their application process, so you'll want to get yours in around September or October—almost a full year in advance.

Effectively this long "to do" list turns the first few weeks of your junior year into a serious brainstorming session. To make life a wee bit more complicated, you'll need to back this session up even further—to the end of your sophomore year—should you decide to study abroad during the fall of your junior year, since life won't wait for you to get back and unpack.

SENIORS

If you've played your cards right, there shouldn't be an unmanageable load left for your senior year. Don't be surprised if you see comrades scurrying to finish their test prep and quickly take the GRE or folks just realizing they have more major requirements to fulfill than they do time. These things happen. But you are on the ball, so you have the whole year to look forward to.

▶ *What do you want to be when you grow up?* It is not uncommon for seniors to quickly come to hate the question "What will you do after you graduate?" It will become increasingly annoying by winter of your senior year. Most of the time the question is being asked by people who don't know what else to talk about but who would like to strike up a conversation with you. However, what many seniors hear in the question is either "What do you want to be when you grow up?" or worse, "What do you expect to do with the next forty-five years of your life?"—which leaves them in a tailspin. And who wouldn't be flummoxed? It's an unreasonable question, and most folks aren't even asking it. If they are, then buy them a drink and aim them toward a different corner of the party.

▶ *Expect the future to intrude on the present and adjust accordingly.* Senior year is a tough balance because you want to enjoy it to the hilt, but you also need to attend to some academic requirements that require an intense amount of focus. It may even feel reminiscent of your senior year in high school, only the intellectual opportunities are richer and the cost of checking out early is so much greater.

At this point in your career, interviewing for jobs is itself almost a full-time job. It's easily as much work as an additional whopper of a class, what with all the research, applications, interviews, and maybe even distant interviews on location. Many classes that are frequented by seniors have attendance requirements because professors know how hard it is for seniors to keep up with their course work when their futures are calling to them—so shop carefully when you choose courses if you think your interviews will have you traveling off campus frequently. Choose courses that meet the main priorities for your education but that will also have attendance requirements that are realistic given your schedule. This issue typically affects the fall semester the most, since that is when the competition for top-notch jobs is most intense.

The goal is to arrange a course schedule that will allow you to both interview at companies and pursue your classes. Hopefully there will be some flexibility with the potential employer so that you can request to interview on Friday instead of Tuesday. Be willing to investigate whether or not there is some leeway, and don't assume that by asking for a different date you are ruining your chances of getting the job. We talked with Vivec (an executive of a well-respected international firm that has particularly stringent recruiting habits—at times the firm requires seven interviews from a single candidate before offering a position!) and queried him on this very topic.

Vivec said, "Were a student unable to arrive for an interview due to a course schedule, the best action to take would be one of honest professionalism. Explain to the recruiter why you cannot miss the course, whether it be limited absences allowed or a test that cannot be moved, and ask if it is possible to come at a different time. And—this part is critical—be accommodating. Offer a few times that work for you, but show you are also willing to go out of your way to take red-eye flights or drive at odd hours to make it work for the company. Most firms recognize you have a life beyond the application process, and how you handle the situation could reflect positively on your application should you manage it well."

So there you have it—wisdom from the man himself.

It should go without saying—but we will say it anyway—make sure you keep your professors apprised of your interview travel and any other distractions from your studies. Professors will be more accommodating if you've been courteous by informing them in advance that you will be absent. However, that doesn't necessarily mean they will be indulgent. Actually the advice offered above from the executive could just as easily come from the professor in terms of making absences work for everyone involved as much as possible.

▶ *Understand that you are not making "forever" decisions.* As you search for the perfect job, try not to stress out too much about signing your life away: "What if my first job is a disaster? What if I don't like it? Will it look bad if I change jobs too quickly?" The bottom line is that you can always change, and if you're like the average American, you will—many, many times. PJ is a recent graduate who—though he was a promising student—could only find a job selling Internet satellites when it came time to graduate. It wasn't his dream job. Three years and two job changes later he is working in higher-level management in a prestigious bank and loves it. How, you ask? Short of providence, the best reasoning PJ gives is that each job change highlighted a set of talents or strengths he wanted to develop in himself—as opposed to staying in a field simply because the job training was similar. So, even though the industries varied, the leadership skills he was honing at each company improved from one move to the next.

> As you search for the perfect job, try not to stress out too much about signing your life away. The bottom line is that you can always change, and if you're like the average American, you will—many, many times.

▶ *Take workshops that will prepare you for life after college.* One last thing to look for are workshops geared toward seniors and life after college. Many colleges offer brief forums on topics such as medical insurance, how to buy a house, how to handle credit cards responsibly, how to plan for retirement, and other topics of interest. Most often these sorts of practical life courses are offered in . . . where else? The career center. (It's too bad you don't get a dollar every time we mention that place. Your college loans could be paid off by now!)

SURPRISE!
How Not to Be Caught Off Guard by the Big Stuff

Until now, we have focused on positive things you can do to position yourself for success after college. You also need to play some defense, avoiding mistakes we have seen too many recent graduates make.

THE CAR

As much as it may pain you to hear this, don't rush out and buy yourself a "happy graduation" car. Even as a gift, a car involves major ongoing expenses. We've seen it happen before. The happy graduate heads to the dealership and signs up for a car he can barely afford, which in turn limits his options because he can only take jobs that ensure that he can meet those payments. (And chances are he'll buy a fun car versus a practical one, so just about the time he finishes off the payments, he'll have to sell it for something better suited to real life.) Even if the student takes a well-paid position and he can afford the car, he may be relocated to a large city (as many recent graduates are) where he won't even need a car.

On the other hand, the lower the salary you can afford to accept (because you don't have car payments), the more tantalizing your career options will be. Many exotic jobs involve low pay in the beginning and often open tremendous doors later on. So, depending on where you land, what you're doing, and how much you're making, a car can become more of a burden than an asset.

LIFESTYLE

An all-too-common trap for recent graduates is trying to live by their parents' standard of living. This may seem reasonable because they grew up with it, but this standard is in fact not reasonable at all—at least not for a recent college graduate. Their parents may have achieved that standard of living only after many years in the salt mines. Students who try to live as if they had their parents' financial status (without their parents' paycheck) quickly plunge into debt, which in turn narrows their career options since now there are hefty bills to pay.

The twenties is a great time to be relatively poor. (It's certainly a lot easier than attempting it later should you be married with kids.) We've been encouraging you from the beginning to experiment, and this is another place to take a calculated risk. Try out something you've always wanted to do that may involve low pay now but that has a long-term payoff. The job that provides great professional networks or learning experiences or public exposure can be risky but rewarding—more so than the job with a higher starting salary and dead-end prospects. As you head into your job search, draw up a budget of what you think you need to earn given your spending habits (and savings). If jobs aren't available with that sort of pay scale, adjust the budget as needed—or consider different jobs.

> **The job that provides great professional networks or learning experiences or public exposure can be risky but rewarding—more so than the job with a higher starting salary and dead-end prospects.**

There are numerous books and seminars on the topic of financial planning, so we won't go into all that here. We will, however, draw your attention to two important facts that seem to underscore their point:

- The miracle of compound interest means that saving in your twenties is turbocharged when compared to saving in your thirties, forties, and fifties.

- Good financial management is 90 percent discipline and habit and 10 percent wisdom and luck. You can't control luck, but if you are wise enough to set up properly disciplined habits, then your investments (and dividends!) will most likely reflect that.

INSURANCE

Health insurance can be another doozy. Upon graduation, most students are no longer eligible to be covered by their parents' policies. Health insurance can be one of the toughest things to nail down since you won't know what insurance plan your company has available if any (not all jobs these days come with health insurance) until you've been offered a position. Figure that if you're going into a traditional career, it's likely you'll have some sort of coverage. If you are in the fortunate position to be offered a job at more than one company, take a close look at their benefits when evaluating compensation.

Should you end up joining a smaller company, the benefits may not be what you had hoped. Regardless of what your insurance plan turns out to be, we *strongly* advise against having a lapse in coverage. We repeat: there should be absolutely no window of time when you are not covered by some policy because of the major risk to your health (though, some hospitals *will* treat you even without coverage) and because of the crippling financial burden it would become should you become seriously injured or ill. Your life can change for the worse in an instant if you have no insurance to provide for those unforeseeable situations. The good news is that you are exactly the kind of person insurance companies are looking for: young and thus more likely to be healthy (which makes for a great policyholder from their point of view—the Holy Grail of insurance is to sell policies to those who won't need to make a claim). At your age, it makes sense to have major medical coverage, but unless you have a chronic condition (and if you don't know whether you do, get yourself checked out while still at college and covered by good medical insurance), you probably don't need a gold-plated policy just yet because, chances are, you won't need it.

RETIREMENT

Another surprise to meet head-on: saving in your early working years for retirement. It may seem like eons away but before you know it, it will be time to retire. When you turn to look for that nest egg, will it be . . . shiny? Cracked? That depends. It's *never* too early to start investing for your retirement. Early on, one of us was given this excellent piece of advice: once you earn an income, be sure you pay your future self immediately. Practically that means that with every paycheck you contribute as much as you can either to a retirement plan or a savings account that you *don't* touch. It's not that we expect you'll be making a lot of money early on. Heck, you may only be able to put in $5 a month. The value of that $5 goes beyond the principal to the principle of the matter (a little financial humor there, ha-ha). You are cultivating an important lifetime habit that will have positive returns for many years to come.

Another surprise to meet head-on: saving in your early working years for retirement. It may seem like eons away but before you know it, it will be time to retire. When you turn to look for that nest egg, will it be . . . shiny? Cracked?

Alumni Clubs

Fancy Bumper Sticker or Future Investment?

As graduation nears, peruse the fine print of your campus map and seek out the alumni office. More than hosting stylistic flair and beautiful furniture, it could prove to be an invaluable resource. If you attend a large university, your alumni website will most likely have information to connect you with alumni and alumni clubs across the nation (and, nowadays, perhaps across the globe). If you are moving to a new city, it could even be helpful in getting to know people and build some new networks. If you attend a small college or an elite university, your alumni office will probably keep files on alums and their careers. This information could be very useful in the event you need a few introductions—and could possibly lead to job interviews or suggestions on your own career course.

The alumni office is a great resource. In addition to helping you maintain a tie to your college and connect with other alums wherever you live, it may also offer discounts on cool extras like travel or car insurance. Since the network you develop in college is almost as valuable as the college itself, wouldn't it make sense to keep those lifelines alive and kicking by keeping your contact info updated in the alumni files?

Don't worry about giving them your phone number. Most colleges know better than to beleaguer recent grads with requests for money. (They assume you don't have it yet—you're probably still paying off tuition loans.) In fact, beat them to it. Plan to make a gift to your college somewhere around your ten-year reunion. (And, no—your alma mater didn't pay us to say that.)

Why give away your hard-earned cash? Well, for starters it is a privilege to be one of the well-educated few in this world and as such it's our responsibility to share. Helping the institution that helped you become who you are is a good way to share some of that success with the next generation. Plus, it makes a nice tax deduction, not to mention an investment in yourself at the same time. How so? As long as your alma mater continues to fare well, the school will maintain a respectable reputation, which means your diploma will maintain its value. Are you seeing the connection?

DILIGENCE AND INTEGRITY

Ready for the last big surprise? It's not about titles or company flash. Just as we've said that it's not so much where you attend school as what you accomplish while you're there, we reassert that it's not so much what your first job is as how you perform in that job. Good recommendations (and bad) will follow you wherever you go.

We knew of one businesswoman—let's call her Matilda—who directed an online start-up company, which we will call Lousy BusinessPlan.com. Despite her initial goodwill, she turned out to be a snake and sold the company downriver, making off with the profits and leaving the employees out in the cold. It was infuriating and the rest of the management team was helpless. A year or so later, Matilda applied for a prestigious role in another company—the sort of position she'd been working her whole career to reach. In looking over Matilda's impressive profile, one of the board members of that company happened to recognize the name LousyBusinessPlan.com (his son's best friend was the former COO). Wouldn't you know, that board member got an earful when he gave the former COO a quick call to hear his impressions of Matilda, and she lost out on a major career move. Your performance has a way of keeping track of you. See that as a good thing, and your devotion to excellence will make you a success.

One Last Thought Before Sending You Off into Success

As hard as you have worked to put yourself through school these past twenty-two years, and as hard as your parents have worked to support you in your ventures, don't kid yourself. That you are standing here today on your way to receiving a college diploma is still providence. You have just won the genetic lottery. True, it's not irrelevant that you were up all night preparing for your anthropology midterm or merely luck that you passed your biochemistry class. (Or maybe that biochem final was . . . look, you see where we're headed.)

None of us chose to be born into a privileged nation. None of us selected our family or our upbringing. None of us even selected the era in which we would live. But somehow we were born here and now, and here you stand ready to begin your bright future having been given more than most individuals in this richly populated world will receive in a lifetime. You have been given vaccinations, taught to read, trained in a healthy lifestyle, given clean air to breathe, and are now blessed with a life's education. It really is awesome when you think about it.

Find a way to financially or personally give back to the world a portion of what you have been able to take thus far—it will never be easier to give back than it is now. You have a lifetime to cash in on the prestige that comes from being in the upper echelon of educated people in the world. For now, use your innate talents and your college-honed skills to right someone's wrong, to confront a global challenge, to create a new opportunity, or to meet a local need. Who knows, this sort of giving back may become a wonderful addiction. And someday, when you have family responsibilities or your own kids to put through college or you're retired and your energy just isn't what it used to be, you'll be glad you were not just another well-fed person on the sidelines pointing out problems; you were part of the solution.

Index

About the Authors

Peter D. Feaver (PhD, Harvard, 1990) is the Alexander F. Hehmeyer Professor of Political Science and Public Policy at Duke University. He has over twenty years of teaching experience—as a teaching fellow at Harvard and as a professor at Duke. He won the Harvard Certificate of Distinction in Teaching (1985–86 and 1986–87), the Trinity College (Duke) Distinguished Teaching Award (1994–95), and the Duke Alumni Distinguished Undergraduate Teaching Award (2001). He has published numerous scholarly books and articles on national security issues, and he has served on the National Security Council at the White House, first as Director for Defense Policy and Arms Control under President Bill Clinton and most recently as Special Advisor for Strategic Planning and Institutional Reform under President George W. Bush. As long as his knees will let him, he can be found waddling up and down the basketball court—or more often these days, cheering his daughter and two sons from the sidelines.

Sue Wasiolek (more commonly known as Dean Sue) is assistant vice president for student affairs and dean of students at Duke University. She was premed at Duke (she never got into medical school), completed a Master's of Health Administration at Duke (only worked in health care for eighteen months), completed her JD at

North Carolina Central University and her LLM at Duke (only practiced law for nine months), and has been working at Duke for the past twenty-eight years. Sue loves the classroom both as a teacher (she teaches education law) and as a student (she plans to complete her EdD in 2008). Sue encourages students to study what they love and base their careers around what they love, even if those two are totally different things. Her time with students is not a job but a way of life. In her free time, Sue can be found jogging around Durham or working out at the gym with students.

 **Anne Crossman** studied at both Stanford and Duke, earning a BA in English and a Certificate in Education. After teaching for public high schools, colleges, and the military for five years, she gave up her day job to pursue authorship and motherhood. A poet by trade, her work has been published in journals such as *Nimrod* and *Margie*, and she is currently finalizing a book of poems about Alzheimer's disease entitled *Trying to Remember*, which is due to be published the summer of 2008. Her third book, a humorous educational series addressing life as a high-school student, is on deck and, if all goes well, will be hitting shelves by the end of the decade. Anne currently lives with her husband and sons in Seattle, Washington.

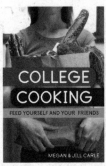